COUNT ME IN

A trailblazer's triumph in a world not built for her

Susan Allen

Susan Allen

This book reflects the author's present recollections of experiences over time, and all content within regarding companies, persons, and experiences is strictly her opinion. Some names and characteristics have been changed, some events have been compressed, and some dialogue has been recreated.

ISBN (Hardcover): 978-1-7782973-2-8
ISBN (Paperback): 978-1-7782973-3-5

Printed by Kindle Direct Publishing and Ingram Spark in the United States of America. First printing edition 2022.

Editing by Dustin Bilyk @ www.authorshand.com
Cover Design by Emily @ emilys_world_of_design

Visit: www.countmein.info

All proceeds from the sale of this book will go to support pediatric cardiology needs in Toronto and young women in STEM programs.

To John, Danielle, and Andrew,

You have always counted me in and taught me what matters most.

"To my dearly loved and first granddaughter, Susan Lynn Allen. May she always be true to herself and her parents in the years to come."

— Xmas 1970, Grandfather Todd

Contents

Part V: Taking a Risk or Staying Comfortable?

Part VI: The Transformation

Part VII: Blazing a Trail to Pay it Forward

Part VIII: Completeness

Prologue

There is heaviness in this task. Writing this memoir was a much larger undertaking than I originally estimated. Sharing the truths of my personal journey was akin to ripping off the band-aids of my past. They left scars and the skin is still tender.

But my purpose became clear.

I want to share the significant events and actions I took that shaped my life as a successful woman in business. But I also wish to explain how, as a wife and a mother of two children, I was forced to make impossible decisions between work and life, and how I balanced (or failed to balance) the two.

My successes and failures have become my life lessons, and my inner-voice is begging me to share my reflections to help you, my readers—aspiring professional career women, guilt-ridden moms, and exhausted spouses—to learn from my doubts and misconceptions, and benefit from my experience as I blazed my own path in the world of business. Use my learned lessons to your advantage. Trust me, it will make your path that much easier to navigate.

My journey begins on the wrong side of the tracks, in a lower middle-class suburb of Rexdale, Ontario, Canada where girls like me graduated from high school, got married, had a family, and took a 9 to 5 job to make ends meet. Girls like me weren't supposed to crave a life beyond the dusty, beaten-down road our mothers and grandmothers took. Naysayers waited at every turn to discourage our dreams and quash our ambitions. Girls like me weren't supposed to perform better than boys in math. And pursuing it as a professional? Get the hell out of here! Girls like me didn't dare venture off to university to compete with the boys in engineering, science, or accounting. Girls like me were not the breadwinners of the family.

But I'm not like most girls. I am a trailblazer, a leader, a mentor, a coach, an FCPA, and an Audit Committee Chair on several corporate boards. I am a woman of many firsts: the first female partner in PwC's Mississauga office, the first woman elected to PwC's global board, Catalyst Canada's Business Leader Champion, and one of Canada's 'Top 100 Most Powerful Women.'

And even though I am all of those things, I am also a dedicated mother and spouse.

If you think racing to attain lofty goals and achievements before other women was an intrinsic goal of mine, you'd be dead wrong. If I had grown up in a world that expected great things of me, and had I, from my early years, directed all my energy towards these achievements, I could, perhaps, understand why I've accomplished these many firsts. But my life took a number of unexpected twists and roundabouts, and I even slammed into a wall or two along the way. With all the insecurities I held and the mistakes I made, I still ask myself how I, of all women, made it from Point A to Point Z to achieve my wildest dreams.

But I did, and I want to show you how I did it.

I would be remiss if I omitted the part of my story that deals with the intersection of career and family. Nor could I exclude the heaping tablespoon of guilt and anxiety I felt due to the persistent conflict inherent in raising a family while advancing my career. Work/life balance and work/life flexibility remains, and may always be, one of life's unsolved mysteries, especially as a woman. How did I navigate these murky waters? Did I strike a *realistic* balance between a rewarding career and a fulfilling family life? Do I have regrets? I defy you to find a parent that feels otherwise.

Being a trailblazer was not my intention, nor do I even like the term. For me, it conjures up visions of crossing uncharted, wild terrain in a covered wagon with scorpions, spiders, and snakes nipping at my feet. I can do without those, thank you very much. But my disdain for these insidious creatures aside, I will take you on a wild ride into my frontier.

The trailblazer label also comes with a heaping tablespoon of responsibility. As honoured as I feel to be called one, it is daunting, if not exhausting. Too often, trailblazers aren't given the chance to make mistakes—we must do it right the first time, with eyes fixated on our every move. This is a difficult cross to bear and that is not okay with me. I challenge this perception. Therefore, I want to show you that even when you are mired in a maze of missteps and self-doubts, you *can* still achieve greatness and leave a lasting impact. Doesn't that make you feel better?

I want to make your journey easier than it was for me, and while my experiences have been told through my own personal lens, they will have meaning for you. You will relate to my personal truths, because my failings, triumphs, and experiences have been shared without reservation.

Prepare to feel seen and heard. Prepare to feel like you are not alone.

You are not an imposter, a hopeless perfectionist, or a guilt-ridden mom who can do better.

You are a strong, capable, successful woman, and as I share my vulnerable inner feelings and thoughts with you, I encourage you to reflect upon your experiences and misconceptions; those behaviours you learned a long time ago when you were playing in the sandbox. It's time to stop them from holding you back and reaching your full potential!

I promise to arm you with the courage to ask for that promotion, to give you tools to take ownership of your future, to set your sights higher, to find balance on your terms, and to accept a dash of risk… for the fun of it.

Count yourselves in.

And count me in for the ride.

Part I:
The Influencers

Our early experiences in childhood and young adulthood shape the people we become, the values we live by, and our approach to purpose and meaning in life.

This urge to write what you're about to read, I freely admit, was prompted with gentle, encouraging nudges from friends and family long before today. For years, I've heard my daughter's millennial friends, as well as other bold, young professional women ask:

'How did you do it, Sue?'

Yet, this is not what you think it is. I am not who you may think. If you want to read about a famous, grab-the-bull-by-the-horns, rags-to-riches tale of triumph, stop here. This protagonist has fears, failings, delusions of inadequacy, and has a history of lacking confidence and direction. I have made mistakes (who hasn't!), and I have regrets (who doesn't!). I never asked for the trailblazer moniker, but with the support from people who believed in me, I did triumph in a world that was not built for women. Even to this day, I continue to surprise myself.

When I considered where to begin my journey, I became acutely aware that my life didn't start with my first job or my first promotion. I was not born on the right side of the tracks, nor did I come from a background where you were expected to get a university degree. I didn't grow up with the drive or goal to propel myself into a professional career full of promotions and leadership roles that would catapult me up the corporate ladder to smash the glass ceiling. In those days, that glass ceiling might as well have been rock-hard concrete!

Those things did eventually happen, but if I started my story there, I wouldn't be accurately answering that nagging question: 'How did you do it, Sue?'

Therefore, my journey begins with my earliest memories—my childhood, my fears and insecurities, my wins and losses, and my socioeconomic upbringing. Our early experiences shape the people we become, the values we live by, and our approach to our purpose and meaning in life. But as you will see, our past or starting point doesn't have to dictate our future. When we take ownership of our future, we can change our outcome.

Similarly, I cannot overlook the initial influencers of my behaviour, character, and core values any easier than I can change the colour of my eyes and the greying of my hair. These are integral parts of what makes me, me. My earliest experiences and relationships are the catalysts for the woman I became.

So, I start from the beginning, covering a diverging tale of love, joy, growth, surprise, and celebration, bounded by disappointment, failure, self-doubt, and fate. Let's all take a deep, cleansing breath—gloves off, shields down—and take this journey through my life so that you may learn from it.

Get ready. This is the straight goods.

1

The Early Years

Today is my living hell, my new reality. It's playing out in my head on repeat. Yesterday, the day before that, and the day before that... my inescapable Groundhog Day. I never imagined I would find my new job at the company of my dreams so unconscionable.

Four male interns—my new 'friends' and soon to be colleagues —saunter towards me, pleased with themselves and their cutesy little inside jokes carried forward from four years together in college. They're playing grown-up in an exciting adventure with their buddies.

They are oblivious to my subtle Lady Diana gaze from afar, so I follow up with a more penetrating stare as they approach my desk, wishing my unique female presence would telepathically force these guys to acknowledge my existence. I long to share a joke, be included in conversation, feel the warmth of their smiles, and answer the simple, but central question, 'Would you like to join us for lunch?' But they look past and through me.

Every damn day at 11:55am they form a bee line from class to venture across the street to enter their new favourite watering hole:

a 'men's only' club to grab… *lunch*. I couldn't even follow them if I tried.

How can this be happening? It's 1981 for God's sake, not 1951.

I feel invisible, but I toss my hurt feelings to the curb and settle on a nearby bench for my lunch break. I stuff an overpriced, pre-packaged hotel sandwich in my face and notice each passerby gawking at me.

Why am I not invisible now? I know they're thinking, *Who is this loser and why is she eating alone?* Or are they? In my fragile state, am I overreacting to what I fear most?

I'm an imposter. I don't belong here.

Overthinking and clutching my sandwich too hard, I narrowly avoid spilling mustard on my blouse, instead dropping a small piece of lettuce on my winter-white jacket that lands on my winter-white skirt. *Damn.* I wore this same outfit to twelve job interviews—it was all I had and all I could afford—and today, I chose this same outfit to be seen, to stand out.

But not here; not like this.

After lunch, the 'boys' and I return to class. We are halfway through our ten-day training program on how to be nerdy number crunchers. While we learn to ask probing questions, we are becoming astute detectives who analyse gobs of related data to find *one of these things that's not like the other*. We've come to audit.

The lessons I hear, the case studies I read, speak to my soul. The numbers on the page don't.

I'm not like the others.

It feels like I'm learning Swahili with our new language of acronyms and terms like g/l's, provisions, bad debts, reconciling items, and PBC schedules flowing freely from the mouths of our instructors. I'm in over my head, and it's becoming more difficult to hide this embarrassing fact. As one of very few women in a sea of commerce graduates, *and* the only non-accountant, I clearly don't belong. I am so naïve to think this could have been my career, my life.

I need a kind word of encouragement, or support from someone, anyone. A welcoming lunch with my new workmates would help. I need my nerves to calm, to be less fearful, more confident.

Where is that woman? Was I ever that woman?

I must stay strong. But when will I feel like I didn't just make the worst mistake of my life?

That was forty years ago. Today, I have different worries, but I still sometimes wake up at night thinking about those first harrowing days in a career that would shape the rest of my life. Today, I see creases on my forehead, laugh lines when I'm not smiling, and stubborn dark circles under my eyes. I wear bifocals, and grey peeks through my centre part every six weeks. My health is fair, but osteoarthritis and my degenerating cartilage prevent me from walking the golf course like I long to. I *have* to give blood every six weeks for the rest of my life—an inherited disease, hemochromatosis.

Let's face it: aging sucks. I have to beat this gradual decline for as long as possible. I owe it to my older self to exercise regularly, eat healthier, sleep in (always), and treat myself to massages when my body says, 'Enough is enough.' I'm also banking on my grandmother Mimi's 98-year-old genes to help me stay as young as I feel.

I answer to Susie Q, Big Al, Sus, JR, Mom, and more recently, Nanna. But when asked what I *like* to be called, I say, 'My friends call me Sue.'

I did not come from privilege, power, fame, or fortune. My siblings and I grew up in a poor neighbourhood in an education system that never expected you to dream big. As a young woman, you found a job out of high school, got married, had kids, and that seemed to be the end of it.

My father, Stan, worked two jobs to make ends meet, keeping him busy days, nights, and on weekends. His second job grew out of his knack for recognising an entrepreneurial opportunity when he saw one. He was fascinated with all things electronic, and he combined his lifelong love of learning (which I inherited) and his boundless curiosity to teach himself about the inner workings of the television set.

Keep in mind that colour televisions were a brand new, must have commodity in the materialistic, post-war era of the 1960's. He capitalised on this, and his company 'S. Allen TV Repair' was born. Known around the neighbourhood as the nice man who brought TVs back to life, he was fully booked nights and weekends, bringing in the extra cash we needed.

Even though his own mother, Mable, had forbade him to further his education beyond high school, my dad was the engineering/math whiz of the family. When I was ten years old, my brother and I would join Dad on the couch to absorb his latest math tricks, learning how to solve for X, answer logarithmic equations, and use a slide rule. He would quiz us on our comprehension and was delighted at how quickly I caught on.

Even though she prevented my father from furthering his education, my dad's mother, Mable, was a loving, 'practically perfect in every way' grandmother to me. 'Nanna' was the definition of matronly, with short and curly white hair, thick glasses to match her wedge-heeled, sensible black shoes, and loose-fitting print dresses tied at the waist which only served to accentuate her full figure.

She had a grade six education from the suburbs of London, England, and was convinced that bookbinding was the only career choice for her only son. As everyone seemed to appreciate but Mable, a bookbinding career would soon find its place in history alongside the blacksmith and the carriage maker.

Henry, my dad's father, and the man we all called Grandpop, was a different sort of man—the opposite of his wife and very different from my own father. A short and stout World War I veteran sporting a full head of white hair, he was unapproachable and scary for a child like me. He wore eyeglasses and spoke in a fast, low, and gruff voice which sounded like one long, rambling mumble, made more difficult by his slight Cockney English accent. He laughed unpredictably, which was the scariest part, and would tell inappropriate jokes young ears shouldn't hear. He was one of those men who was hard for children (and adults) to warm up to.

As we came to find out years later, Grandpop had a scandalous and sordid past. He'd knocked up his boss's daughter at the butcher shop and fled England, then upon arriving on Canadian shores as an off-the-boat immigrant, he worked illegally as a bartender during Prohibition. Trying to make something honest out of something crooked, he invested everything he had into the stock market. But fortune looked unkindly on Grandpop, and he lost every last penny on Black Tuesday when the markets crashed, and the infamous Great Depression took the world by storm. He was forced back into his old trade: a butcher.

However, Grandpop *was* famous for one lasting achievement. He had developed a recipe for pork and sage breakfast sausages the entire family loved, but the only time we were destined to savour Grandpop's sausages was when we visited him, because he would share his recipe with *no one*. This, as true to human nature as it gets, made the sausages and the recipe even more desirable! We all thought he would go to his grave with his sausage recipe crimpled and clutched tightly in both hands. That was until I tore it from his grasp.

When I look back on this moment, it's so clear in mind. I think it's because this was the first time I used my feminine wit and charm to negotiate successfully and deliver a result that would make my team (my family!) all happy.

My plan was simple, but effective. I patiently waited until Grandpop was in a particularly good mood one day. Alcohol may have been involved in loosening him up a smidge. So, upon seeing him in this state, I seized the opportunity to pounce, and I bashfully jumped up on his knee just to talk—granddaughter to Grandpop.

First, I stroked his ego a bit with generic small talk, and as soon as I mustered up the courage, I asked him the zinger, 'Tell me, Grandpop, what ingredients go into your oh-so-delicious sausages?' and in between our meaningless small talk, he would let an ingredient slip out and I would excuse myself every so often to write it down in the amounts I could remember.

One innocent question after another and kaboom! The detective in me had extracted what others far older and wiser than me had tried so many times before to get their hands on: Grandpop's sausage recipe! My dad couldn't have been happier, and I couldn't have been prouder of my sorcery!

My mom, June, was the artist of the family. Her soprano voice presented her with the lead singing roles in her high school musicals. But it didn't stop there. She could also draw, create graphic designs, paint, and produce metal art known as copper tooling. The Ontario College of Art would have been the place for her to attend and excel, but that wasn't in the cards for her either—a married woman in her snack bracket didn't venture off to college in the 1950's.

Our walls were adorned with scenes of oceans crashing into rocks, a far-off sunset, trees in a fall forest, or a lighthouse on a pier. She used a wide flat knife as her paint brush and was not afraid of colour. Her large canvasses created stunning pieces with their unique, uneven surfaces, and the colours she selected matched the room they were designed for.

Even though I managed to inherit my dad's logical math abilities, I have the artistic aptitude of a two-toed sloth. I draw stick people. My soapstone art project from grade eight shop class was supposed to be a long, slender cat, sitting tall. If you saw it, you would swear it was an injured soup ladle.

My mother's parents, Mimi and Douglas, were close to our family both in the geographic proximity and continuity of our daily lives. Although they were born and raised in Canada, they too had English roots just like my father's parents. Mimi and Grandad spent their hard-earned wages on vacation experiences and the best gifts they could afford for their six beloved grandchildren, but they were only able to do this by living frugally in a one-bedroom, high-rise apartment complex on the border of Toronto.

'Mimi' was a perfect nickname for my petite, no nonsense, and fashionable grandmother... but she was nobody's grandma! She was far too cool for that. Regrettably, like my mother, Mimi was born at the wrong time and place in history, and after trying her hand at a couple of careers, she accepted her fate as a stay-at-home wife and mother. Stuck in an age where women were not supposed to be working outside of the home, she resigned herself to stop work and take care of her small apartment, her husband, and her grandchildren when they were sick. I think that's why she could relate to and understand me when she was well into her nineties.

Mimi was my second mom. She just *got* me. She was an empathetic listener, a great model for me and my future behaviour, and there were many times in my young life I selfishly used her to vent, because hearing her voice made me feel better. Until her dying day, she was a lucid, remarkable woman with an upbeat attitude and zest for life. I know there is a place in heaven saved for her.

As for my Grandad, I fondly remember one day, when he was taking care of me during one illness or another, he presented me with a foot-high, cylindrical-shaped brass container. He told me it was an artillery casing from World War I, and it was heavy to lift because it was filled to the brim with quarters. He asked me to count his change and tell him how much he had, whereupon I dumped the quarters onto the floor and put them in neat stacks of four.

I still have no idea what the hell he did with this information, but I loved performing this duty for him. I pretended I was Mother Goose's king in the counting house, counting out his money. To this day, I smile at the joy I found with this WWI artillery casing every time I visited their home. Talk about foreshadowing a career as a bean counter, hey?

Grandad was the wild one of the family. He reminded me of Walt Disney, the distinguished, successful man I watched on the *Wonderful World of Disney* every Sunday. In fact, he could have passed for Walt's brother. He was of similar size and build, wore his hair slicked back, and exuded charm with his warm heart, kind eyes, and friendly smile.

One of my fondest and longest lasting memories ever involves a gift Grandad gave me when I was thirteen. It was Christmas, and when we were alone, Grandad approached me carrying a black, leatherbound book. He whispered to me to come and sit with him in our living room. Once there, he presented me with his book, *The Holy Bible*. Grandad asked me to open it.

I carefully opened the leather cover and read aloud:

'To my dear son, Douglas on his tenth birthday, December 9, 1918. Hoping he will read and study it well for his mother and father's sake. God so loved the world He gave His only begotten son that whosoever believe in Him should not perish but have everlasting life.'

Grandad's mom had written her eloquent inscription on the inside page of this beautiful book. *How extraordinary,* I thought. *But why am I sitting here reading this to him?*

He then asked me to turn over the page and read it.

'To my dearly loved and first granddaughter, Susan Lynn Allen. May she always be true to herself and her parents in the years to come. — Xmas 1970, Grandfather Todd.'

I looked up at him, smiling from ear to ear. Carefully turning the crisp, fine pages with gold edging, I could see its pristine condition even though he had owned it for 52 years. A very special gift from his mom was being gifted to me. I gave him a big hug and hoped he could tell how grateful I was, and how 'dearly loved' I felt in that moment.

But later that evening, alone in my room, I reread the inscription, trying to make sense of it. It must have been important for Grandad to choose that sentence of all sentences to write in such a significant book, but I didn't understand what I should 'always' do or what being 'true to myself' really meant. Did he think I was living a lie? How was I hiding my true self? Who was I supposed to be for my parents? These were deep thoughts for a thirteen-year-old, and they would follow me for decades to come.

Several years passed before I assigned meaning to the words Grandad inscribed. At first, I concluded that 'being true to myself' meant acting consistent with my values and ethics, as well as setting a moral code for myself with boundaries to live by. As I grew older, 'being true to myself' came to mean being my *authentic* self by speaking up and not regretting decisions I'd made in the past or paths I'd choose to go down in the future. I had decided that my values directed my priorities, and if I stumbled, I held myself accountable and took responsibility for my actions—especially when my decision was a poor one.

I have tried to live by these words when I have a difficult decision to make; a fork in the road of life or a choice that pushes against the margins of my principles. Being true to myself means looking back on my life, being proud of the person I am, the friendships I've made, the kindness and support I have provided, and the love I have shared. You may be surprised to hear that I am not a religious person, but I have come to understand the basic lessons and principles of a Christian. I cherish Grandad's gift and what he was asking of me. I hope, when I look back on my life, I have made my parents and my Grandad proud.

While Grandad passed far too soon, Mimi lived a long and happy, grateful life. She measured her good fortune by her relationships, her family, her friends, and her health—the simple things in life. In her late life, she didn't dwell on her limitations as a blind woman, or on her long, lonely years as a widow. No, Mimi was a remarkable woman, and her attitude taught me how the power of a positive perspective feeds one's life with far more meaning and purpose than material things and money. She is my litmus test when I need to reframe my circumstance and consider how bad things really *aren't*. Even after her passing, she's kept me grounded in my good fortune. She has been my lifelong inspiration.

My parents were married in their early twenties and were soon raising a family with two kids under three. We lived in a modest, six-room bungalow in a lower-class suburb of Rexdale, Ontario. My parents both had jobs outside the home to pay the bills, and all this at the age of 21 and 23. I often reflect on how hard it must have been for them to establish a strong foundation for their relationship and marriage.

At some point in my childhood, sitting down to dinner together as a family no longer became a priority for my parents, so I became a latchkey kid who entered an unlocked home after school to do as I pleased.

I remember my after-school ritual well. At five o'clock, I heated two frozen Swanson TV dinners, gave one to my ravaged, skinny, older teenage brother and slapped a second unappealing aluminum tray of processed food in front of myself. I choked back the bits of mystery meat, the baked curly fries, and the apple sauce dessert, and then went straight to my homework (or to watching original episodes of *Star Trek* on TV!). I was twelve.

Despite this freedom, I missed when we dined as a family, even if my parents had a standing order that 'children should be seen and not heard.' Before those years, family dinners, boardgames, backyard corn roasts, costume parties, and vacations were a bit more common. The simple traditions these events created were and still are the glue that holds families together. These are my fondest memories of childhood.

In contrast, my latchkey years were lonely, missed opportunities that left a scar on my heart where cherished, family memories should have been.

Years later, in my two-career marriage, these feelings of loss and regret resurfaced, and they weighed heavily on my adult heart during my first years with my son and daughter. To avoid history repeating itself, I made myself a promise: to fill my home with fond memories, special occasions, and family traditions. This was non-negotiable.

However, any latchkey kid will tell you that there are certain benefits living away from the watchful eyes of parents. In fact, I bet some of you reading are thinking, *Damn, if only my parents gave me the freedom at that age!* It definitely had its perks.

During these years, my brother and I were involved in what would forever be known as the 'Great Potato Chip Scandal of 1968'. My mom had ordered a subscription for potato chips which, while unhealthy and completely unnecessary, was delicious. Why we needed a bi-weekly delivery of potato chips in a bucket is a mystery, but who am I to judge the wisdom of the 1960's?

A couple of months into our chip subscription, I accepted the chips at the door from the delivery man, promptly carried the bucket downstairs, and watched the latest *Star Trek* episode. Before I could say 'live long and prosper', I had devoured the entire bucket of chips!

When my mom came home from work and enquired about the chip delivery, I explained, 'Well, it's like this… the chip guy delivered the bucket, but IT WAS EMPTY! Can you believe it?' My brother Doug backed me up, and what was more stunning than my hokey lie was that she actually believed me!

I was feeling good about my cover-up until I heard Mom on the phone berating the chip company's receptionist who had no explanation for our chipless delivery. After a heated exchange, my mom cancelled our subscription! I may have fooled her, but Doug and I paid the ultimate price for my fantastic lie—no more chip feasts.

Doug keeping this secret was an anomaly, however.

My image of an older brother was to be my protector, wiser and stronger, someone to lean on and look up to. Instead, my brother Doug was shy, sensitive, naïve, and trusting which clashed with my competitive, sharp, and ambitious nature. Growing up, we were 'frenemies', constantly pushing each other's buttons, his brawn often overpowering my brains.

I was selfishly disappointed and hurt he could not live up to *my* vision of a big brother. I should have accepted him for the easygoing, caring man he was—a big, gentle teddy bear who loved me unconditionally despite how intimidating I must have seemed. Instead, I expected him to be an all-powerful, super boy with powers to defend and outsmart his little sister. My Type A personality found fault in his naivety, kindness, and sensitivity. To this day, I regret not telling him, 'You are all I need, I love you as you are.' All he ever needed to be was my brother. He passed at 55 from a heart embolism, having suffered for decades with unresolved health issues that led to his fate.

My younger sister, Cheri, on the other hand, arrived just in time for me to assume she was all mine; a living baby doll whom I was thrilled to play with, dress up, and fuss over. For years, my sister did anything I asked and believed everything I said. As Sheryl Sandberg's book *Lean In* explains, I was not bossy... *I was demonstrating leadership!*

Sharing a bedroom with my sister strengthened our bond that continues to this day. I took the job as big sister seriously, and Cheri accepted my advice and warnings when I thought she was veering off course. As the mentor in this unofficial mentor/mentee relationship, I hoped to be a good role model, and I believe I too gained from this experience and was able to draw upon it later in life.

My proudest act of influence was convincing Cheri (and her naysayers) she *was* smart enough to attend university. Having been there and done that myself, I knew she had the chops for it, and that it would lay the foundation for her future. All she needed was the courage to believe in herself.

In a mentor/mentee relationship, it is said 'reverse mentoring' occurs. I am a better listener, am more willing to accept opposing views, and remain grounded because of my sister's influence and our shared life experience. Never underestimate the power of sisterhood—sisters understand you, care deeply for you, are intensely proud of you, and can act as your advocate, mentor, and protector if you're open to it.

So, with both parents working, three kids left to their own devices, microwaved food on the table, and a roof over our heads, it wasn't a terrible existence by any means. Many kids had it better, but many kids had it worse than us in Rexdale.

Then, one unremarkable summer day in 1973, my father asked his three children to come to the living room and sit down. Tears were welling up in his eyes—I'd never seen him look this somber. I feared something bad was about to happen. He began slow and deliberate, choosing each word as if a dagger was lodged in his heart.

'What I am about to say is the hardest thing I have ever had to do or say. I love you all very much, but I have decided to leave our home and live somewhere else. Your mom and I are going to live apart now because we don't love each other anymore. That doesn't mean that I don't love you, but I have decided it is best for me and your mom that I leave.'

There were no options given, no reconciliations to consider, no hope. In choosing to leave her, he had chosen to leave us.

My brother stormed out of the room, unable to contain his anger and rage. But my dad continued, trying not to create a scene with my brother's exit. He had rented a sketchy apartment (all he could afford) clear across the city, over an hour away. He didn't say when or if we would see him again. He asked if we had any questions, and of course, I had many. But my throat was dry, and it felt like there was a lump in it the size of a baseball. We met his gaze with stunned silence, and I just watched him pick up his bags from the hallway and walk to his car. My sister, my brother, myself, and my dad each suffered in our own way, all in tears.

It was devastating, even though it should have come as no surprise to any of us. My parents' marriage had been falling apart for years. Words had escalated into arguments, tempers were short, voices were raised into screams, and doors were slammed. They were both unbearable and miserable with the status quo.

My dad's departure was the end of our family unit, and we became another statistic all too familiar in the years and decades that followed. My parents separated when I was 15, my brother 17, and my sister 10. At this time, the idyllic 70's, divorce was a four-letter word, not publicly accepted by the generation that grew up watching *Leave it to Beaver*. We were the first and only kids on the block to come from a broken marriage, with a dad who came to visit us every other weekend for outings he hoped would keep him connected to our lives.

But try as we might, distance and time were not our friends. Our exchanges with Dad became polite, shallow conversations with awkward silences. I kept asking myself, 'When is life going return to the way it used to be?' My brother, refusing to join our charade, stewed at home, keeping peace with Mom who played the victim, furious and hurt. For years she would struggle to raise three kids on her own with inadequate support payments (in her mind) and a full-time job that was no longer an option.

Being among the first families in our 'circumstance', there were no support systems in place to deal with our sorrow and confused emotions. On one occasion, my mom asked my younger sister to lie about our 'situation' so strangers wouldn't be aware that there wasn't a man living under our roof. We were a common statistic of the one parent family of the 1980's, but we just happened to be dealing with it a decade earlier.

Because I am too much like my father, I soon got into my own heated arguments with my mom, picking up where Dad left off. Mom and I fell into a pattern of fighting over petty, irritating things that should have been left unsaid.

I constantly fought a losing battle to protect my sensitive and naïve brother from my mother's scorn for her husband. But with each passing day, Doug was becoming less neutral and more infuriated with our dad. It incensed me that my mother berated my father and made herself the victim while Dad wasn't there to defend himself. I didn't want Doug to hate his father, but my mother, now a bitter divorcee, needed an outlet for her rage and chose her kids to soften the blow. We were there to lick her wounds.

Unfortunately, I was a persistent, negative reminder of the man who left her stranded. I knew how to push her buttons and she could definitely push mine. We brought each other to our breaking points, said things we didn't mean, and regretted them later. It was a tough couple of years for both of us.

The pinnacle occurred when my mom was knee deep in her divorce settlement. Predictably, her lawyer argued she could receive larger support payments, so Mom was to appear before a judge privately to argue her case. He would then deliberate the facts and announce the final settlement.

I learned that she intended to take Doug with her to testify in court *against his father*. I was mortified. How that translated into higher support payments made not a shred of sense, but her manipulation of my brother was the proverbial straw that broke the camel's back.

I blew a gasket. It was wrong on so many levels. I was enraged as I pressed her to explain what the hell she was thinking! Exasperated and uncomfortable, she snapped at me, shouting, 'I want you out! I want you out!' An unnerving silence fell over us as we both thought about what this meant.

The timing of this couldn't have been worse. I was thick in the final weeks of exams in my last year of high school. Thankfully, as often happens after a collision course of angry words said in the heat of the moment, cooler heads prevailed. I was not sent packing that day or that week. Nor did I attempt to leave home before school was officially finished.

However, in the weeks that followed, the sting of her words (I want you out!) were not retracted, so I looked for and found a one-bedroom apartment in a cheap, rundown Mississauga neighbourhood thirty minutes away. As soon as high school was finished, I moved myself and a suitcase of clothes—the total sum of my personal belongings—into a cramped, decrepit space, and waited, impatiently, for a room to free up in a four-bedroom townhouse near the University of Toronto in Mississauga campus I planned to attend in the fall.

I truly regret the timing of this. Leaving home when I did felt like I was abandoning my impressionable, younger sister. I had been there in the past to support her, direct her, and even parent her, but this time, I was too busy dealing with my own challenges to help her with hers.

I don't blame my mother. The experience of moving out, abrupt as it was, was bittersweet. It gave me time to reflect on relationships and how important a mother, *my* mother, was to me. I knew I could not let this define us or our future relationship, because I knew how lonely and painful that would be for both of us. So, I chose to accept her for who she was and was not, grit my teeth, and be thankful I had a mom who loved me. I had to remember that she had shown me, time and time again, that she would do anything for me.

Her words, and my subsequent actions, ended up being a blessing in disguise. I was forced to deal with my new reality and attend the school of hard knocks whether I liked it or not. The experience of living alone in a new city on a meagre income taught me how to survive and flex my independence. I fretted on a daily basis about whether my government loan (intended for university living costs) and my minimum-wage, part-time pay cheque would cover my rent *and* my food.

I learned how to do more with less, to budget, to be thrifty, and to leave something for tomorrow. The cost of everyday things my parents had managed to provide for me, that I took no notice of, gave me sticker shock! The price of a winter coat, a pair of no-name running shoes, or dining in a family restaurant were all suddenly massive expenses. I quickly learned how things added up without my notice, so I learned to do without, ate at home, searched for deals, clipped grocery coupons, and avoided waste. I put $5 of gas in my Volkswagen Beetle for my weekly excursions—no more. This meant by midweek I was driving with the low fuel light on and ran out of gas on a regular basis.

It was time for me to be a responsible adult, whether I was ready for it or not. Living frugally, working jobs, and making personal sacrifices became an important step in the next part of my journey.

My biggest lesson, however, was appreciating the things that cost me nothing—a positive outlook, humility, kindness, gratitude, spending time with friends—all things Mimi personified. As I passed fellow apartment dwellers in the lobby—middle-aged, pleasant, new immigrants—I was made acutely aware of their plight and how hard beginning a new life in a new country must have been. There they stood in their hand-me-down clothes, carrying multiple plastic bags in each hand containing all their worldly belongings alongside their week's groceries. They looked mortified when their kids (just being kids) ran amok in search of space to play, while disapproving adults shook their heads. In time, I saw a way out for me and hoped there would be one for them too.

I knew I had my health, my intellect, my dad's logic and discipline, and a deep sense of self to apply to my advantage. Moreover, I was fortunate to be accepted by a university, and I had the ability to commit to hard work and achieve great things.

I decided I would be accountable to no one but myself, because no one was helping me, and no one was coming to my rescue. My success or my failure would be no one's responsibility but mine. The seed was planted to forge my path as an independent, hardworking, and successful woman.

I have come to realize, in an odd and surprising way, I should be thanking my parents for having the strength and courage to try and make their marriage work for as long as they did *for the sake of the family*. I should applaud them for being honest with themselves, admitting failure and defeat, in order to search for happiness elsewhere.

Both my parents remarried in time, and they lived to experience many years in healthier relationships with better-suited life partners. I'm thankful that my dad had the courage to call it quits, for his own wellbeing and for the rest of us. When he fell out of love, he was strong enough to accept his fate and let it go.

Life is not meant to be spent in a miserable, unhealthy, or toxic relationship. This was something that I chose to never forget.

2

For the Love of Dance (And Learning to Fail)

As I stare into the rear-view mirror at my childhood, I cannot gloss over my childhood without sharing one of the most important facets of my early life and how it affected me in the many years to come.

My character was shaped by the hours upon hours I spent in a dance studio. While I was busy learning, practicing, and performing dance routines, I was developing the valuable life skills I would draw upon time and time again in later years.

The courage to use my voice in the boardroom was rooted in the stage confidence I acquired performing in front of hundreds and, later, thousands of people. My desire to excel, amplified by my inherent competitive nature, took its first steps on the dancefloor. And my pursuit of passion in my work and life was fueled by the emotions I experienced with my first love.

Can you look back at how your childhood and teenage experiences sculpted you into the person you are today? Did you play team sports, spend time at the back of the classroom drawing in your notebook, find a place on the debate club, or did you prefer spending nights at home with your nose buried in a book? What have you faced in your past that you draw upon in moments of insecurity or doubt?

Being aware of and reflecting on your strengths, your behaviours, your attributes, and your passions is critical. This knowledge allows you to understand what makes you *you.* Self-awareness gives you the ability to build upon your innate skills, rather than dwell on or be paralyzed by your limitations. When you merge your potential with your experiences and learned skills, your superpower is born.

Dance—the lessons it taught, the passion it ignited, and the behaviours I developed for my growth as a woman—was my first positive step towards self-discovery.

I've been told, at five years old, I was a clumsy and shy child. Who knew? So, my mom, convinced dance was my ticket to grace and confidence, marched me up the street to my neighbour's bungalow, where my dance teacher Mrs. Boynton lived.

Mrs. Boynton had a makeshift studio in her basement—no mirrors, no barres, no space. I learned to dance on a cold, concrete floor, with records playing in the background. These days I think about Mrs. Boynton as an incredible example of a woman who made so much out of so little—a woman who followed her passion to teach dance, doing whatever it took to do so.

Regardless of the small space, I immediately loved it, and in my mom's own unique way, she gave me the opportunity to pursue something she had not and could not have afforded herself—something I would use to draw upon in spades throughout my life.

I performed my first solo at six—a bunny hop tap dance sporting a white leotard with a fluffy bunny tail pinned to my butt and stand-up bunny ears my mom had sewn herself. My dad captured my premiere performance on his trusty 8mm camera, including my bunny bootie shake with Mrs. Boynton shouting in the wings of the school auditorium, 'Shake it baby, shake it!'

I performed my second solo a few years later after my successful audition with CHCH TV's *Tiny Talent Time*. This local show aired on Sunday afternoons and featured talented local kids performing their acts of dance, music, singing, and magic. I performed on the very last black and white show to be aired, missing my colour TV debut by a week! I had to wait another decade for my next chance.

The hardest part of this ordeal was not what you might think. My dance was perfectly executed, and had there been an audience in the studio, the pre-taped clapping would not have been needed!

No, what terrified me more than dancing alone in a daunting, barren studio on live TV, was my interview with the show's host, Bill Lawrence, prior to my performance. His question-and-answer banter was supposed to settle my nerves so I could put on a great show for the other dorky kids and their parents watching in the Greater Toronto Area.

Bill asked me my name, which of course I was ready for. But then he asked me the zinger... the name of the dance studio I attended! Now you would think this would have a simple answer: 'Mrs. Boynton's Basement.' But no, Mrs. Boynton would have none of this. She instructed me, in no uncertain terms, on the day of the TV taping, to say I danced at *Stewart's Dance Studio.*

Whaaaaat?

This made absolutely no sense to my nine-year-old brain. Where did this name come from? Who is Stewart and when did he pop into my class? It took every ounce of my energy and focus to remember her meaningless, fake dance studio name when I should have been preparing for my upcoming performance. But, as the ever dutiful, conscientious student, I answered, 'Mr. Lawrence, I go to *Stewart's Dance Studio.*'

Had Bill stopped there, all would have been great. I had completed the monumental task.

However, he asked me one more innocent question, 'Susan, how old are you?' My head was ready to explode. I blurted out, 'I'm eight.'

I was 9, damnit! I cracked under pressure all because of that Stewart guy I'd never met. The shame, the lies... how could I forgive myself?

Shortly after my TV debut, I felt like I'd hit the big time (hah!), and I stopped taking lessons with Mrs. Boynton. I enjoyed what I had learned in her basement, and dance came easy to me, but I had outgrown the Boynton's *and* the Stewart's.

So, my mom found a real dance studio, with space, mirrors, barres, elaborate recitals, national dance exams, and accredited teachers. Edwina's Dance Studio became my home away from home for the next ten years, and as every hour of my spare time was absorbed in dance, I began my steady transformation into a fit and graceful teen, just as my mom predicted.

As one of the studio's elite dance troupe members, I performed at gala events around Toronto and in competitions as far away as the Big Apple: New York City! I was given my first leadership role as captain of the studio's competitive Dance Twirl Troupe, comprising a subset of six of the best dancers from the baton corps I belonged to. I can't recall how I may or may not have inspired my team, but my young, growing ego adored it. Responsibility and titles made me feel special and important, and like a bear to honey, it was something I found myself attracted to achieving again and again in the future.

Dance became integral to life outside my home. It provided an important escape from my parents' unravelling marriage and a welcome relief valve from my self-induced pressure to excel in school. These were lessons I drew upon as an adult, but I need not wax poetic on how important exercise is to both physical and mental health, though it is incredible what a little sweat can do for your world perspective.

At 15, I took a big step and auditioned to be a Hamilton Tigerette: the baton twirling, professional cheerleaders for the Canadian Football League's Hamilton Tiger Cats. And I was successful!

Performing on national television when the Ti-Cats won the Grey Cup is my claim to fame—a huge step forward from *Tiny Talent Time!* My least fond memory was my costume... a skimpy, sequenced mini dress with white go-go boots (it was 1972), not to mention twirling a metal baton in Canada's frosty November temperatures.

After the Ti-Cats big win, the Tigerettes performed in Walt Disney World's Mickey Mouse Parade. It was much warmer in Florida for that silly costume, and although the park's visitors had no clue who we or the Ti-Cats were, generous crowds of smiling faces on vacation clapped as we twirled by.

I was living on cloud nine, and just when I thought my teen years were going to breeze by without a stumble in my step, life kicked me in the kneecaps, and I went tumbling ass over teakettle. The bruise from this fall was embedded so deep in my soul it took years to remove. I'm sad to say that a single moment dominated my inner voice for a very long time.

I believed with all my heart that my combination of dance, baton, choreography, and stage presence would translate nicely into a coveted cheerleading position for my high school sports teams, the Cougars. In my freshman year, I had attended every home game, both basketball and football, sitting in the bleachers with my long-time friend, Sandy. Together, we would belt out the words and clap to the rhythm of the cheers. So, it was only natural that the logical next step in Grade 10 would be to take this teeny, tiny little risk and try out for the North Albion Collegiate Institute's (NACI) cheerleading squad.

In my mind, a place on the cheerleading squad was the icing on my high school cake. I knew it was something I could excel at and have tons of fun with—a welcome diversion from mundane academics and much easier (for me) than trying out for a sports team. No doubt, I was influenced by the status that came with being an NACI cheerleader. They were unmistakably the most popular girls in the school, second only to the guys on the basketball and football teams they hung out with (and dated). I loved the fact that these girls didn't have to smoke cigarettes or drink alcohol to be considered cool. They were cool because they were talented, athletic, outgoing, and pretty.

I wanted to be like them. I didn't have a boyfriend, or really any experience dating at this stage, but I accepted this because I had a heavy schedule of dance lessons and studies. For this reason, I saw absolutely no harm in being a cheerleader hanging out with the popular crowd!

Tryouts were at the start of the school year and took place from 4-6pm every day for three weeks. The two teachers who managed the squad gave plenty of time for all the girls to learn the ropes, especially those with no prior dance or cheerleading experience. I liked that everyone would have a fighting chance to learn the routines, the jumps, and the cheers. I assumed they were looking for fit girls with coordination and personality.

I learned the routines, cheers, and jumps instantly; they were simple, and I performed them effortlessly. Many of the other sophomores struggled to execute the star jump and the side jump fluidly in succession, and I saw how this could be tough for a non-dancer. I was empathetic, so I spent much of my practice time teaching my friends how to become great cheerleaders, as did many of the experienced, returning squad members.

The tryouts took place in the gymnasium, each of us performing our routines individually for a group of five judges, which included three teaching staff and two students. The sixteen chosen girls would be posted on a bulletin board outside the school's main office. We all knew the results were to be posted later that night, so we waited with bated breath for the news.

Finally, a teacher appeared before the anxious crowd to pin the list on the wall. I will never forget that moment. I searched for my name, and then I searched again and again, struggling to peek around and over the heads and shoulders of all the other girls who had stayed late. All around me there were screams of joy, hectic jumping up and down, and clapping.

When the Red Sea of frenzied teenage girls finally parted, my stomach sank. I stood immobile, mortified, and shocked. My name wasn't on that list. I can't recall which sophomores made the squad, but the ones I taught were among them—another stab to my tender heart.

I simply couldn't make sense of how this could happen. Why was I rejected? I had coordination, I had talent, I knew the cheers backwards and forwards, and I had performed them without a mistake. I projected confidence in my voice as I bellowed out 'Go Cougars!' when I leaped high in my jumps. I was in great shape; I had a dancer's body. Surely, I had personality and stage presence? I was a professional cheerleader for the Hamilton Tigerettes for God's sake!

What were the judges looking for that I didn't have? What was I missing?

Then, I reached a heartbreaking conclusion… the only one left.

I'm not pretty enough.

Around this time, like most teenage girls, an emerging sense of self was developing as I constantly compared myself to others and asked, *How do I measure up?* My inner voice was a ruthless critic, and this was without pressure from social media's pretense of beauty, slimness, and the 'my life is grand' façade placed on the impressionable youth today. I can't even imagine growing up with those added pressures!

Instead of social media, I had my bedroom mirror. My hideous, oversized bump on the bridge of my nose (teenager voice talking!), a feature inherited from my mom, stared back at me, ugly and eternal. I'd always felt it was my Achilles heel, and failing to make the squad reinforced that fatal flaw. My feelings of inadequacy had been validated, along with the destruction of my vulnerable teenage self-worth.

I was a loser.

I trudged home that evening in tears. I cried and cried. My parents tried to comfort me, telling me the judges had made a huge mistake, and it was their loss. They told me I *was* pretty enough, that it was not meant to be, and I was better than this tryout. I tried to pick myself up and face the music, but all I heard was my inner voice crying out:

Sue, face it: you're not pretty enough!

My ego and self-esteem suffered in silence for years before I could overcome that rejection and believe that I could be pretty enough for any *one* or any *thing* again.

The following year, as a high school junior, I was encouraged by everyone—the cheerleading squad, the teachers, my friends, you name it—to 'please try out again!' But I couldn't bring myself to do it. In fact, hell would freeze over before I subjected myself to that embarrassment again. Even at that age, I subscribed to the saying, 'Fool me once, shame on you; fool me twice, shame on me.'

As it happens, in both my junior and senior years of high school, I was elected to the NACI Student Council as the Social Convenor by fellow students. This was a popularity contest, as most positions among teenagers in high school tend to be. I soon found this position was more about developing leadership and execution than beauty, which suited me just fine. As Social Convenor, my duties were to plan, advertise, oversee, and execute entertaining, sold-out student social events, which was easy-peasy for the extroverted, social butterfly I paraded as on the outside.

With the help of the teacher liaison, Mr. Hamill, who was also my geography teacher, we selected bands and DJs for the traditional Sadie Hawkins dance and the Sock Hop, as well as half a dozen other annual events which incorporated students dancing in the gym and secretly necking in the janitor's closet. For our lunchtime entertainment, Mr. Hamill cleverly sourced an old jukebox for the school's cafeteria, which we filled with my favourite 45s (records), but what I am most proud of was hiring The Stampeders ('Sweet City Woman' their claim to fame) for the annual spring dance while keeping within my frugal student budget. It was totally rad!

I built skills such as budgeting, building a team of volunteers, delegating, fundraising, and project managing. It was an opportunity to be responsible, get some practice at public speaking with my regular spot on the morning announcements, influencing and cajoling my peers into involvement, and I believe it was one of my first steps towards becoming a leader.

So, while the cheerleading fiasco left me with a hidden bruise that would take years and years to heal, I plowed ahead and made lemonade out of lemons with the time that would have been otherwise used to cheerlead. It was the painful rejection that allowed me to build upon my skills as a manager of people and set myself up for future success.

In an ironic twist of fate, at the start of my senior year, I was asked to be a judge for the cheerleading squad selection.

Oh, how the tables have turned!

It was high time for just retribution. I made a pact with myself: I was not going to let a talented, confident young woman—a diamond in the rough, so to speak—be overlooked for any squad that I had a hand in selecting. *No way.* Not on my watch.

Today, I can admit that I was borderline obsessed with this opportunity. I was in search of my mini-me in that group of young hopefuls: an ordinary, average-looking sophomore who performed the routines perfectly. And as luck would have it, I found her—the perfect match. Her name was Kelly. I hope I made her day. She definitely made mine. Righting the wrong by granting someone else the opportunity went a long way to repairing my soul.

What did I learn from this setback? Life isn't fair—some days it sucks. But when you are thrown off course, it's what you do next that counts. As my golf partner and bestie, Christiane, reminds me, 'Get over the bad shot you just made. It's how you react and recover for the next one that matters.'

Today, with all that I have experienced since, I reflect on how I should have put my disappointment in perspective. After all, it wasn't life threatening, and it rarely ever is. The setback did not break me or define me, because I found courage to move forward at something I was great at: organizing and leadership. I built resilience, and in it I found a lesson to learn from. I was learning to fail. I had also gained a friend and a mentor: Mr. Hamill.

During and after high school, I had two part-time jobs: one as a cashier at a nearby liquor store, and a second as a pseudo pharmacist's assistant/cashier in a drug store, keeping me extremely busy as I learned how to fend for myself. Nonetheless, I longed to return to dance class. The problem was that I could no more afford to pay for this fantasy on my dime than fly.

I missed the lift I received from exercise and the profound ability dance had as a social and spiritual outlet for my escape. To bridge the gap of my reality and my desire, when I started university, I asked the Sports Director if I could teach beginner adult jazz classes to my fellow students, and just like that I had two classes a week—an outlet for my passion, and a third part-time job to pay my bills. Bonus!

During this time, I learned of an opportunity to audition for a 'Cheerdancer' position with Toronto's first professional soccer team, the Toronto Blizzard. My inner voice shouted, *Don't do it! You know what happened last time; this is high stakes!* However, I knew I was stronger now, and I listened to my heart to overcome my fear.

I was elated to find the audition was assessing dance ability (my wheelhouse) more than cheerleading, and I was selected as one of twelve elite Blizzard Cheerdancers. At $35 per week for the full seven-month soccer season, our annual salary exceeded the pay of the Dallas Cowboys Cheerleaders!

The NASL's Blizzard soccer team was owned by Global TV in Canada, so to drum up interest and support for Canada's only team and their Cheerdancers, they produced a twenty-minute film called *The Making of a Blizzard Cheerdancer.*

As you can imagine... riveting stuff.

I was chosen to be filmed at the University of Toronto's Blind Duck pub. They framed it as a touching story of a part-time waitress working to pay her way through university, only to be chosen as a Cheerdancer and ripped from poverty.

Uh huh. I was swimming in coin like Scrooge McDuck over here…

What they actually filmed was a dark, seedy pub that was vacant, save for the college drunks and regulars who had skipped class to play pinball… and of course *me*, the starving student turned Cheerdancer. It was another classically Canadian TV appearance to add to my growing portfolio that will never see the light of day again.

At 21, I auditioned for a high-paying, summer dance job that surprised even me! I was hired to perform Greek folk dances at an upscale Greek restaurant in Toronto, seven nights a week with at least a two-hour return commute each night. With zero nights off, this job destroyed my social life. I put up with it because I discovered my new favourite food: anything that sounded remotely Greek! In addition, I learned to add a smidgeon of Greek, 'parakalou' and 'efharisto,' to my vocabulary, and I performed the *Hasapiko* like a pro!

To truly understand how big of an impact dance had on my life, you need only know that my high school yearbook stated that my ambition in life was to become a professional dancer. Dancing on Broadway under the footlights of New York City was my fantasy; a pipe dream.

Truthfully, there wasn't a snowball's chance in hell I would have had the courage to leave my little world in Rexdale to try something that risky and uncertain, but to see my dream in writing… well, it *inspired* me, and any time a chance came up to make even a smidgen of that dream come true, I took it.

So, what did all my years of dance teach me about myself? This is what I know for sure.

Dance prepared me for my greatest performance: the stage of life. From my countless performances, I learned to speak as the meeting chair in front of my superiors, and eventually give keynote speeches in front of hundreds of people, almost without butterflies. Often as the only woman in the room, I was poised and composed with C-suite executives, because dance taught me to think on my feet, literally!

Dance taught me to be prepared. Winging it invited intolerable embarrassment for me. Forgetting my dance steps on stage was a recurring nightmare I would wake up in a sweat over! That kind of outcome was unacceptable to me, so preparation became my mantra.

Dance developed my trust in others and the importance of showing up for them. Competition channeled my ambitious nature and energy in a positive way. These life skills helped me become a valued member of a team in the workplace.

I bet the saying 'practice makes perfect' was created by a dancer. When I had a challenging tap sequence to learn, a double pirouette to master, or a baton to catch after multiple revolutions in the sky, dance taught me to never give up. What I would have once considered impossible feats were eventually performed with ease after countless hours of focus, determination, and practice. I drew upon this learned strength and perseverance when I faced a taxing exam or when my resolve was tested.

To me, dance is math in an art form. Geometric shapes are made as your body moves in jazz or ballet, while tap dancing creates intricate sounds, taking the counting of full, half, and quarter time musical beats to a whole new level. My love of math was accelerated here.

I found what made me truly happy. It stirred my soul and I embraced it. Dance will always hold a special place in my heart, my body, and my mind. Did it help me become more poised and outgoing? Did it give me stage presence, and teach me discipline, time management, and confidence? You bet it did. But what matters most is how immensely happy it made (and still makes) me feel *inside*.

3

Hard Work: Does it Always Pay Off?

I inherited the hardworking gene from my father. I also have the perfectionist gene. Whatever I do, *it's never good enough,* which presents its own challenges. I'm not proud of this, but I have come to accept this is who I am, and I deal with it.

There are pluses and minuses to the hardworking and perfectionist genes. The *plus* is what you can achieve when you set high expectations for yourself, believe in yourself, have intention and purpose, and perform to your fullest potential. You can accomplish anything you set your mind to. The *minus* is the toll this kind of intensity takes on your health, your family, your colleagues, your friends, and anyone else who is dragged onto this merry-go-round of yours. Someone or something is always at risk to pay the price.

Growing up, I completed my homework and school projects without prompting or bribes. (I thought parents were supposed to offer bribes now and then?!) I didn't need external pressure; I applied plenty of my own, thank you kindly. I took pride in my work and found nothing wrong with spending countless hours and evenings working through my homework to get it *just right.*

As smart as I may have appeared on the outside, sciences and languages didn't come easy for me. I am a slow, methodical reader. I don't skim. I read every word repeatedly, going over one sentence again and again until I completely absorb its intended meaning. As you can imagine, this is time consuming, but I brought home glowing report cards, and developed into a conscientious honour student.

I thrived on praise and recognition from my parents. Pleasing them was very important to me. Their approval or accolades, no matter how often they dished it out, was never enough. I was also competitive, and I liked to compare my results not only to my peers, but also to my older brother. I carried a heavy dose of sibling rivalry, and any praise he received for completing his projects just-in-time with his average performance was not fair; I had higher marks and a better performance. I felt the limelight belonged to *me.*

I can't believe I remember this, but in grade two, I brought home a report card that I was very proud of—five As and two B+s. These were the best results I had ever received, and I expected a biblical flood of praise from my parents. Noah, gather the animals, prepare the barge!

The fleeting 'good job' I received didn't quite match up to the streamers and balloons reception I'd concocted in my young head, and like a sugar addict, I craved more.

Instead, I had to listen to my parents' exaggerated praise for Doug's report card of Cs, Ds, and his one oh-so-wonderful B. This was my parents' way of encouraging my brother to try harder and *be more like his hard-working sister* (my emphasis!). I understood why they did this, but I deplored them for it. My fragile, young heart was hurting.

However, whether they realized it at the time or not, my parents' outward restraint on celebrating my achievements taught a valuable, grown-up lesson to the needy and egotistical eight-year-old girl I was. I continued to work hard for their affections, but over time I learned not to let this bother me so deeply. I began setting goals and standards for myself, rather than for my parents, my teachers, and later, my bosses. I learned to be the best version of myself *for me*. I found satisfaction knowing that when faced with any project, goal, or roadblock, I would give it my all. It has served me well.

Although others may disagree, I don't believe I'm a workaholic. I consider myself highly disciplined, ambitious, driven, and competitive. You will never catch me apologizing for this.

In spite of my strong belief in my non-workhorse nature, for much of my working life I would be the last person to leave the office. On a yellow sticky note pinned to my office bulletin board, you would have found the phone number for Building Security, which I called regularly to get the lights turned back on. Cue thumb and index finger making a capital letter 'L' on my forehead.

FYI: Knowing the cleaning staff by name is not a good sign.

My thoughts typically go, *If I finish this assignment to my satisfaction, next time it will be easier; I won't have to work so hard next time.* But that next time never comes, so I replace next time with this time and appreciate the opportunity for another challenge; a chance to be more perfect.

My father was the same. After several years as a linesman climbing telephone poles, my dad's work ethic and capacity for more challenging work was recognized by his supervisors. His efforts paid off, and he was provided with an opportunity to work in the office as a Tester—a promotion from his blue-collar livelihood. In fact, a trailblazer himself, my dad developed the first 911 emergency call system for Canada! This led to a white-collar middle management position where he was considered a valued, loyal, dependable employee of Bell Canada until his retirement after 35 years.

Although I admit to my bias, my father was capable of more responsibility and a more senior management position at Bell Canada. He dreamed of improving his standing in life and, by inference, our family's, but his limited formal education trapped him. His progression took him only as far as a high school graduate could go. Nevertheless, his experience was a perfect coaching moment to ensure history didn't repeat itself for his ambitious, yet naïve, adolescent daughter.

It was the summer of 1976—my first as a high school graduate. I spent my summer working at Xerox, clearly impressing everyone I came in contact with as their competent Girl Friday. They wanted more of this bubbly, fresh-faced perfectionist, so I was offered a full-time position for a growing division in the Canadian head office of Xerox as… a Girl Friday.

My definition of this job, to be added to Wikipedia, is, 'To do odd jobs in the office for anyone who asks, including filing, delivering mail, xeroxing (at Xerox, no less!), and other tedious tasks no one else wants to do because they have *marketable* skills.'

My genuine desire for a steady income, more time with friends, and the end of spending late nights and weekends studying had me excited for this opportunity. Who could blame an 18-year-old for thinking this way? I was seriously considering this posting to be a viable career prospect, and this was in no way strange for people from my neighbourhood.

However, when this opportunity came knocking, I had already accepted a place at the University of Toronto in Mississauga (UTM) for the upcoming fall to pursue a Bachelor of Arts degree. Yet, my mind was suddenly focused on stashing money in my pockets versus three years of school with no plans for how my tuition, books, or rent would be paid for.

To be honest, I was sick of being poor. I wanted a fast track to gainful employment. I wanted to enjoy my life on *my* terms, instead of hustling with no end in sight.

My parents, but especially my father, were horrified by the thought of me entertaining this idea. But Dad kept his composure, and calmly explained how incredibly bright his daughter was, how proud he was, and how much more potential I had than this job at Xerox was offering. My dad believed in me more than I did, and this would be a recurring theme throughout my entire life.

I was a lower middle-class child living in a lower middle-class neighbourhood from a lower middle-class family. That's all I felt I would ever be. I didn't believe or know that I could pull myself out of Rexdale, because it was a big deal to dream big and dreaming big just wasn't something people like us did. No one in my family, nor anyone close to me, had gone to university or even tried to get out of our hometown. No one I knew had dreams about rising in society to be something more.

And then there was Mr. Hamill, my geography teacher/student liaison, who took me under his wing to teach me so much more than just his subject matter.

Looking back, I was blessed to have him as my teacher. Mr. Hamill must have seen something in me worth nurturing. I was living in my disrupted, one-parent family home, and though I was good at hiding my internal troubles, he must have seen through it when he took it upon himself to be a male role model. He supported and encouraged me to apply to university, listened empathetically when I needed to talk to someone other than my peers, and related to me in a non-preachy, non-teacher kind of way. He was the first of many mentors who subtly shared his years of wisdom with me, and by posing reflective, non-judgmental questions, he taught me to think for myself.

Beyond that, I became the proud owner of his 1968 Volkswagen Beetle which he 'sold' to me for $250 (not nearly what it was worth). He painted it a feminine Pepto Bismol pink for my maiden voyage to university life in Mississauga. But, most importantly, as a friend, he gave of his time generously and held me to the highest of expect-ations.

The respect I had for Mr. Hamill, added to the sage advice from my father, led me to be the first Allen in family history to attend university. I was soon followed by my younger sister, Cheri, after I pressed her to do the same.

My decision to get a post-secondary degree was a pivotal choice that would change the course of my life. I often wonder what my life what would have been like had I taken that Girl Friday job.

UTM was a friendly, lowkey campus on the western border of the Greater Toronto Area, its population a fraction of the downtown University of Toronto campus. The more traditional downtown Toronto campuses were certainly where the fun and action could be found, but that scared me more than interested me. I was afraid of what I was getting myself into without a single, trusted, 'been there done that' friend to guide me.

I decided to take a mixture of generic courses leading to a Bachelor of Arts degree, letting time decide what I would specialize in. With my dad's solid endorsement and encouragement, I was leaning towards becoming a schoolteacher. He liked the fact this would give me a professional designation and I could take the summers off—clearly an advantage, he thought, for a woman who may want to have a family one day.

I agreed, but also liked the thought of teaching because:

1. I am proficient at breaking down complex concepts into understandable chunks of information. *If I can understand this, anyone can.*
2. I like children and have a decent degree of patience.
3. I get inspired when I make a difference. I like to see a struggling student change from confusion to understanding, and I wanted to offer challenges to the gifted ones.
4. I wanted to emulate my teacher mentor, Mr. Hamill.

However, I had a black cloud hanging over me. My senior year grade of 54% in English class was shocking. How could this be? It was the lowest mark I had *ever* received, so much so that I thought a great conspiracy was afoot.

My English teacher, Mr. Smith, was a thinning, grumpy old man in a baggy, grey suit that hadn't fit him since World War II. He'd told me, in no uncertain terms during my senior year, that I was not cut out for university. If he'd heard I said no to the Girl Friday position, he might have had a stroke.

Mr. Smith shook my confidence. How was I going to succeed at university if I could barely pass my mother tongue? To make things worse, I had no one to ask what would be demanded of me in university, because no one that went to my school *went* to university. I didn't know whether I had the chops for the challenge. It terrified me.

My first university essay was due six weeks into my first term. This, I decided, would be the tell-all answer to Mr. Smith's dark prediction. The essay was 5000 words for my second year Urban Geography course, which I had elected to take in my first year because it sounded interesting and cool.

I chose to research, analyze, and write on the topic of the 'Staple Theory of Economic Development in Canada.' Captivating stuff. I considered the topic with intellectual curiosity and gravity. I allowed myself plenty of time to produce a report that was insightful with convincing arguments.

Although I was proud of my first essay, I submitted it with the trepidation of a child dipping her toes in sea water for the first time. I placed my faith and my fate in this essay—this was my answer to whether I was good enough for university.

But my worries were all for not. The stars aligned, and with an 89% on my essay, I'd received one of the highest marks awarded in the class. Take that Mr. Smith... along with a big, fat raspberry! Would you be surprised if I told you I mailed him a copy?

Well, I didn't, but you can be damn sure I thought about it.

What did I learn from this? That I shouldn't be surprised when I encounter naysayers. I learned that they weren't my allies, and they never had my best interests at heart. If I avoided them and steered clear of their negativity, I couldn't get caught up in their pessimism. Instead, I had to rise above them, listen to my heart, and trust in myself.

Yet, as I look back at myself, with more essays written, late nights studying, classes attended, and friendships made, I see a naïve university student trying to obtain a Bachelor of Arts degree in Urban Geography and Drama. What the hell was I thinking? How did I end up with this unlikely combination of subjects? More importantly, what was I going to *do* with that?

Although my journey through university was full of excitement, personal growth, making friends, and building memories, I was no closer to knowing what I wanted to be when I grew up. Moreover, I was up to my eyeballs in debt with government-funded student loans.

But I'll have you know my original plan was not *completely* flawed. I thought a teacher with a Geography and a Drama specialty could be an asset, an economical hire, justifying one salary for a teacher performing the work of two, especially given how unrelated my two fields of study were.

But the cards did not fall my way. In 1979, when I graduated, there was a surplus of university graduates who, like me, were choosing the teaching profession. Besides, I required another two full years of study in Teachers College, and I was apprehensive about graduating in two years with no better prospects for a job. This sounded risky and, frankly, I was worried about compounding my university debt.

Strike One.

Okay, so if teaching wasn't in the cards, maybe I could be an Urban Planner for a municipality? After all, I obtained a specialist degree, and that had to help, right? Wrong. A master's degree in Urban Planning was required before a prospective employer would even look at my resume. I couldn't even work as an intern without further education (or connections). That seemed like a lot of time studying for a career I wasn't convinced I would like or even be good at.

Strike Two.

The 1979 job market in Toronto was finicky at best. Highly qualified, engineering graduates and MBAs were moving west to work in Alberta's oil sands with Calgary offering the best opportunities for employment in all of Canada. These jobs were offered to our engineers and MBAs, not your run-of-the-mill Urban Geography/ Drama types.

Strike Three, and I'm out on the street with a boatload of debt and no career prospects.

I was lost. I'd put in the work, and I was the first Allen to graduate from university, but what good had it done me? I was no closer to a career than when I'd started. Girl Friday at Xerox was starting to look pretty darn good right about now, *Dad.*

At first, I blamed others for my predicament. Why had my dad and Mr. Hamill failed me?

I began to question just whose dream I was following. Was I becoming a teacher for my dad or taking a geography specialty for my teacher? When push came to shove, teaching and geography didn't draw my heart in deep enough to take the risk to practice either of them. Had I blindly accepted others' suggestions?

Thinking back on those days, I know now that something went wrong. I was going through the motions of being a university student, not knowing what I was doing and letting the chips fall as they may. I was too busy working and being perfect at something I didn't even care about. I was blind to the long term.

Finished with university and desperate to find the silver lining in my misguided journey, I sat down and justified my time and debt, if only so I could sleep at night:

- I developed writing skills useful to just about any field of work. (Maybe even a book someday...)

- I learned how to research, take a position, and argue it.

- I learned how to prioritize competing demands on my time between work, school, and my social life.

- I learned to live on my own as well as with others and became more tolerant and accommodating of other people.

- I had a bachelor's degree from a world-class university.

When I accepted responsibility for my actions, or in this case, *my inaction*, I saw the glass half full. So, I set a new lifelong game plan.

Passion would be my new guidepost. I would carry on with my positive attitude to comfort my bad days, be open to where the bus I'm driving takes me, and I would find work that made me happy and fulfilled. One caveat to all that? This plan had to help me rise above the economic status I was born into.

It was time to put it into action.

REFLECTION

How our earliest memories and experiences shape us

There is a lot to unpack when you consider what is learned in childhood and how deeply this influences our view of the world. It's more than we realize, and certainly more than I ever realized until I took the time to breathe, sit down, and write this book. You have no idea how cathartic this has been for me. I wish someone had told me to reflect on my formative years and write down my thoughts forty years ago.

I guess I'm the one telling you now.

Family, relationships, upbringing, mentors, successes, and setbacks have a profound impact on how we see the world. They shape our values and our outlook. As young adults, often without realizing it, we begin to set goals that ignite (or dampen) our passions and nurture (or obliterate) our ambitions. As our frontal lobes are still forming, half-baked judgments and weighty decisions made in haste bear consequences. We begin to carve out a life and a future to be proud of, or regret.

But here's the best part. While our early experiences and the life we are quite *randomly* born into shape us, we are not fixed by them.

Our past doesn't have to dictate our future. We can change our outcome. I am proof of this.

These are the lessons I learned from my childhood:

- Appreciate the many things in life that cost you nothing: a positive outlook, humility, kindness, and gratitude. Let's call it 'The way of Mimi.'

- Have the strength and courage to recognize when you are in an unhealthy, toxic relationship and get out before it takes you to the dark side with it.

- Reframe your circumstance and take time to consider how bad things really *aren't*. When you find the silver lining, you will learn how to put your disappointments in perspective. You will learn how to fail, because failure really isn't that monster under the bed that you've made it out to be.

- Don't let your choices paralyze you. Neither should naysayers dissuade you from your dreams. Admittedly, whatever path you choose may involve regrets. Move forward, grow, and learn from your choices; recover from your mistakes. Once made, hold yourself accountable for your actions. And by all means, celebrate your successes; I'm betting there are more than you give yourself credit for!

- Try to be self-aware. Build upon your innate skills and your learned experiences to develop your full potential. This is what you do well and likely what you enjoy most. When you merge what comes easily to you with what is the most fun, you have found your passion. Go for it! This is the end game.

I really want you to work on the self-awareness bit, so I've provided you some optional reflective questions to help you find clarity on what you have just learned. If you just wish to keep reading, please do so. But I encourage you to revisit these questions when you are ready.

Reflection Questions

1. How have your experiences in childhood shaped the person you have become?

2. List your strengths, behaviours, and attributes. How will you become more self-aware?

3. Are you living your most authentic life? Are you being true to yourself? What tweaks or adjustments are needed today for you to be better aligned with your values and your wants?

Part II: Setting a Course

Never underestimate the power of purpose and passion to set (or reset!) your compass.

I am fascinated by the twists and turns life can take—it's never a linear path.

If it was, life would be boring, wouldn't it?

Still, sooner or later, our lives have a way of falling neatly into place, the way they were always meant to be. But who or what is guiding us towards the path we are meant to take?

What is the secret sauce that brings meaning and purpose to our lives? Is it chance, coincidence, accident, karma, or destiny?

I believe it is only when we grant ourselves the freedom to look past self-imposed limitations and society's expectations that we can spot new opportunities as they present themselves. It is only when we draw upon inner strength to bolster our confidence, listen to our gut, and maintain a mindset that says, 'You can do this!' that those new roads are forged and diverging paths are revealed.

In my experience, all new opportunities deserve a fresh look, even those that appear to chase dead ends, are surprisingly far-fetched, or carry uncomfortable risks. *If you don't buy a lottery ticket, you can't win the lottery.* It is only when we let down our guard and choose new possibilities that we allow ourselves to experience new beginnings.

When I think about my university years, I am surprised by the unexpected maturity I demonstrated at twenty-three. Despite my continuing naivety in life, I *was* understanding and kind to my shriveled self-esteem. I cut myself slack for veering off track, and I resisted the temptation to rush into anything new because, frankly, I was fresh out of ideas on what I wanted to be when I grew up. Although a complete but inapplicable bachelor's degree weighed heavy on my spirit, I granted myself the luxury of time to push pause and reconsider my future before I ever considered pushing reset. The next step was to ask myself some tough questions. Questions I wished I had asked my younger self. Questions I didn't have the answers to.

What am I good at? What motivates me? Is there a job out there that I would be proud to go to every morning? If that job exists, how do I find it?

My long and winding road of life has taken many twists and turns—too many to count—and I am better for each of them. However, the most surprising and essential fork in my road, the one you are about to read, is my home run.

4

Working to Live or Living to Work?

At the start of my first College semester, I randomly applied for and was hired to assist the University Registrar's Office with their overflowing workloads. My job was to process student tuition cheques and match them against their outstanding fees and course load. It was an easy role that paid an above average hourly rate for a keen (starving) student.

I worked at the Registrar's Office for six semesters, so when I graduated without a job in hand, the Registrar asked if she could help. There was a job opening in her department, and she encouraged me to apply. Ironically, this position at the university only required a high school degree as its prerequisite. Go figure.

I needed a job. I needed the money to pay back university loans. I needed to feel I was working towards something better, and I also needed a freakin' break from school. I thought I could use this opportunity to pause, breathe, and figure out what I should do next with my graduate cap on.

I was hired in the summer of 1979—my first permanent job paying the paltry sum (even for 1979) of $10,000 annually. It included health benefits and free tuition towards any courses I might take while employed. My title was—*drumroll, please*—'Cashier, Erindale College.' How incredibly ordinary and unappealing for someone obsessed with titles, but I had to start somewhere, and this was a steppingstone. It was my time to grow up, be responsible, and reflect.

I learned the duties of the Cashier position within a few weeks. What surprised me the most, however, was that I found the whole concept of *debits* and *credits* exciting! This was my first exposure to bookkeeping, and I enjoyed learning about how everything must balance and how various transactions then flowed into their rightful place in the bigger picture. In the past, I never had occasion or the slightest inclination to ask what accounting was and therefore, never gave it a second thought. Yet, accounting was a natural extension of my love of all things math related—my favourite and best subject in high school.

You may be asking: If math was such a love of yours, and you were good at it, why didn't you get a Bachelor of Math or a Bachelor of Commerce degree? *That is an excellent question.*

Rather than receiving the critical pieces of guidance counsellor advice I desperately needed, my fate was determined by three other factors:

1. As a female, I was not *supposed* to pursue science, technology, engineering, or math (the 'STEM' fields), because these were reserved for the more capable male students.

2. I, along with the rest of my high school graduating class, were not *supposed* to go to university. Community college or full-

time work were the recommended post-high school options we were expected to follow.

3. I had limited access to professional career information or role models who had been there and done that. My only positive exposure was to Mr. Hamill, a geography major, and look what I went and did!

My high school guidance counsellors never bothered to gear me towards my obvious strengths. I was never granted so much as a meeting with either of the two guidance counsellors hired to help kids like me decide what I should do after high school.

And why should they give me the time of day? I wasn't expected to go anywhere, or ever work or live more than a few kilometers from where I'd grown up. But I had thrown a monkey wrench in the typical fact pattern they'd always followed, and apparently, they didn't know how to deal with me.

One thing they *did* insist on preparing me for was a life behind a secretary's desk. Given that it was the 1970s, all girls were required to take typing (really!) along with a course in shorthand. These clerical subjects were offered with the practical purpose of preparing fine young women like myself for a career as a trusted secretary for male bosses in leadership positions who sported the science, business, and engineering degrees.

Ironically, I had the last laugh. With the introduction of personal computers and their indispensable role in our future, my forty words per minute on the QWERTY keyboard created a distinct advantage. How many two-finger typists wished they were required to take 'Introduction to Typing' when they were freshmen? Enough said.

In the beginning, my cashier work was new and interesting. I gravitated to the office environment and enjoyed working with the older women, learning what they did for the Registrar, seeing the big picture whenever I could, and trying to help as a member of a larger team. We all reported to a man, who was the only male in the office.

Accounting came easy to me. In record time I was looking for more challenging projects around the office to entertain myself with, because I was typically finished my entire day's workload by 9:30am.

Unfortunately, I started my day at 9am. Standing around waiting for something to do was like holding my feet over hot coals all day, just grinning and bearing it—I was going insane! I needed to keep busy doing something, anything, and after a few weeks, the honey-moon was over. I was desperately bored, restless, and frustrated.

Enter my friend and saviour, Bess. She graduated with a teaching degree with no immediate prospects of a job and was hired as the Fees Officer for Erindale College. The best part of this arrangement was that she sat just outside my office!

I already had my own office due to the fact I dealt with heaps of cash on the regular—Erindale's very own queen in the counting house, counting out the money; a bizarrely similar task to stacking and counting my granddad's quarters. Who could have seen that coming?

Within a few weeks, Bess too was desperate to add challenge to her routine. So, I taught her my job responsibilities and she taught me hers. We took turns doing each other's work and would still be hungry for more by 10:00am. Seriously, I don't know how the rest of the office kept busy all day long at their jobs! What were they doing that took up so much of their time?

It was the peak of our Canadian summer, and neither of us cherished being stuck inside and twiddling our thumbs from 10 to 5.

So, we devised a plan. We went to our respective bosses and negotiated a job-sharing arrangement. I worked two consecutive days one week and three consecutive days the next, while Bess worked the alternating three days and two days. We covered for each other; two positions for the price of one overqualified employee.

This was a win-win for me and the College. I basked in the Canadian summer sunshine during my extra days off, reclaimed my social life, became more serious with a fellow university grad I had been dating, and Erindale College saved on their budgeted salary costs. Unfortunately, our negotiations didn't include paying us on our days off. We weren't *that* good.

It was great while it lasted, but once student registration ramped up in early September, Bess was shifted back into her role completing her busy work as a Fees Officer, while I remained trapped in the most undemanding job on the planet.

The one perk? The job gave me exactly what I needed: oodles of time to think about what I wanted to do next.

This job also taught me a very important lesson.

I would never, *ever* settle for unchallenging work again—it made me feel miserable. I made a promise and a commitment to keep myself busy and challenged from that day forward, and this would remain top of mind for me, regardless of what came next, because the alternative was agony. You could call it a curse to crave this type of work, but for me it was deliberate and sanctioned; a decision I would never regret.

However, I don't regret my time at the Registrar. There is a benefit to performing work beneath one's capabilities, be it tedious, manual, clerical, repetitive, or labour intensive. It gives you first-hand knowledge about yourself and helps you decide how you want to spend your future and make a living.

I believe many students found their second wind, and kick-started their motivation to work harder at university, after working a repetitive summer job that didn't challenge them. What better way is there to motivate yourself and find a renewed sense of commitment and determination to improve your study habits and marks?

Of course, there is nothing wrong with accepting or preferring tedious work. I know many people that find great joy and comfort in repeating a task over and over to perfection. What matters is that you find work that *fulfills* you, work that doesn't feel like work. In doing this, you are more likely to exceed expectations, and find joy in your day.

But for those of us who crave challenging work in a demanding, ever-changing environment, we must always be prepared to ask more of ourselves.

I was only three months into my first permanent job since graduating, and I decided it was time to take advantage of the benefit I received as a college employee: free tuition!

So, without further delay, I enrolled in an 'Introductory Accounting' course. I wanted to explore what I liked most about my Cashier position and to see what else I could learn about the exciting field of debits and credits. If I wasn't going to be kept busy with my day job, at least I could pass the time improving my skills while completing my homework on Erindale College's dime.

Little did I know this course would be the catalyst I needed. A few weeks into my class, I had my 'aha!' moment. I learned, quite by accident, over small talk with a classmate, that there was a professional business designation that used accounting as its foundation. What? Amazing!

It seemed the entire class knew about this business designation, and they were tackling this difficult entry-level course as a prerequisite to becoming a Chartered Accountant. (In Canada, now called a Chartered Professional Accountant or 'CPA').

Within a few short weeks, we were barely past the first few lessons in the textbook, and I realized I was just scratching the surface of this field in my Cashier position. I learned there was a *whole world* of accounting I didn't know existed. I felt like Lucy stepping into the wardrobe and plopping out the other side in Narnia—there was just so much to learn, and I was chomping at the bit to explore this new field more fully.

While making friends with my classmates, I learned future CPAs took intern positions with accounting firms. There were eight Global Firms (called the Big 8), several mid-tier firms, and smaller sole proprietorships accredited to take students for internships.

I learned the Big 8 Accounting firms recruited for intern positions on my college campus every fall. How fortuitous! I registered for two more prerequisite courses in the CPA suite: 'Introduction to Economics' and 'Introduction to Computer Science.'

If you've ever been in this position, then you'll understand this well. I suddenly had purpose, intention, and a clear vision in mind, and my studying took on new meaning. It was difficult, but it was also exciting, eye-opening, and it filled me with a vigour I had never felt in my previous four years of university. Best of all, as long as I was working as a cashier, class was free!

I applied to each of the Big 8 Accounting firms, and to my complete surprise, I received a first interview with five of them! To this day I'm convinced the interviewers just wanted to meet the dancer with a Bachelors in Geography/Drama trying to become a bean counter. I'd ask a few questions of that person too!

I was pitted against Bachelor of Commerce graduates with accounting skills and experience I was sorely missing. I had three *introductory* accounting courses under my belt, with fifteen more business courses to go just to be eligible to write the CPA exam. Both the recruiters and I knew it would take a minimum of two to three years to complete these courses while working full-time with their firm.

I was clearly a long shot, but time and time again, I made it to the next stage of the interview process. They started to enthusiastically sell to me on why I should accept an offer with their firm over the others I was interviewing with. For some reason I couldn't fathom at the time, they were competing for my acceptance. Astounding.

I found out later that the recruiters saw passion oozing from my veins and sensed my determination. I sat in their office, a ball of energy, asking for a chance to prove myself and for them to believe in me. I had found my passion, and they noticed.

So, do I think it matters if you go through high school and even university not knowing what you want to be when you grow up?

If you've been paying any attention, then you know the answer is *no*.

However, when the time comes that you do find your passion, a university degree still goes a long way. You learn life skills such as perseverance, sticking to and making priorities, developing study habits, and finding a balance. A degree gives you credibility and a solid foundation to prove you are worth the risk. It's a clear advantage when choosing between two similar candidates, because the university graduate will always have the upper hand.

What my experience has also taught me is that age is generally irrelevant when it comes to pursuing your passion. I am torn when I see twenty somethings forced into fields of study to fulfil their parents' dreams, while often ignoring their own. Or when I see these young minds, like sheep, apply to colleges where their friends are going, work toward degrees their friends are taking, and accept the same jobs their friends are being offered.

How strongly can I say this...

You are truly, really going to be fine if you're 25, or even 45, and you don't have your entire life mapped out for you!

Moreover, and this may come off as blasphemy to any of you fellow baby boomers raising a young adult, perhaps parents shouldn't be the ones directing their child's future? Perhaps children should be nurtured in an environment of discovery, rather than forced down a path that is not their own?

Consider the consequences of this forced approach.

A creative, well-spoken teenager loves to read historical fiction, writes poems, and keeps a diary. She wants to be an award-winning journalist one day, but instead of pursuing this, she listens to her parents who tell her she is better off becoming a doctor. She doesn't have the mind for science, nor the chops to stick to such a demanding program, and she flunks out after several desperate years trying to make her parents happy. She's depleted her parents' bank account along with her resolve to continue post-secondary anything. She has disappointed her parents and herself, choosing neither medicine nor journalism, and the world is deprived of her talent as her abilities and her passion fall to the wayside.

Think of the well-intentioned dad with an exceptionally high aptitude for a sport; as a proud Canadian, let's say hockey. He was encouraged to pursue this, but was passed over for the NHL, because like the majority of really good hockey players, he wasn't *good enough*. Dad, however, has visions of raising an elite, Olympic athlete from his DNA—his offspring. Sadly, his protégé doesn't get the chance to be a child or decide if this future is what *they* want. But it is all they know, because they've been training in their dad's sport from the time they could walk. What if they don't make it either?

It's your decision and your life. If you rush into something because it's what your parents want or what your friends are doing, you shortchange yourself. And if you have to push reset to start over? *So be it.* You owe it to yourself to become the person you were meant to be.

I was 23 years old with an irrelevant degree, guided down a path that wasn't my own, but I made that 'late' course correction. So, it stood to reason that I could hardly believe I had a choice of which firm to select.

After multiple interviews and sales pitches, there was no contest. Though it wasn't the reason I chose them, I picked the only firm whose name I had actually heard of: Price Waterhouse. It had international recognition for its part in balloting the gold standard of award ceremonies, the Academy Awards.

There was, of course, more to my decision than the Price Waterhouse brand. I met friendly, open, and engaged staff working in their office, and most impressive was the Audit Partner, David, who interviewed me in the office. Just a few weeks earlier, I had the privilege of hearing him speak at the university about why he had become a CPA, and I was inspired by his journey with Price Waterhouse (now called PricewaterhouseCoopers LLP or PwC). He epitomized everything I wanted to be as a professional. In fact, he blew my socks off, and I knew I would be proud to tell people, 'I work at PwC.'

Two years to the day after I landed my first permanent job with Erindale College, I happily resigned from my Cashier position, and on June 5, 1981, I entered the Mississauga office of PwC to begin my 'Student in Accounts' intern position with fifteen other fresh young faces—three women and twelve men. My starting salary was a whopping $15,000 (a 50% increase from my Cashier salary!). I accepted my written offer with gratitude, signed on the dotted line, and so began my dream come true.

5

Trauma, Growth, and Renewal

When I accepted my intern position at PwC, the idyllic fairy tale I had conjured up in my mind was flawed. That shouldn't surprise you. In spite of my sunny disposition, I was profoundly naïve. I under-estimated how exceedingly difficult this career thing would be.

My deep-seated insecurities, inexperience, and imposter syndrome arrived just in time to stomp on me and my dreams. Thankfully, they were soon quieted by the most supportive and considerate managers I had ever known. As my feet were sinking in quicksand (i.e., I was freaking out), colleagues came to my rescue and pulled me out. I watched and learned, and years later, I would pay this forward.

Life is never black and white, is it? Just as my career was beginning to take shape, my home life with my university boyfriend was rife with conflict. White had mixed with black, and a repulsive dark grey had formed. My heart and the promise I made to my grandfather to be true to myself could not be quieted. But with everything else going on my life, I pushed it aside as best as I could.

It didn't help that my first two weeks at PwC were traumatic. I, like everyone else who had accepted job offers, was required to attend *Level 1*—PwC's training course for new starts.

The problem, however—completely manufactured but thoroughly ingrained in my mind—was that my wealthy peers were Bachelor of Commerce (BComm) graduates from reputable universities across Canada, while I was a lowly, uninformed, wannabe accountant with a geography major who was just scraping by and knew nothing about what we had just signed up for: *auditing.*

My inferiority complex against the BComms plagued me for years, despite my best efforts to ignore the negative inner voice whispering in my ear every chance she got:

Sue, you aren't good enough.

The last thing I wanted to do in this training course was leave a bad first impression on my esteemed PwC colleagues, so I didn't dare show how green I was. I could recite aspects of the 'Staple Theory of Economic Development in Canada', but this was not the forum for my dissertation. My inexperience in all things accounting was about to be exposed.

On the first day, we were seated in prearranged table groups and asked to 'develop the correcting journal entries for the provision for doubtful accounts and post to the g/l' after which we would be called upon to give our solution to the rest of the class.

Uhhhh, what? I looked to the door. My inner voice was deafening. I was in serious trouble now. *What the hell is a g/l and why are posts involved? Are we building a fence or learning to audit?* There was no way I was going to participate in this discussion, and this was the morning of the first day!

I faced my imposter syndrome on overdrive. *How did I get here? I shouldn't be here. I don't deserve to be here. Get me out of here!* I was a bundle of nerves, gripping the edge of the table to quiet my shaking hands. Worse, I drank *a lot* of coffee, which just made me more jittery, though it did also make for frequent trips to the restroom where I could take a moment to myself and breathe.

There was another thing bothering me, however, that was beyond my ineptitude, though I should have seen it coming.

As was typical in the early 1980's, fewer women graduated from university than men, and even fewer graduated with business (or engineering, law, or medicine) degrees. Hiring 'the brightest and the best' candidates often involved hiring predominantly men. This meant there were very few women hired for accounting and even fewer in PwC's introductory class. I had no one to bond with.

I didn't know a soul in the Level 1 course. In my class of thirty-five interns, five were destined for the Mississauga office, including me. Everyone else knew at least someone in the course, and many knew the majority. Why wouldn't they? They had spent the past four years together obtaining their BComms!

However, I set my sights on making the most out of a bad situation, attempting to introduce myself and possibly make some friends with the four guys hired to join me in Mississauga. I hoped they felt the same way about getting to know me.

Instead, it went from bad to worse. For ten excruciating days, these four guys went to lunch together, and it wasn't just any lunch either. Our course was held in a hotel near the Toronto Pearson Airport, so there were plenty of 'men only' eating establishments in the area. Yes, that's right, the 'brightest and best' of my esteemed colleagues chose to go to The Men's Room, a bar *for men only*. It never dawned on them to ask me to join them for lunch, not that I would have accepted *that* invitation. I was the only female, and I felt invisible.

So, there I sat in class, paranoid and wondering how the hell I earned a place at PwC—a fraud and an outcast, eating lunch *alone* every day. Had there been a single other woman in the Level 1 course, I knew we would have made each other feel more comfortable. However, to my great disappointment, the two other women slated to join the Mississauga office, Kathy and Laurie, were not starting until the fall.

I didn't know them, but I couldn't wait to meet them. I believed, as women, we would find common ground in our gender and would *want* to support each other in our climb up the corporate ladder.

I got the opportunity to test this theory when Kathy and Laurie joined the rest of our cohort three months later. I was so right. They became two cherished, lifelong friends, and we joined several other bright, ambitious young women in the office, each of whom had their sights set on climbing the ladder with me. We had much to overcome as women in business and just as much to celebrate when we did.

As women, we owe it to ourselves to support, not criticize or undermine, our female colleagues. I believed that then, and I believe it now. Many of us are already our worst internal critics, afraid to put our hands up or ask for a promotion. There has never been any room in my world for the fire-breathing dragons of Corporate America who feel their ride to the top involves stepping on other women along the way. That is so 1950.

Our path is hard enough without backstabbing. I've seen those dragons, who climbed the corporate ladder decades earlier, attempt to squash other women, dumping their pain from their years of adversity on us because we have it 'easier.' We should never have reason to pounce on the brave women who come after us; they deserve to be encouraged, mentored, and supported to succeed.

To be clear, an underperforming female colleague should be called out for bad work. Her performance must be addressed, just as it would be for an underperforming male colleague. What I *am* saying is women shouldn't be *harder* on their fellow women than they are on the men—cut them some slack for Pete's sake! Women have enough to overcome in the workplace without malicious backroom gossip, and helpings of 'It's hard out there! So, suck it up, buttercup!' to toughen them up. If we are concerned about facing competition from our female colleagues, good for us *and* them.

Before my female reinforcements arrived, there were three *long* months to hold down the fort as the only female intern at PwC Mississauga. I felt like I stood out from my group, and while this was not the last time I was the only female in the room, it was the *first*, and it was incredibly difficult.

I pondered whether I was on equal footing with my peers. Was I being placed under a microscope more than the men? I had no way to know if my intuition was correct, but decided if this *was* the case, I would do whatever it took to manage others' perceptions of me. I would be evaluated on my strengths as an individual rather than letting my natural feminine qualities, whatever those were, hold me back or get in the way. I decided that unconscious biases in my workplace would not govern my future or any other woman's future at PwC if I had anything to say about it.

Little did I know how true those words would become.

To my relief, the rest of my summer in the PwC office was infinitely more bearable than those first two weeks of training.

As an entry-level auditor, my physical place of work was not the PwC office. I worked in the field (i.e., the client's premises). In fact, at my level, there were only two reasons I should have been in the office at all: to complete my administrative tasks, or if I was *unassigned*. To be unassigned meant you had no billable hours to invoice, which meant you were not adding revenues or profits to PwC's bottom line. At any level, this is a recipe for a pink slip.

My PwC colleagues recognized I was behind in my business acumen and accounting knowledge, so they did a smart thing to support me. They assigned me to client work that was relatively straightforward and 'clean,' which meant my clients were easy to work with, well prepared for our arrival, and had accounting staff often consisting of other talented CPAs. Moreover, my immediate PwC supervisors were technically strong and considered to be the most respected teachers and mentors in the office. My team did everything in their power to set me up for success, and it was up to me to make the most of it, so I damn well did.

With patience and mentoring, I grasped the basics—the technical concepts of auditing, what tasks I was to perform, and what was expected of me. I asked probing questions to better understand my duties and how the client's business risks affected our audit scope. Fortunately, my role predominantly involved documenting my client's answers to PwC's tried and true questionnaires, which were then verified with my independent testing. I had a good roadmap to follow, along with last year's files where similar steps were performed.

Learning was 100% practical, just-in-time, and on-the-job. This was instrumental to building my auditing skills from the ground up in a way that made the work easier to understand and apply. I had no preconceived notions, and I accepted what was asked of me, whether that was getting coffee, proofreading tax returns, testing bank reconciliations, or adding columns in a financial statement. It was easy to be positive and enthusiastic! This job was lightyears ahead of my Erindale College cashier duties, and I was never bored.

In some ways, a completely irrelevant geography degree served me well. I knew nothing, and out of necessity, I asked a ton of questions, never holding back. This was my chance to learn as much as I could from the best teachers in the office while there were no expectations. I knew that, in twelve short months, I would no longer have that luxury. Expectations would be placed upon me, and I would be asked to train the next crop of newbies in the office. The time to ask questions was *now*.

There are no stupid questions. I would rather risk asking a stupid question, if there is such an animal, than lose valuable learning time struggling on point A, while others have moved on to points B, C, and D without me. In all the classes and meetings I have attended, I don't blame myself for not grasping a concept. I'm not stupid. There is a 99% chance someone else is struggling along with me. That goes for you too!

Asking questions to clarify understanding is not a sign of weakness, but a sign of strength and confidence.

As the weeks went on at PwC, I realized I was born to audit. I am curious—a prerequisite for auditors whose secret weapon is to ask questions in nauseating detail. It was my job to understand how a company's internal control systems worked, to look for weaknesses, and to identify compensating controls to prevent them. After I completed the audit, I would check to ensure the financial statements were free of material errors. That was what the firm and my clients were paying me for.

I may have been born to question, but as an auditor, my questioning techniques needed perfecting. My earliest clients dealt with my misguided, probing questions which were misunderstood. I shrunk when the finance staff's answers were a waste of my time, taking me down a rabbit hole I had no desire to enter. But I listened and nodded politely. *Practice patience, be patient.*

Sometimes, I would speak to a junior accounting clerk, and during their innocent explanation of a journal entry they made, I would uncover an error that seemed obvious to me—a significant one. This would take diplomacy and thinking on my feet. What words do I use to explain how they have made such a blatant error? Who's going to tell their boss? *I hope I haven't sealed their fate with this company*. How tragic that would be! Whose job is it to ask them to correct it?

At other times, I identified a weakness in my client's system of internal controls, because I quickly learned that I have a mind made for finding loose chinks in the chain. There were many times I saw that a control my client was relying on could easily be exploited by a dishonest employee, or when computers were introduced into the workplace, an outside hacker.

How was I supposed to explain my devious criminal mind at work, finding holes in places they thought were airtight? It took me some time to navigate these waters professionally, but I needed to expose the chink, make them understand why they needed to change their process, segregate roles, and develop alternative procedures to compensate for it. No wonder auditors have a reputation for coming in after the war to shoot the wounded!

As I found my groove in the auditing world, I realized Peter Falk's approach from *Columbo* was highly effective. My exchange with the 'suspect' came from a position of naivety.

'Sir, can you help me understand this? This is confusing to me.'

This insinuated that I was stupid, so could they please enlighten me?

Being vulnerable, no wiser than them, helped them let down their guard, open up, and lead me to issues they never knew existed; issues I was meant to expose, solve with them, and correct. It worked like a charm.

Learning how to audit was not the only thing I had to worry about during the summer of 1981. I also had to start completing the *twelve* courses I was missing; the prerequisites needed to write the CPA exam. PwC was not going to let me coast without my CPA forever.

I created a master plan, with my goal being to finish school in the least amount of time possible. In case you missed me droning on about my BComm paranoia, I was *forever* concerned about being inferior to my peers. The sooner I could write my CPA exam, the sooner I could scream from the rooftops, 'I am equal to you guys now!'

My plan was simple. Find the twelve courses I needed to take, wherever and whenever they were being offered, whether that was night school, correspondence, half course, full course, springtime, summertime, or winter. Then, I was going complete those twelve courses in exactly two years from my PwC start date, come hell or high water. This meant non-stop class on weekends and nights in the fall, winter, spring, and summer for the next two years, while I worked full time. I wanted to write the CPA exams with my peers. No, I *planned* on it.

My plan required PwC's flexibility, support, and endorsement to work. They agreed to the time off I requested, so I took three of my twelve courses in my first summer while working a four-day week. This was the second flexible work arrangement I would design, propose, and successfully negotiate with an employer, and that became a common theme throughout my life.

Now, if you think this education plan sounds like too much work and not enough play, you are correct. It was a grind, but I was persistent and determined. I found a method to my madness, and like a dog with a bone, I was resolute on getting to the finish line and obtaining my CPA designation. I looked upon those three letters like the holy grail, and only once I had attained them could I ever reach enlightenment.

There was also an unexpected silver lining to this plan. I found a surprising degree of consistency between what I was studying and what I needed to know to perform an audit and understand my clients' business. Imagine that? Learning something useful and relevant at school!

If my plan was successful, I would write my CPA exams with my BComm colleagues. That in and of itself was enough to keep me going. It was what drove me to say, 'No, not tonight, I can't. I'm studying' to my friends and colleagues who were enjoying life, partying hard, and managing their stress by letting off steam in the bar scene.

On my most difficult days, I stood alone outside on the balcony of my tiny townhouse I could not afford, and gazed across the street at the large, detached, two-storey, four-bedroom homes adorning the beautiful, residential neighbourhood I didn't feel like I deserved to belong to. At the time, it was a constant reminder of what I was working so hard to achieve. I dreamed of crossing the street to a grand home with a backyard, and this image was my north star—albeit a shallow, materialistic one. But the young, immature woman in me saw this as the blue ribbon at the end of the race; my rise above the station I was born into, and an accomplishment that the women (and men) in my family could only have dreamed of.

But not everything in my chaotic life was going as planned.

I promised to give you the straight goods. Though many of you may have been through this (the statistics would agree), this part of my journey is painful for me to recount. Not only is it *the* biggest mistake of my life, I knew it was a mistake while I was making it, yet I felt powerless to prevent it.

The professional wedding photographer captured my helplessness in full colour. Like a tragedy, where I am the protagonist, his photo, the proof of my mistake, has haunted me for an eternity. Was his lens revealing my falsehood to him? Did the photographer see more than he let on?

All I know, is that when I see my lost self in that photograph, it hurts my heart to see that 21-year-old girl submerged in her innocence and youth, standing at the back of a church, linked arm in arm with her proud father. I remember him patting my forearm softly, then receiving a sincere, encouraging smile, like a warm embrace. It seemed to me like he was asking, 'Are you ready?'

How I wish he asked me that question six months prior. A father's gift is to steer his children in the proper direction when they can't see it themselves. Why didn't I take the time to meet with him face-to-face and ask for his guidance? But it wasn't the time to stop the parade and have a father-daughter huddle. The music was playing; it was too late.

'Yes, Dad. Let's go.'

It was an empty lie I would live to regret.

And so, we began our long, slow, arduous walk, my mouth downturned, far from a smile, with sad eyes watery, trying to stop myself from bursting into tears. Is this the face of a blushing bride? No, this is the photo that upsets me so, foreshadowing a destiny I wish I could erase.

As I approached the altar, I didn't see a church with the midday sun shining through its gorgeous stained-glass windows. Instead, I felt a layer of dense fog descend upon me, weighing me down like a heavy, cold blanket.

I had started dating this man in university, and now I was living with him. Once upon a time, in the not-so-distant past, I affectionately admired him. I didn't love him, I couldn't have. Love feels different, better than this. I know that now.

But I reasoned that this was how everyone felt on their wedding day. I thought that my groom could once more be the mysterious, ambitious, funny man I had come to know in university, and despite the past few horrible months leading up to this moment, he could once again be worthy of my devotion, time, and attention.

Take a deep breath, Sue. You have vows to say and a party to attend where you are the guest of honour. You can do this!

Those thoughts became my inescapable regrets. Several months and years passed in a marriage doomed to fail from its inception. I could no longer push aside my destructive feelings; the dense fog of the church had found a permanent home in my mind, penetrating my every waking hour with despair, cloaking my sleepless nights in guilt.

This man, my husband, had his faults, and naturally, I had mine. However, living together as husband and wife exposed the worst of him to me—his life of partying, his contentment with an uncertain future, his lack of ambition, his gradual withdrawal from meaningful conversation, and ultimately, his retreat into a world I was not part of.

I suffered in silence remembering my vows and imagined that our silence, cross words, and escalating fights were not insurmountable. I empathised with him. It was obvious to me he had lost his way. Or had I changed, and he was being who he always was: a man I never truly knew? Either way, there came a point where he was a man I could no longer stand to be around, never mind be married to.

When we married, I was a Blizzard Soccer cheerdancer, and a recent UTM graduate with my impractical degree, finding my way in my first full-time job as the College Cashier. Now, I was maturing into a serious young woman with bold, new goals and dreams. I was no longer the naïve, happy-go-lucky girl he was attracted to and decided to marry.

When I joined PwC, we were a few years into our tenuous marriage, and I was nothing short of a workaholic by day and a boring academic by night. On the weekends, I did homework, studied, and worked some more. It was clear I was no fun to be around. Hell, *I* didn't want to be around myself!

Meanwhile, he worked the late shift as the manager of an upscale restaurant and bar until 1am. He was in a field that did nothing to propel him into the leader I thought he could become, and his late hours worked just exacerbated the distance between us. We had grown apart in our life goals, desires, and aspirations, and we didn't spend enough time together to even understand how far we had already separated.

It was over, I was done, and I needed to move on.

Living the biggest lie of my life was eating me alive from the inside out. I feared my extreme anxiety would affect my health. How could it not? I witnessed my parents' marriage and their lives together in contrast to their more meaningful lives apart. *Life is not meant to be spent in a miserable, unhealthy, or toxic relationship.* I thought this was something I chose to never forget? History was repeating itself. How could I have let this happen? How had I failed to learn from their mistake?

May she always be true to herself.

My grandad's creed was given to me for a reason.

In the spring of 1982, with all the strength I could muster, I asked him to leave me, our mortgage, and our debts behind. He was free to fly from this cage we called a marriage and start anew, no questions asked. He must have been suffering as much as I was, because a simple 'Okay' was all he could muster.

The weekend arrived and… *poof!* He was gone. On Monday, with a mortgage and other debt I had to somehow manage on my intern PwC salary, I looked around the empty spaces and fragments of a life I had the courage to walk away from. I felt the thick, grey fog clearing, making a path. I took a few more steps through the living room, the dining room, and the kitchen. Tentative, I soon found myself standing on my balcony to greet the fresh spring air. I looked up at the clear blue sky and closed my eyes. It was comforting to feel the warmth of the sun's rays on my face.

I took a slow, deep, cleansing breath—*in and out, in and out*—and instinctively outstretched my arms towards the sun, accepting its warmth as it gently absolved me of my sins. I heard a cardinal nearby whistling its familiar song and opened my eyes. I stared ahead at the familiar houses across the way—the beautiful homes I was now more determined than ever to one day own and live happily ever after in. In this moment, I felt free of the chains that bound me.

6

Survive to Thrive

An intense drive, a positive attitude, *Columbo* questioning techniques, technical knowledge, and practical on-the-job experience pays off. Six months into my career as a staff assistant and I had gained a reputation as a high performer. Audit Seniors were requesting *me* to be on their audit teams, and that old, fabricated stigma of being a geography and drama graduate had been kicked to the curb. I should have been shouting from the rafters, 'Come on, throw anything my way. I'm all in!'

But the only person struggling with my performance was me. I couldn't accept that I was performing at least as well or better than my BComm counterparts. *Managers must be mistaken; they're giving me the benefit of the doubt. Or, worse, they feel* pity *towards me.*

However, my irrational, negative inner voice worked to my advantage. My inferiority complex pushed me to keep proving I had earned the right to be an intern at PwC. I had to earn the respect I imagined, rightly or wrongly, I was being given unconditionally.

This drive to outperform, no matter the cost, may have been what saved me only months later.

I experienced my first ever 'busy season' in 1982, and if the previous six months hadn't been a shock to the system, this most definitely was. Busy season represented three months of 60- to 80-hour workweeks, whereby I was asked to cope with unrelenting deadlines and mounting responsibilities. It meant long stretches of work every day, which could extend into the weekend if I wasn't careful.

This is the moment every new accountant wonders, *What the hell did I sign up for?*

In spite of the hell that busy season could be, some of my dearest friendships were made and fondest memories had while attempting to survive this demanding time of the year. My social life became inextricably linked with my fellow PwC colleagues—those brave souls as foolish as I who subjected themselves to these unreasonable hours in the dead of winter.

During busy season, one's resolve can be tested, and morale can suffer. Staff turnover or sickness in the middle of this period can exacerbate what can already feel like an impossibly tight work schedule. I'm not the first, and I won't be the last, staff member at an accounting firm to have this experience. To be fair, however, this was my experience thirty years ago. Today, firms, including PwC, embrace more flexible and hybrid working models and offer programs to support their staff and partners in managing overtime, stress, and their overall wellness.

Why would I or any reasonable person stand for this volume and intensity of work? Personally, all I had to do was remember the boredom that came with my cashier position at the university. As much as I may have complained at the time, on balance, I enjoyed being busy way more, and I loved to be challenged.

Then, just days after my first busy season ended in 1982, what we knew around the office as Black Friday (not the shopping-induced American holiday!) hit PwC like a tidal wave. I remember that morning so well: many of my colleagues had their sights set on a liquid rehab recovery regime from busy season, and there was excitement in the air. But that all changed.

One by one, PwC managers would come into our open concept work area called 'the bullpen', where my colleagues and I were sitting together without productive work to do. A manager would ask one of us to join them in their office and, thirty minutes later, that same individual would return, pack up his things, and leave the office, not saying a word.

Call me crazy, but this looked like a whole bunch of people were getting fired.

I was holding my breath with trepidation, always expecting to be the next one summoned. The afternoon came and went with rumours about how there was only one person left to be fired. Managers were waiting till Monday to do the nasty deed to that last poor soul, and I didn't breathe a sigh of relief until Monday afternoon, when the poor guy who had just returned from vacation learned of his fate.

There were so many BComms at my level that had been fired, but somehow, I was still there. How could I have survived this deep cut at all levels? It was mind-boggling at the time, but typical of me to deny that my strong performance had anything to do with it.

Black Friday layoffs were PwC's reaction to a very real risk and threat; too many staff members for too little work as Canada slipped into a drawn-out recession. Five of my twelve peers were let go, along with several second-year staff accountants and third-year seniors. The fallout of jobs in every sector had begun.

I felt fortunate I had decided to apply to PwC in the Fall of 1980 while the economy was booming and inspiring earnings forecasts were the norm. When I consider the unlikely chance of my being recruited and offered a position with *any* firm, I could only wonder: *Is this good karma or a remarkable coincidence?*

I survived my first year at PwC—Black Friday and anxieties be damned—but I still had to finish my accounting courses and write my CPA exam. This would prove to be one of the biggest challenges of my life. Four intense months of planning, studying, exam-writing, positive self-talk, endless worrying, and sleepless nights would be my life before the three letters would dare take their place after my name.

But before I could shut myself off from the outside world, I had my first hurdle to overcome: a four-hour, multi-subject exam chocked full of questions on advanced accounting, tax, and auditing theory. This tested my endurance even more than the technical material we had already stuffed in our brains. It followed four exhausting weeks at a postgraduate 'School of Accountancy' which was Ontario's method of weeding out the unfortunate 'would be' accountants who couldn't hack the intensity. I passed with a mark in the first quartile compared to my peers. *Check.*

I was only two months away from writing my biggest hurdle: the Uniform Final Exam (UFE). The national pass rate was only 50%, and this statistic unnerved me.

Would I be one of the lucky ones to slay the UFE dragon? There were no guarantees and no way for anyone to predict who passed and who failed. Some very capable, smart people I worked with hadn't figured out how to properly arm themselves and slay the dragon.

But I couldn't bear to fail—the expectations I placed on myself were too great. Nor could I bear to do this more than once—the sacrifice had been too great.

When my mind wandered over to the dark side, and it often did, I worked hard to convince myself, *You* are *smart enough. You've been smart enough every step of the way, so why stop now!* I'd provided the same corner talk to my sister, and it had a similar effect on me. I'd come this far; I had to keep going.

I made copious notes from source materials and read them over and over; that's how I learn best. On the other hand, I only wrote a single practice exam... which was about five practice exams and fifteen multi-subject cases shy of the suggested amount.

I didn't join a study group to bounce questions off colleagues, but this was simply because I didn't know the study groups were out there. I came to learn those dreaded and astute BComm students *did* gather often. This made me feel alone, isolated, and lost in my anguish.

So, I persevered with my personal study plan, and tailored it to my weaknesses, of which I believed there were many. These weeks of studying over the summer were tough slugging, one of the most grueling processes I have ever put myself through. But, as I have mentioned, failure was not an option.

By the time the UFE exams were closing in on me, I believed I had given my heart and soul to it and had nothing left to give. If I didn't pass, there was nothing more I could do. For some people this might have given them peace. For me, this thought was paralyzing. If I failed, there was no 'trying harder next time.' My tank of effort was on empty.

I wrote the exam, and there was nothing left to do but wait.

For three excruciatingly long months, I waited to discover my fate in the early morning edition of the *Globe and Mail* newspaper. It was Friday, December 7, 1984. As I feverishly searched through the list of several thousands of other successful CPAs from across Canada, I finally zeroed in on 'Susan L Allen, Mississauga' in the full-page ad congratulating the successful new Chartered Professional Accountants of the Canadian Institute of Chartered Accountants.

This remains one of the happiest moments of my entire career. I was the proudest I had ever been to that point in my life. I felt like I had achieved my impossible dream.

From the moment I found out I had passed, I celebrated Results Day with my colleagues, friends, and family. All the accumulated steam and stress from the past months was blown out of me, and I replaced that with a heavy dose of booze and celebration. At 7pm, my grandmother, Mimi, called to congratulate me, but I was already being plunked into bed. Too much cheap wine and a vague memory of smoking a cigar had knocked me down for the count.

As I tried to keep the room from spinning, the thought of passing my CPA exam, and the opportunities I imagined this would bring, surrounded me like a comfortable blanket.

It was all worth it. Dreams usually are.

7

The Decision to Stay

Two demanding years of night school, compiled with weekday and weekend studying, passed like watching the last drop of honey fall from the honey pot. Winnie the Pooh might have the patience to wait for his dinner, but I was exhausted, hangry, and edgy.

My free time had been virtually non-existent. In perpetual study and work mode, I had pushed pause on my home life, ignored potential dating opportunities, and lived on a steady diet of salad, canned soup, cheese, and crackers. But it was all my doing. I put myself at the mercy of all this mayhem just so I could place those three significant letters behind my name: CPA.

It was all worth it, but now I longed for a slower pace and change of scenery. I wanted some semblance of my former, carefree life back. And I was single, again.

I was not alone with my feelings—my colleagues were also dreaming of their alternate realities. It is and has always been the norm for newly-minted CPAs to look up from their desks and think, *I have so many options open to me now that I have my designation. This job is no picnic, and if I don't* have *to be an auditor, I don't* want *to be one. I need a change.*

I've said it before, and I'll say it again: auditing is not for everyone.

For many of us, this would be the first, but not the last time we would be hotly pursued by headhunters. Headhunters prey on the tough slugging they know new CPAs have been through and use this to lure us away from our auditing jobs to (what may seem to be) a more fulfilling career with new and exciting opportunities. They also know that once we attach those three letters behind our name, we are no longer tied to the firm that helped put them there.

So, off goes the new CPA, free as a bird, accepting their dream job in the corporate world with entry- or mid-level positions in the private or public sector, often at one of PwC's clients. They leave for the title of Corporate Controller, VP Finance, VP Marketing, Internal Audit, or an operations role. The job comes with the promise of a better work/life balance, a more predictable work schedule, a sizable jump in salary, a bonus, shares, and the chance to do something radically different. Moreover, unlike the auditor role, they are suddenly *welcomed* and not feared by companies. Many see it as that place just over the rainbow where Dorothy is singing on a fence and the Lollipop Gang are kicking their heels in glee.

I watched as many of my friends, new CPAs that PwC had *recruited and trained,* immediately walked out the revolving door in search of their utopia: the promised land of new, different, and better. This is not a new phenomenon for PwC or any accounting firm, and they hire a surplus of entry level graduates because of this.

So, when the experienced CPA decides to leave the firm, PwC's hope is that these individuals will think fondly of their time with the firm, be PwC proud, and continue to be connected to PwC as valued alumni. Not a bad strategy. Who better to be a future client or refer work to PwC than happy, loyal alumni?

Many of these talented CPAs find their calling in industry as Senior VPs, CFOs, Presidents, CEOs, and board members, but there are always others who return to the firm to pick up where they left off. Many make the private discovery that the grass wasn't greener outside the walls of PwC.

Then there are others, mostly women in my experience, who leave their financial careers altogether to stay home and raise a family—a rewarding, but difficult job.

For decades, I saw a mass exodus of upwardly mobile, professional women in my industry. It was often justified by others saying, 'It's a personal decision. She must decide what she feels is right and just. Of course, we'd love to keep her, but she's made up her mind.'

This thinking was flawed. I noticed well-intentioned career moms leave with no other choice offered. There was no blueprint to navigate a demanding, professional career and deal with the pressures of motherhood at the same time.

What women heard if they considered being a mother *and* a professional was, 'If you want to succeed, you need to work beyond 9-5, be ready to travel, and self-sacrifice... *like the men do (implied)*. That is how you survive around here.' This left women with no option, and they were often pushed into their 'rightful place': the home.

It deeply troubled and saddened me to see women work so hard to obtain their professional designation, begin their arduous climb, get married, have a child, and *poof!...* abandon their career to raise a family. *What a waste,* I thought, careful to keep my unpopular opinion to myself. I knew better than to throw stones at a mother's decision to stay home. I was not living in their shoes.

But I wasn't yet a mother, nor was I even married, so these difficult decisions weren't yet mine to make. Instead, I was faced with a much easier decision, though looking back, it was one of those choices that shaped the rest of my life.

As much as I felt like I might burn out as the Audit Senior in Charge, I didn't want to leave the firm to feel the change I needed. I loved working with the staff, managers, and partners I had been exposed to. They were my friends and family—my home away from home. I had developed strong relationships with my clients, friendships with their finance teams, and I was developing a rolodex of professionals and executives who respected my opinion and valued my contributions. I was making a difference for my staff and my clients, one audit at a time.

At PwC, I was surrounded by the smartest people I had ever known, each one of them only too willing to teach me new skills and gently steer me straight when I stumbled. I had so much more to learn. How could I leave my latent potential behind when I could be coached, mentored, and moulded by the best and the brightest, doing work I loved to do?

I decided to stay with the firm, and while this wasn't the *safe* thing to choose, it was the *smart* thing to choose, even if I didn't realize it at the time.

So, while I wasn't looking to leave the firm with my CPA designation in hand, I was looking for a change—something different with new challenges to energize me. I formulated the perfect solution to my predicament: a promotion. With four years of work experience behind me, why shouldn't I reach for the stars? How else would I get invited to an office with a view of the glass ceiling? My dream of becoming something better was within reach. It was time to get recognized for my accomplishments.

The best part of my strategy? I wouldn't have to leave the firm.

I was now just as good as any BComm (Well… *almost*. I will never outgrow that obsession). I was no longer the naïve, insecure geography/drama student waiting to be found out, fearing the worst. I was not a fraud—I had the added credibility of my CPA, and I was a highly-rated senior accountant responsible for challenging, high-profile client work.

There was just one problem: I didn't have the courage to *ask* for a promotion. I was afraid to put my hand up and scream from the rooftops, 'Pick me! I'm ready! I'm excited to try this. I won't let you down!'

As I came to learn in time, I was not alone. Many women assume their managers and partners can and will magically figure out when they are ready and interested in a promotion. It's obvious, isn't it? All any boss needs to do is notice our solid work ethic, our strong relationships with clients, and the mature and empathetic way we manage staff. Oh, and of course, they must *read our minds* telepathically screaming, 'I am so ready, willing, and able to accept more responsibility!' As I have seen over the decades, this attitude fails women, and it is one of the fundamental differences between men and women in the workplace.

Not that I knew anything about that at the time. I thought everyone felt like me, and so I waited and waited, in silence.

Thankfully, on July 1, 1985, PwC announced their promotions to staff across Canada, and to my surprise, my name was on the promotion list! It looked like my managers and partners *had* noticed my efforts, my growth, and my performance, and so they put their reputations on the line and convinced others that I was more than a dancing geography major. I was worthy of becoming an Audit Manager!

I did not, for one minute, take for granted the risk that PwC took in hiring me, nor their persistent confidence in me. My gratitude manifested itself in a powerful urge to pay it forward. Harkening back to the time I gave the plain, but worthy and capable girl a spot on the NACI cheerleading team, it became a passion of mine to root for the underdog, take a risk on other young hopefuls, and then mentor, sponsor, and support them.

To many, the manager role is the first *real* promotion one can receive at PwC. Although I had received more responsibility in each of the last four years, this promotion was the real McCoy.

It couldn't have been sweeter. Me and my dear friend, Kathy, who began her journey at PwC a few months after mine, were now the only two in our office on the manager promotions list— two women, a year in advance of our *male* colleagues. Overnight, I had leapfrogged the BComms.

It was time to accept the new challenge thrust upon me, and I longed to be a consummate professional, just like my mentor, David. He was the role model I had met years earlier at UTM, whose powerful words and stoic demeanour inspired me to become a CPA in the first place. I wanted to emulate this man by personifying the female version of my hero.

David didn't have the slightest idea he had made such a lasting impression on me. If he had, he would have been embarrassed and, I think, a smidge proud. He was modest, yet confident, and so, so brilliant—the youngest person ever promoted to partner in the firm.

I chose to keep my hero in the dark for years. But thankfully, I came to my senses when it mattered most. Nine years later, something inside begged me to seize the moment and share my gratitude in the most unlikely of moments.

While David and I were waiting to take an elevator down to the lobby, I interrupted our silence. 'David, I don't know if you know this, but I have been meaning to tell you something for a long time. You are the reason I joined PwC and why I wanted to become a CPA. You gave a presentation on campus at UTM that inspired me so much it changed my course. Afterwards, I came up to the podium, you probably don't remember this, and asked you if I should get my MBA degree before my CPA. You convinced me that my CPA was all I needed, and the rest is history.'

David was staring intently at me, trying to recall this time, and reflecting on the impact he had on me. He didn't know what to say, so I continued.

'Coincidentally, you were also the partner who interviewed me during my in-office interview, even though you didn't remember meeting me beforehand.' Apparently, he had made a bigger impression on me than I had made on him. We laughed together over this, and this was the last time I spoke to him, just the two of us, uninterrupted, face-to-face.

Our careers took different paths in the years that followed this encounter, and then he was diagnosed with a terminal illness. Within months of discovering this, his health took a turn for the worse and he passed away, too early, suddenly, a shocking loss for his family, friends, clients, and PwC colleagues. I will never understand how cancer chooses its victims. This one was unbearable for me to comprehend.

With the support of David and several other partners behind me, I began to grow into my role as a manager and mentor for the new PwC hires. I wasn't perfect, but I knew I was getting better as I learned through trial and error, tweaking my approach with each mistake I made.

Often, it was difficult to tell if the mistake was mine or theirs. Did I ask something that made them nervous? Even though I thought I was perfectly clear, sometimes I could tell I was speaking audit nonsense by their furrowed brows and deer-caught-in-the-headlights looks. So, I learned to break it down into easy steps and explained the 'why' to give them context.

When I received work from junior staff, and they missed the key point, whose fault was that? I would have to take a deep breath and ask myself to stay calm—it does no good to let them see you sigh or your eyes roll. I remembered to apply one of Steven Covey's seven habits, 'Seek first to understand, then to be understood.' I would stand in their shoes, then remind myself not how *green* they were, but how far I had come in four short years.

Naturally, as a new manager, I made mistakes too. An embarrassing moment that stands out in my mind was when I missed a major error in David's client's financial statements. He leapt into my office at the eleventh hour just before his signed audit report was to be released, and announced, 'There's trouble in River City.' I looked up in surprise to find him concerned, but not intimidating nor demeaning. This was his way of letting me know, *You screwed up.* I was horrified.

However, by deflecting the error away from me (i.e., you are a failure!) and onto the problem itself, I was saved, and he kept our working relationship intact. I was his ally as we worked through the issue together. In essence, he addressed my mistake by reframing it and separating the person from the problem. I figured if someone like David could be patient with me and my daily dose of questions and mistakes, I could be patient too.

The new hires had a lot to learn, but it was not an impossible journey. I enjoyed teaching and watching the lightbulbs go on. Their success was my success, and I learned to recalibrate my message, and restate my expectations. I became a better listener and watched for clues of their comprehension.

I learned soft skills like empathy, how to teach not tell, and how to be a better listener from the role models who took me under their wing. I tried very hard not to project my work habits on others; my work was a high priority for me, but my way was not necessarily the *best* way nor the *only* way to get through life and be happy and successful.

One of the greatest teaching moments, however, came from outside PwC long before I ever thought about accounting. How often in life do bad examples teach us more than the good ones?

As an underage fourteen-year-old, my first job was part-time work in a drugstore. I was hired to sell soft ice cream scoops... yes, in a *drugstore*. Before long, I was asked to work in the back of the store and assist the pharmacist. He was a lazy man who hated his job.

I had to teach myself to read doctor scribbles and fill prescriptions, and while I was preparing the prescriptions, the pharmacist was hidden in the back office, asleep and lying as far back in his chair as the small room would allow, with his feet on his desk. On his best days, he could be seen reading a book or the newspaper, his face a straight line, eyes dull and expressionless. Clearly, he didn't want to be there.

I was constantly torn between waking him up to serve his customers or leaving him be. When was the line of customers long enough to bother waking him? What if there was only one prescription waiting? How long should that customer wait? The hardest part of my job was picking the right time to bother him, because once I peeked my head into his office, there was no turning back. It had better be a good reason.

I swear he never said a pleasant word to me the entire time I worked there. He never got to know me, and never gave me the chance to get to know him. He performed his tasks begrudgingly, hated his customers, disliked me, and worked a job he loathed.

That was my first experience with a boss, and to a fourteen-year-old girl, not only was he terrifying, but I also thought *that* was what a boss was.

But this man taught me more than he realized. I would never emulate his behaviour or be in a job that I hated, and I would never ever treat employees like I was better than them.

Still, despite all the training and solid mentorship I received at PwC, I found the manager role surprisingly difficult. Though I was more confident than ever, I would still get a familiar pit in my stomach when I found myself playing the leader, chairing a meeting, meeting a client for the first time, dealing with a controversial topic, presenting my ideas to my superiors, or giving difficult performance feedback to a staff member. I'm not convinced this ever gets easy.

Moreover, with increased responsibility it meant I was *always* on. Some days I felt like my inner stress would result in an uncontrollable, embarrassing explosion. Or, worse, it would bubble up inside and create chronic health issues that could not be reversed. These were real concerns, and yet, when I had a successful meeting, a new client was pleased with my work, or my staff were inspired by my words, the stress would peel away and I would feel so energized, so valued, so proud, and so happy to be doing what I was doing.

Part of my intense anxiety at this time stemmed from my inherent need to be liked, and I know now that I am not the only one who deals with this. There are others (more often a trait of women than men) with a deep-seated need to be liked. Whether it stems from our nurturing soul, society's lens on the value of 'likeable' women, or our less-confident demeanour, when people like me feel accepted and liked, we get our boost of assurance. In our quest to nourish this need, we tread softly on what we say and how we say it, and we instinctively read the room for others' non-verbal cues of scepticism or irritation. This is empathy in action, but it can be torture when you're in a managerial role.

The more I felt a project reflected me, the harder I pushed myself to reach for and exceed my high standards. My goal was to make my report better and my recommendations more practical and precise. I wanted to be the one to present the smartest solution and deliver the most inspirational address. This was the 'never enough' gene playing out in all its glory and wickedness.

Often, I had to sit back, give my head a shake, and force myself to apply the 80/20 rule: getting whatever I'm working on 80% of the way to perfection, while reminding myself that it was 'good enough', rather than taking the extra time to perfect the last 20%.

Many people don't work well in a company with the type of intensity, risk, uncertainty, and pressure I faced. Repeated 60-hour workweeks, immoveable deadlines, extensive technical knowledge to keep abreast of, precise documentation, and focusing on never missing a key audit risk are not for the faint of heart. If we screwed up, there was a damn good chance our client could end up on the front page of the *Globe and Mail*.

Those who don't like this work intensity should and do leave for a more predictable work pace. Those who do like this work often sink or swim, then learn how to flourish in it, and with time and perseverance, get promoted.

Maybe this is wrong. Maybe this is perpetuating the wrong behaviours and makes a work/life balance unattainable. Still, all these years later, I feel privileged to have worked in a profession where quality and excellence was endorsed, recognized, and celebrated. I was glad to be among friends—the other Type As in town.

So, with these tendencies, how did I manage to survive without wreaking havoc on my personal health and relationships?

Maybe I didn't. My family must answer that question. I will say, however, after too many late nights spent pouring over my computer, half asleep, making tweaks on working papers that didn't make a damn bit of difference, I eventually matured. With this maturity, my priorities were better aligned with the things in life that really matter.

I worked at turning off and unplugging when I could. I wasn't perfect, but my mental health was helped by anticipating vacations, planning them, and spending time and savings on life experiences—a trait I learned watching my mom's parents, Mimi and Grandad, who spent their limited earnings making lasting memories in far-off, sunny places.

It was also important for me to take time for simple diversions. One of my favourites was the mindless task of making banana bread on Saturday mornings, while encouraging my kids to play an active, messy role as 'banana boy' and 'flour girl'. Moreover, I relished the time I spent cheering them on in the after-school activities and weekend sports clubs they belonged to.

Later in my career, when I had a more flexible schedule that I could control, I snuck out for extra-long lunches to exercise with a personal trainer. (I wish I had the courage to include this type of stress relief much earlier in my career.) When I rose in the PwC ranks, I was able to afford housekeepers and nannies, which gave me that flexibility to have meaningful connections with family and friends that I craved. I was content having less money so I could free up the many hours it would have taken me to clean house, do laundry, then prep and cook meals.

Regardless of the measures I took to ensure a healthy work/life balance, top of my mind were the client deadlines I had to meet; I didn't want to let my bosses down. But was it their fault?

No, my bosses were not my problem. *I* was my problem. I had to learn to manage my own unrealistic expectations and live with my 80%. In time, I learned how to take better charge of my time, leaving blocks of blank spaces throughout the week for the inevitable crises that would crop up, derail my to-do list, and require my complete attention to solve. As I grew into professionalism, I was considerate of other people's time and came prepared to meetings with a clear message of what I needed from them. My hope was that they would do the same for me in return.

When my days got out of control, I asked myself, 'What would happen if I didn't get to this today? Can this wait? Can I say 'no' if the alternative means spending less time with my family? Alternatively, can someone else deal with this? Why not?'

As Marcus Aurelius advised, 'Ask yourself at every moment: "Is this necessary?"'

But these skills took time to develop. In my early years, my priorities were work, then work, then more work. My own health, mental and otherwise, took a back seat, and it was only through the emulation of others, and the development of my managerial skills, that I learned to leave work at the office, keep my sanity and health in check, take time for myself, and be present for my family.

As much as I showed intensity towards work, I tried not to pass judgement onto my colleagues. They had other commitments just like

I did, and I didn't expect them to follow my work habits—particularly the bad ones.

Looking back on the role I played managing teams and individuals, I believe in my heart I did not tread too hard. But honestly, I can only hope they saw me as the patient teacher I strived to be. I wanted to teach them to have pride in their accomplishments, to throw their best selves into their work, to accept there are other ideas worth considering, to make light of their mistakes, and never to take themselves too seriously. Above all else, I wanted them to have fun. If they recall their days with me in this way, I succeeded. This is what I hope I will be remembered for.

REFLECTION

Setting the course for your future

I often imagine I was struck by lightning when I knelt in my grandad's home, counting quarters and playing *King* in my counting house, loving it so much that I remember it more vividly than the breakfast I had this morning, or the time I broke 90 in golf. All the signs for a future in numbers were there throughout my childhood, but I refused to pay attention.

Then, against all odds, the bolt struck me a second time, and this time, I leaned in to feel the *zap!* So began a career that inspired the latent passion within me, and so firm was my conviction in this new future that I felt okay pushing reset and starting all over.

Passion has a way of igniting a lifeforce within you to keep going despite the odds. When you find what you are meant to do, you don't settle. You go the distance, even when this impacts your personal, physical, mental, and emotional strength.

During the hardest times, I dredged up visions of the alternative: experiences in jobs that did not challenge or recognize me. So, I *chose* to spend my days with Type A intensity, accepting challenges, demands, and increasing responsibilities, no matter the cost.

So, do I think it matters if you—yes *you,* the person reading this—still don't know what you want to be when you grow up? Now you know the answer to this.

I present my lessons learned to help you set the course for your future:

- When you hit an uncomfortable fork in the road, take a step back and reflect upon what you are feeling and why. Just remember: the best actions and choices are those that align with your values, your needs, and your passions.

- If you crave challenging work in a demanding environment, be prepared to ask more of yourself. This means you may be expected to attain higher education, develop specialized, technical, and leadership skills, and be a continuous learner while consenting to a dose of self-induced stress. Go in with eyes open.

- There are no stupid questions. This is especially true when you begin a new job in a new field. Asking questions to clarify your understanding is not a sign of weakness, but a sign of strength and confidence. Use your time as a newbie to your advantage.

- Pay it forward, and don't pounce on the brave women who come after you; they deserve to be encouraged, mentored, and supported.

- Separate the 'urgent' and 'important' tasks from those that can be delegated, deferred, or ignored. Apply the 80/20 rule whenever possible. Getting 80% of the way there is more than often 'good enough'. The time and effort it takes to achieve the last 20% is futile. It is ugly perfectionism at work.

- Have the courage to ask for a promotion! (*More on this to come.*)

Reflection Questions

1. What are you good at?

2. When you face imposter syndrome, what do you do? How do you convince yourself (and truly believe) that you are good enough, you belong here, and you are ready for this?

3. How do you keep Type A perfectionism, stress, or anxiety under control? Do you apply the 80/20 rule to your tasks? What other tools do you employ?

Part III
Motherhood: Learning to Troubleshoot

Life involves weighty decisions. One of the heaviest is the evolving balancing act of work vs. life.

It's all well and good to achieve higher education, be success driven, and make a deal with the devil to get there, but at what cost? For years, all work and no play had made Sue a dull girl.

As I re-entered the dating scene for the first time since my divorce, I discovered that when the social and personal pieces of our lives are invited to the party, new priorities have a sneaky way of making themselves known.

Deeper questions arose, and they'll come to the table for you too—if you let them.

But what if, in reaching for personal goals, you are forced to give up career goals? Which goals do you chase? How does a shift in priorities align with your beliefs?

An emotional, difficult transition emerged that I wasn't prepared for. I wasn't ready for the drag of guilt that came with motherhood.

When my life was blessed with a child, I truly understood the difficult decisions working moms dealt with *daily*. How naïve of me to think otherwise? I asked myself, *How do I make these two separate but significant pieces of my life integrate with each other?*

As I share the next part of my journey, I hope my story helps prepare you for the conflict you may one day face. Or, if you are currently going through this, I hope it shows that you're not alone with your thoughts, and that finding a healthy work/life balance *is* hard and has never been easy for us working moms.

8

Everything Changes

On Friday evenings, after a long, challenging workweek, PwC rank and file routinely met at a local pub for our ritual 'Drink Up'. These impromptu social gatherings gave us our much-needed release from the pressures of our day jobs with time to let down our hair, unwind, complain a bit, laugh a lot, and most of all, bond with our peers who were destined to become our closest friends. It was a night such as this, on October 22, 1982, that I found myself there, relaxing with my colleagues, enjoying a glass (or three) of wine.

For no other reason than to make a mockery of myself, I began to broadcast my hard luck emphatically and passionately to anyone within earshot. 'Listen up, can you believe this? Next Saturday is my 25th birthday and I have absolutely nothing to do! I will be at home *alone* on my quarter-century birthday! I am such a *loser*!'

Before a minute passed, one of my peers, seated clear across the other side of the bar, ever-so-calmly proclaimed, 'I will take you out.' His retort to my droning on, which I am known to do, was heard loud and clear in the noisy bar, so, of course, everyone else heard this too.

There was a deafening silence. Heads turned in my direction and my friends waited with bated breath for a response.

Uh... I definitely wasn't expecting that! Time stood still. What had I done? I was taken aback by this young man's confidence and the serious look on his face. Did he really mean what he just said?

I found myself uttering my most embarrassed, sheepish reply ever, 'Okay.' Then I thought, *Oh my God, I accepted a pity date. What is wrong with me? I'm an even* bigger *loser now.*

Little did I know that this unassuming 'Okay' would mark the moment I accepted a new man into my life... forever.

This young man, my friend, my colleague, and my peer, was also someone I had come to truly admire and respect. He was handsome, of average height, thin, with a small frame. He dressed impeccably well in tailored Armani suits of the finest Italian cloth, wore matching ties and crisp white shirts which had been freshly pressed each morning by his doting mother (what?!). I believed he dressed for the job he wanted, *and the girl he wanted,* not the job (*or the girl*) he had.

Unlike me, with my business wardrobe comprising of a single winter-white suit, this guy had options and dressed like he meant business. It was the 80's, and business casual wasn't a thing.

His full mane of thick, wavy black hair was his calling card—the physical feature that unexpectedly defined him amongst his peers at PwC. It was never out of place, and this would inevitably prompt colleagues to try to muss it just to tease him. He was nicknamed 'Tony Vaselino' which was a tribute to his beautiful head of hair and his heritage. His Christian name was John Cerisano.

I had never dated an Italian before, and I never intended to date a PwC colleague. I was told nothing good could come of that. It is messy and uncomfortable mixing your personal life with workmates, especially when things don't work out. How awkward would it be to work together and pretend nothing happened?

But there I was, psychoanalyzing my situation and, a split second later, accepting a pity date with one of my peers.

Although my interactions with John had been fairly limited, what I did know about him impressed me. He exuded confidence and was technically proficient at both accounting and auditing. He personified an efficient, no-nonsense, consummate professional, and I was envious. I often compared myself to his demeanour, and asked myself to try, *please try,* to be more like he was.

Although John and I had only worked together a few times in the past year, I had the opportunity to observe his work ethic first hand and wished to emulate it. I was inspired and thankful for his willingness to help me on the job and witnessed how he would offer to help others on our team without prompting.

Before our date, I remembered a conversation I had enjoyed with John's ex-girlfriend ten months earlier at PwC's annual holiday party. She made a point of seeking *me* out to share how incredibly encouraged and fascinated John was with my pursuit of the CPA designation given my atypical geography background. John had evidently impressed upon her how much he admired my determination and my commitment, and explained to her the substantial, arduous road I had in front of me. I found it interesting that John was following my personal journey closer than he let on.

So, the following Saturday arrived, and to my great surprise, so did John! He was at my Mississauga townhouse on time, with flowers, a card, and a gift: *L'Air du Temps* perfume by Nina Ricci. To say that blew me away would be an understatement. He went above and beyond to make my birthday special, and we had yet to leave for our date! He brought me to his car, and like a true gentleman he opened the passenger seat door and said, 'I've booked a restaurant downtown. I hope you like Greek food.'

We had an intimate dinner with authentic Greek food and traditional Greek dancers performing the Hasapiko with roaming musicians to serenade us. How did he know I was a huge fan of Greek food? Or that, in my teens, I worked as a Greek dancer performing that very same dance? *Smooth operator.*

Although we ordered the dinner platter for two, I devoured the lion's share of scrumptiousness placed in front of us. I'm pretty sure my entire side of the conversation centred on that huge platter of food under my nose.

'Are you going to eat that last Spanakopita? I think that Mouss-aka has my name on it. Do you know how much I love Dolmodakia? Are you going to finish the lamb? What about the rice? Okay, I will. But don't you hate to leave it?'

Since this wasn't a *real* date, I didn't pretend to be someone I wasn't. I didn't eat like a bird, move food around on my plate, or look all coy and mysterious like a maiden in distress. (Aren't those the behaviours to model from a 1980's first date manual?) No ma'am! I sat back, relaxed, and enjoyed my feast. After all, it was my 25th birthday, and I was spending it with a PwC colleague who pitied my single life!

Following the delicious dinner, and just when I thought things couldn't get better, John asked, 'Do you want to go dancing?'

Wait, what? You dance too? Who is this guy and what planet did he fall from? 'Yes… yes, please… I would love to go dancing.' Besides, I needed to wear off my overindulgence. Bring on the disco ball, it's Saturday Night Fever in Mississauga!

And so, my first date with John, and my 25th birthday, will be forever noted in the history books as a smashing success. John got me home before midnight and remained a complete gentleman. He brought me to my front door, waited till I was safely inside; no hug, no kiss, no plans for another date, just, 'Goodnight.'

It's fair to say he had me at *Greek restaurant*, and by the end of our date, I was captivated and curious. This Italian colleague of mine with the great hair deserved a closer look.

John and I began dating exclusively a few short weeks later, which coincided with the release of his CPA exam results. Of course, John succeeded in passing, and a few nights after his results party, I decided to treat him to a romantic homecooked dinner.

This is more of a big deal than it sounds. I could make a mean tossed salad, but my oven was almost exclusively used for warming up someone else's meals. In retrospect, I didn't think anything through... in particular, the part about him being *Italian*. I should have known there was a high likelihood he was used to *really* good homecooked meals. But how hard could this really be?

I purchased my first fresh whole chicken and roasted it with potatoes. I made my own gravy, steamed some vegetables, and of course, made my reliable tossed salad to start. Let's just say my heart was in the right place.

So, there we were, enjoying each other's company in my townhouse, and I had done all the prep in advance of his arrival. We simply needed the chicken to roast, and my special dinner would reveal itself.

As I took the beautifully browned roast chicken out of the oven to make gravy from its juices, I asked John to carve the bird. As he began to carve it, he noticed there was something in the cavity of the bird.

'What in the name of God is this?'

Inside my beautiful roast chicken was a bloody paper bag oozing nasty half-cooked giblets—the heart, the liver, and the guts. As it happens, I hadn't taken the bag of chicken guts out of the chicken before I popped it in the oven, *because I didn't know chickens came with paper bags holding giblets*!

After much fussing and some choice words over what exactly we should do with this partially cooked mess, we decided it might be safe enough to eat the outer pieces of the chicken; those with no connection to blood, paper bags, or raw giblets. We picked away at what we could, unsure with every bite whether we were going to come down with salmonella tomorrow, then threw the rest out.

Well, at least there was my salad!

As I soon came to learn, John grew up on his mother's *outstanding* Italian family recipes and was doing his best to keep from laughing (or crying?) at my incompetence. However, many weeks passed before I had the opportunity to meet John's parents. Our first encounter was not at all how I envisioned, nor was my introduction set under ideal conditions.

When John informed his parents that he had broken up with his Portuguese girlfriend of several years (whom he had intended to marry) and was instead dating me, a divorcee, his father's first question was, 'Why do you want to be with someone else's wife?'

Ouch. His words punctured my heart like a dull blade. I was going to be a tough sell. I wanted to wait a while to meet them, but my introduction was pushed ahead by circumstances none of us could have predicted.

Just a couple of weeks following John's CPA news, he was struck with painful, debilitating gastrointestinal bleeding, which rendered him bedridden. He was losing weight, unable to keep anything down.

After numerous specialist appointments, ultrasounds, and X-rays, doctors determined his intestinal lesions, bleeding, and overall lethargy was ulcerative colitis and was likely caused by a period of prolonged, chronic stress.

Anyone who knows John knows that he worries *a lot*, even when things are going well. So, one could have only imagined the toll the past year of studying and work, mixed with partying and celebration, took on his body.

To this day, John also believes there was one other factor that instigated his condition:

My romantic homecooked chicken dinner...

Eye roll.

Doctors began treating John for what they stated would be a permanent, lifelong condition he would have to manage through a change in lifestyle and diet. He was given high doses of prednisone ('the wonder drug'), and other anti-inflammatory prescription drugs, and was told to stick to bedrest and a strict diet consisting of bland boiled rice and carrots. Despite how appetizing this sounds compared to *roast chicken à la Sue*, John lost weight at an alarming rate. He was weak, lethargic, and even more worried than normal about his prognosis.

His condition was a cruel twist of fate taking him from his highest of highs to his lowest of lows. John was desperate to recover quickly, get back to work, and live the life he'd always imagined. But the days passed into weeks and the weeks into months as he remained on medical leave convalescing at home, with his loving mother preparing his meals and providing him the comfort only a mother can.

Naturally, when I heard of his condition, I was shocked and concerned, desperate to see John and wish him well, even if it meant meeting his parents for the first time under these most unfortunate, awkward circumstances.

I mean, who the hell was I? The unknown new kid on the block, not of Italian descent, and most certainly their suspected homewrecker. I assumed they were fond of his ex, and I concluded they were not anxious to meet his new flame anytime soon.

Weeks passed before John began to feel well enough to accept visitors. Our relationship had become a long-distance one with the aid of our landline phones. There were no apps like Zoom or Skype to help us stay connected virtually.

It was a blustery, cold Friday night in January when I was given the go-ahead to make the trek to his two-storey, semi-detached home in an Italian immigrant community in midtown Toronto. When I arrived, John was sitting slumped in his parent's living room, a shadow of the man I was dating just a few months earlier.

As I stared at him, my heart sank, and I put on a brave face to conceal my growing fear and worry. He was, however, as happy to see me as I was to see him.

The evening with his parents started out calm enough with small talk and pleasantries. John didn't say much—he just laid on the couch, too weak and tired to participate. But to my surprise, John's parents were gracious, warm, and completely lovely to me.

About an hour into my visit, John received a phone call which he took in the kitchen. When he returned, he quickly dismissed his parents when they asked who it was, so I didn't give it another thought.

It was a call from his former girlfriend. She had learned of John's failing health and was respectfully concerned. However, John didn't give her much information, nor any news to comfort her. He was too preoccupied with keeping his conversation short and getting her off the phone, given I was sitting in the next room within earshot of his conversation. But his lack of detail and uncharacteristic abruptness only made her worry more.

Just when I was getting ready to leave John to rest, there was a knock at the door. To everyone's great surprise, none other than John's ex-girlfriend stood in the doorway. She had hung up the phone, jumped in her car, and driven straight over to his parents' house to make sure he was okay. In fairness, I may have done the same in her position.

So, in she walked. Only she was as surprised to find me sitting there as I was to see her! I will never forget the look on John's father's face; he couldn't believe his eyes. Two girlfriends, one current and one former, perched on either side of John, there to support and comfort him but only succeeding in stressing him out to the max. He found it very amusing.

With all the confidence in her relationship with John and his parents that I lacked, John's ex set out to show me who was boss. Just as soon as she got herself seated on the couch, she jumped back up like a toilet seat, and asked, 'Does everyone want tea?'

Are you kidding me?

I felt sick watching her prance around the kitchen, helping herself to whatever we needed, serving up tea and cookies, making jokes and small talk with John's parents. It was over the top. I was at my breaking point. A monkey could have detected her jealousy and resentment, but I tried to make it clear that I was the girlfriend now, and I was not leaving until she was gone. My eyes said it all. I was shooting sharp darts in John's direction, despite his frail condition.

Having finished our intimate family tea party, John took his ex aside, and in no uncertain terms, told her she needed to go, *now*. She obliged and left discretely and quietly, in tears. I followed her minutes later, also bawling my eyes out. It was too much drama and too much sickness, anxiety, and emotion for me to take in one night. I couldn't wait to get out of there.

But, despite the trauma of that night, we made it through, and eventually John returned to work once he regained some of his strength and weight back.

It was around this time that I made the difficult decision to sell my townhouse. I was riddled in debt from a mortgage and other costs I could not maintain on my salary alone. I needed to start fresh and leave the memories there behind me, so I relocated from Mississauga to Etobicoke and rented a two-story, three-bedroom house with Tasha, my first dog: a scrappy, yappy, chocolate-brown poodle, as well as Sandy, one of my best friends from primary school.

During the weeks of solitude battling his illness, John took the time to contemplate his future. Unlike me, he wasn't thrilled with a career as an auditor. His illness gave him the opportunity to reflect on his purpose, and what would make him happy, less stressed, and more excited to get up in the morning. Within a year of his return to PwC, he ultimately left for a job in industry.

One of John's other revelations was his desire to move from his parents' home and begin a chapter of independence. Sandy and I talked about whether he should move in with us. She enthusiastically agreed to a third roommate, and we happily lived together in our roomy house.

Our relationship flourished under the same roof, and when our lease was up, we bid my wonderful and patient friend, Sandy, goodbye. John and I put an offer on a house, combining our savings together with a generous loan (later a gift) from John's parents for our down payment. To our delight, our offer was accepted, and we became first-time homeowners of a 1,700 square foot, two-storey, four-bedroom house in Mississauga.

We intended to live together for a while as a couple and tie the knot of marriage later, but those best-laid plans were short-lived. I became pregnant within a year of moving into our home, and although John and I were overjoyed with the idea of becoming parents, it was daunting to think of this much change in such a short time. My parents had suffered this same fate—kids in the same breath as marriage—and as you know, that did not end well. Notwithstanding my fear of this, we concluded the prudent (accountant) thing to do would be to get married before having our first.

We were married on December 29, 1985. Noticeably absent from the service was the dense, unwelcome fog that fell over me in my former nuptial—a life I had cast aside. Notwithstanding my burgeoning bulge, our wedding photos show a beaming bride at peace with what I dreamed was still to come: our family of three.

Three months of marital bliss (and another busy season at PwC!) passed by, and on April 1st, I was in the early stages of labour. The *real* contractions began around 8:00pm, and like a hailstorm my baby decided, 'I'm thirteen days overdue, and I will have no part of a scheduled inducement. I want to leave this womb all by myself!'

I grabbed my overnight bag at the bottom of the stairs and, with slow, cautious steps in between intense contractions that stopped me in my tracks, I made my way towards the front door.

As I looked over my shoulder to hand John my belongings, I noticed he was still in the kitchen, taking his sweet ass time. The fridge door was propped open, mayo out, Henkel carving knife in hand. He was slicing thick slabs of leftover roast beef and was placing them on top of thick slices of fresh ciabatta bread slathered with mayo.

'You've got to be kidding! It's time! John, let's go!' I was stunned by his nerve, but John, convinced this was *the most important thing* he should be doing, was headstrong. He wrapped his enormous sandwich in waxed paper, squeezed it into a paper bag, and replied, 'Okay, I'm ready now.'

He gently positioned me into our compact Toyota Celica for liftoff, and seconds later, I was a front-seat witness to a Formula 1 race I did not pay for. John decided to masquerade as freaking Mario Andretti through the streets of Mississauga.

An apparent plan of his all along, John blew through a red light so that, were we caught, he could explain to an officer, 'My wife is in labour! We're on our way to the hospital!' Lucky for me, the hospital was only fifteen minutes away and the streets at midnight were empty.

John blasted onto the emergency department scene to place me in a wheelchair and admit me to the Mississauga Hospital. From there, I spent all night in agony, dilation taking its sweet, sweet time. By morning, sleep-deprived and in a foul mood, I was desperate for news regarding my cervix's journey. However, the new gynecologist on duty informed me, 'Ms. Allen, you are only three centimeters dilated.' I almost swore out loud. This was becoming my worst nightmare.

The doctor, observing my anguish, made an executive decision. 'How about I break your water and get things moving along?' Before I could mutter, 'Can I think about that?' she reappeared with a two-foot, steel crochet hook. With a slight prick and a pop, the deed was done. New, more intense contractions empowered my uterus to turn itself inside out and then backwards. This was the devil's work. I had every intention of delivering my baby naturally with no medication for the safety of the baby, but there was no pride or courage left. I was no Wonder Woman.

'Give me the drugs!'

Meanwhile, sitting next to me, unaffected by my agony, Coach Cerisano decided he was hungry. As he unwrapped his gigantic, messy sandwich and devoured it, I half-expected him to say, 'I wonder if they sell Doritos in the cafeteria?'

For the next ten hours, I coaxed my cervix, my uterus, and my baby to come to an agreement: 'Can't you all just get along in there!' Twenty-one hours of exhausting contractions and a pair of icy-cold forceps were needed to pull this delivery off.

Then, like magic, a baby girl appeared; exactly what I wished for! Weighing in at 7.5 lbs, with a cone-shaped head and a tiny, wrinkled body, she was a sight to behold: precious and beautiful. On April 2, 1986, at 5:30pm, Danielle Kristen was welcomed into our world. We had been blessed with the miracle of birth.

9

Managing the Impossible

In 1986, I took all the maternity leave the government offered, then negotiated eight additional weeks of accumulated vacation and a month of unpaid leave from PwC.

I wanted to be home with Danielle for as long as we could manage, which came to a grand total of six months. I figured this was one of the few times in my life I could take time off, because I had made it clear to John and the rest of my family that I wasn't stepping away from my work. I had worked too hard, and I loved what I did, so it wasn't something I could let go.

Still, I looked forward to the time away from PwC. I hadn't taken a break longer than a day or two since graduating from university, and I was excited to bond with Danielle, just her and I. It was time for me to learn how to be a mother.

Although my maternity leave was a fraction of what Canadian women are granted today, at the time, a six-month maternity leave was not the norm, especially for women holding down a profession. Unlike Canada's paid *parental* leave of eighteen months today, government-sponsored maternity leave in the 80's was a total of seventeen weeks of paid leave, and unemployment insurance reimbursed only a fraction of what I was making as a full-time CPA. However, I was one of the lucky ones who received a small top-up from my forward-thinking employer.

But sadly, there was no such thing as parental *(paternity)* leave. Companies and governments must have assumed, wrongly, there was no need or demand for it.

Why?

Because men didn't *dare* take time off from their careers to look after a new baby. That decision would have sent male colleagues laughing all the way to the watercoolers. 'Who's wearing the pants in this family?' I know that many men would have liked to take paternity leave and spend more time with their newborn child, but they remained silent. They couldn't admit to wanting this arrangement, nor would they subject themselves to the teasing and ridicule from their male colleagues for even suggesting it. Fathers saw paternity leave as a *career limiting move,* just as career women rarely took their full maternity leave for fear of missing out on a promotion or stalling their career.

My experience saw the few senior women in the firm, those who dared to have children in the first place, take one, two, or at most, three months off before returning full time to a full-steam-ahead environment, just so they could continue their demanding climb up the corporate ladder. Some women took as little as *three weeks.* It was atrocious, even painful to see.

Women junior to me, in the decades to follow, were not afraid to take their full maternity leave. However, I never saw many of them again. They left for less demanding positions in industry or placed their CPA designation on a shelf to collect dust, choosing to work in the home and raise their family. I've explained how sad I was to hear this. Post children, very few of my colleagues opted for a reduced work schedule, even though the firm seemed open to flexible, reduced work arrangements and had programs that could support them. But I would learn of the reasons why a flexible, part-time schedule at PwC was considered career suicide, particularly when I examined this issue in detail twenty-five years later.

Even as I broke the norm by taking my six-month maternity leave, it was not enough time for me to adjust to motherhood. I was never sure I was doing the right thing and Danielle sensed it, as babies do.

I was overwhelmed, sending her into John's arms like I was tossing a football. I couldn't stop her uncontrollable crying. There was no internet to research the right way to breastfeed, what to expect for her sleep and feeding routines, and certainly nothing to prepare me for the difficult first six weeks I would endure as a new mom. Doulas, midwives, lactation specialists, and night nurses were support services I had never even heard of. I felt like I was just handed this living, breathing, defenseless crying machine, and then sent home without an instruction manual.

As it turns out, I was starving my poor child for the first six weeks of her life. Instead of a blissful breastfeeding experience, I learned the hard way I had a defective, exceedingly painful 'let down' reflex. (Picture thousands of tiny needles simultaneously stabbing my breast each time she latched on.) I wasn't building up my milk supply or releasing what little milk I produced for her growing body, and as she lost weight, I lost confidence in my ability as a mother.

It was heartbreaking. All I could think was, *What's wrong with me? Why can't I figure this out?* Every day, when John walked in the door after his long day at his new job with Pepsi, I would shove Danielle into his arms. 'Take her, please! I can't do this!'

However, at the advice of my doctor, once I made the switch to formula, Danielle began to gain weight and cried less. This was a blessing, but sadly, I was no more competent soothing her with her full tummy than I was in her times of need. The more she cried, the more tense I became. I was at my breaking point.

She continued to be fussy throughout the day and was completely inconsolable by 6pm, her witching hour, just as I was reaching the end of my tether. Glancing at the kitchen clock, I would tell her (and myself), 'Just another thirty minutes, fifteen minutes, ten minutes. Dad will be home any minute now. He will make you better.'

I remember one night the phone rang as I was looking outside the window, waiting for the car to drive up. Danielle was in my arms wailing. It was 6:50pm—only ten more minutes before John would come to my rescue.

'Hello?'

'Hi Sue, it's John. I haven't left yet.' *Pause.* 'I had to work late tonight.' *Pause.* 'Sorry. I'll be leaving in a few minutes. I'll be home as soon I can.' Tears were streaming down my cheeks as I hung up the phone. For the next hour, Danielle's sobbing matched my weeping tear for tear.

'I can't handle this; it's breaking me in two!'

Was this postpartum depression?

Though I should have, I never saw a doctor about my sadness. I felt that my ineptness as a mother was the root cause, and if I just improved, I would feel better, do better. Classic Sue.

But I was extremely disappointed in myself. I felt like a failure who was unable to calm and comfort her own child, and while it's true that Danielle was colicky, starving most of the time, I'm convinced my Type A-ness stressed her out more. Babies sense that kind of thing.

My hopeless shifting of this little bundle from one hip to the other, bouncing her in my arms, and asking her *nicely* to stop crying (really, you think that's going to work?) taxed me every waking moment of my day. I had no idea how to troubleshoot my latest stretch assignment: a newborn. All I knew is that what I was doing was useless, and I often felt small and inept any time I was around others with Danielle.

One day, as I was showing her off to my colleagues at the office, a complete stranger took crying Danielle from my arms to settle her down in hers. Worse? She was successful. *Ouch.* God that hurt.

No, I didn't classify myself as depressed, but I needed a giant dose of positive reinforcement from friends and family, as well as the constant reminder, 'Sue, you *will* get through this' during my darkest days.

Then, at four months, like magic, Danielle grew out of her colicky behaviour, which was around the same time she was developing her own unique personality. Danielle was full of wonder of the world around her, and I soon reasoned she didn't sleep much because she didn't want to miss one single thing.

Not *one* single thing. God was it exhausting!

But the more she grew, *the more I grew*. I was learning how to be her mother, and how she wanted me to hold her and keep her safe, just as she was becoming a little human. I was finding my stride, my confidence as a mother was growing day by day, and then suddenly, the last two beautiful months of my maternity leave were over. It was time for me to return to work.

That hurt… *a lot.*

I suddenly understood why so many successful, intelligent, and powerful women never returned to the office.

I misjudged how I would feel leaving her in someone else's hands, no matter how capable I knew they were. The possibility of missing her first word, her first step, her first *anything*... I couldn't bear the thought of missing a second of my child's life.

As a willing participant in her laughs and smiles as she laid in my cradled, secure arms in those final two months of maternity, I would gaze down into her loving eyes to see her looking up at mine. It melted my heart daily. Every minute I spent with her was bliss. I never knew love for another human could be this intense. Here in my arms was a little being that loved me more than anything else in the world; a tiny, fragile baby that needed me and loved me as much as I needed and loved her.

Why wasn't I prepared for this slice of motherhood? I was deeply conflicted with mom guilt. My friends, my family, and other mothers didn't use this term specifically, but their curious frowns and questioning tone when I stated, unequivocally, during my pregnancy, 'Of course, I'm going back to work,' was their clear warning. I didn't appreciate how difficult my dual life as a career mom would be. I didn't understand the powerful guilt I would feel until it was too late, and I was knee-deep in the quicksand of motherhood, sinking fast.

It's impossible to appreciate the profound bond a parent and a child feel until you have a child yourself. If there was ever anything strong enough to convince me to leave PwC, Danielle would have been it.

My priorities before Danielle were simple: my health, my career, and, more recently, my marriage. In case this isn't obvious, let me spell it out for you: *it was all about me.* And why shouldn't it be?

And here's another shocker. On (too) many occasions, my career had taken first position. Work meant everything to me. It took strength and courage to move the mountains that had stood in my way to this point—course corrections, personal sacrifices, and resolve. I was relentless in securing my place in the world of business. My husband understood this better than most.

However, with the addition of Danielle, life was flipped inside-out and upside-down. How was I expected to introduce a baby into my pre-set priorities? Was I supposed to ask them to take a back seat to Danielle? She would not understand my established order, nor could she quietly step aside and be anything less than the number one priority. Over the last six months, she had secured her place.

But would this always be the case?

Don't take this the wrong way. I accept and support a parent's decision to stay home; this is no easy feat. When faced with this dilemma, I believe we choose what our heart (and bank account) asks of us. I know a few lucky parents with financial security that can afford to have one parent work while the other stays home. More often, however, I have seen couples altering their lifestyle so they can live on a single parent's salary. They choose the lower income, or less upwardly mobile parent, to take on the caregiver role at home. It should come as no surprise that, in the 80's, this was almost always the woman.

That said, every day I stayed home, I found it more and more exhausting, physically and emotionally. It was hard for me in the stay-at-home-mom role. I don't know how moms or dads do this and keep their sanity.

I knew this then, and I know it now. If I took the stay-at-home-mom route, I would have been shortchanging myself. That life isn't my life. If I remained home to meet the expectations of my extended family and friends, it would have cost me my happiness and my truth. Some might argue I was making a cold, hard, selfish decision to go back to work.

All I know for certain is that I would have regretted staying home for the rest of my life. How would that have affected me? Or worse, how would I feel about my daughter, who I could unconsciously and unfairly blame for giving up my career?

I decided that a fulfilling, challenging career would make me happy—just like the one I chose before I became a mom. I knew I would be a better parent to Danielle if I could be a career woman, *for me*.

But that wasn't it, and I knew the second part of this equation might prove just as challenging. Possibly *more* challenging.

In order to be a better professional for PwC, I needed the *flexibility* to be the best mom I could be. This was very important, and it still is today, because to be successful at one, I had to be successful at both; two lives learning to sway in step like two dance partners supporting each other. This, as so many people in this situation come to understand, would be a constant battle.

So, how could I handle another priority? Truth be told, I couldn't. There was no time left in my crowded 24-hour day. But life doesn't care about that, does it? You *make* time.

A three-legged stool does not collapse with the addition of a fourth leg—it becomes a chair, stronger and able to withstand even more weight. I had to make room for the fourth leg, allow motherhood to equal or even, dare I say, *overtake* my work priority. I needed a perspective change.

Enter my most difficult challenge yet: developing and adhering to a more manageable work/life balance.

I made myself a promise—a critical step for any arrangement to work. I pledged I would not miss a milestone, no matter the consequences or the cost to me or my career. I would never miss something important in Danielle's life for a client or a meeting. I wasn't going to set myself up for that regret. There is no meeting that cannot be rescheduled.

Listening to my child give her winning speech on 'Why we are afraid of bats' in front of the entire school cannot be rescheduled. Neither can watching my child's face when she makes the winning basket, the winning soccer goal, the winning water polo shot, or the winning field hockey goal for her team's school. It's that simple.

I pledged to be at every milestone, tipping point, and special event in her life. If necessary, and it would be necessary, I told myself I would push aside feelings of guilt whenever I told my clients, my boss, or my staff a little white lie in order to attend my child's event.

'I'm sorry, I can't be on that call, or in your meeting today. I have another meeting I cannot reschedule. I will call you later when I free up.'

Unfortunately, in the 1980's and 1990's, it wasn't acceptable for men or women in a client service role to admit they were taking time off during the all-important 9-5pm workday. We would be a laughingstock if we missed a meeting for anything other than a child's sick day. So, I had to lie about it, and when cell phones were introduced to the workplace, I'd put it on silent so I wouldn't be distracted.

Which leads me to one of the most important promises I have ever made to myself, and I would invite you to do the same if you're ever in this position as a working mother.

When I was with Danielle, I would *be present* for her, support her, encourage her, and inspire her. I would bring my best self to her and be the role model I knew I could be, so I could demonstrate, through my actions, that she could be anything she set her mind to. No goal was too big, too impractical, or unattainable. I wanted her to know she was brave, beautiful, strong, smart, and loved. I *needed* her to know she could be an independent, successful woman, just like her mom.

Still, returning to work was difficult, not only because I would miss Danielle, but because we needed to find her a caregiver so I could comfortably ease my way back to work. I set out to find the perfect someone to be her second mom when I wasn't there. Only then could I accept my choice to return to work and live with the guilt I knew I would experience every day.

I spent my summer seeking out a person I could trust and found the perfect match. She was my age and answered all my probing questions well. She had me convinced she was the ideal candidate—married with a toddler of her own—and I believed she would treat Danielle as her own. As a stay-at-home mom, her in-home care for my child was intended to supplement her family income. She lived fifteen minutes away, and it was a short, convenient drive for me to drop Danielle off in the morning and pick her up on my way home from work.

This woman had only one stipulation: *Danielle must be picked up by 6:00pm sharp.*

Uh oh.

She was adamant about this, so she could make a clean break from caregiving for my child to spending private time with her daughter and husband. She wouldn't tolerate a nightly interruption. (i.e., me picking up Danielle during what was supposed to be her personal family time.)

Seeing this as a reasonable ask, I vowed to adhere to her modest request. In return, Danielle would receive her loving care, homemade baby food, and an opportunity to learn how to play and share with another toddler for a fee that worked within my budget. I honest to God couldn't have asked for more.

It wasn't feasible for John to pick up Danielle at 6:00pm considering his one-hour commute in the opposite direction compared to my fifteen-minute commute to PwC's Mississauga office. I went into this arrangement with my eyes wide open, accepting the fact that John would not be able to pick her up. Red flag.

Yet, I was optimistic that I could make it work, but as the weeks progressed, my workday demonstrated its strong hold over me. This should not have surprised me. As flexible as my workday was, it could also be unpredictable. I found myself plagued by last-minute client requests, emergencies, urgent deadlines, and staff who needed me just as I was packing up to leave. I met others' needs at the expense of mine *and* Danielle's, because I hadn't learned how to deal with emergencies or unrealistic expectations. I didn't know how to say 'no' or simply ask, 'Can this wait?'

My repeated attempts to end my day at 5:40pm were missed, and I failed to keep my part of the bargain at least once a week. In those moments, I was a frantic mess, speaking incoherently and describing in greater detail than necessary why I was late. But each and every time my explanation was met with skepticism. As Danielle and I started for the car, I looked back, and announced over my shoulder, more times than I could count, 'I promise this will not happen again.' The front door was already closed.

It was futile. As much as I willed this arrangement to work, it became clear to me, and to the caregiver, this just wasn't going to work. The relationship had scarcely begun.

Caught between a rock and a hard place—an unpredictable work schedule and no feasible solution for childcare—I had exhausted all leads. Daycare was not an option because they have even stricter drop-off and pick-up requirements. God knows how that would play out... a baby left curbside with an angry caregiver...

I also heard stories of how often children contracted colds and sniffles in daycare from the sheer number of children they would come in contact with. What would happen then? Neither John nor I could drop everything to stay home with a sick kid on a moment's notice.

Furthermore, the cost of daycare for a single child was expensive. The benefits didn't outweigh the costs. I imagine this was a huge reason why so many women left their burgeoning careers for homemaking. I imagine this is *still* the case today.

Each of our three sets of parents lived too far away. Besides, mine and John's parents had raised *their* children already. If circumstances were different, and they lived close by (and they had offered), I may have considered it. But they didn't. I saved my asks of them for special occasions: a Saturday date night, a fundraising gala, or any number of weeknight work events I was required to attend.

So, what does the proper childcare solution look like for an 8-month-old when both parents are consumed by demanding work schedules? We were back at the drawing board, crossing out alternatives, one by one, until there was only one option left; something we never imagined we would consider.

We decided to hire a live-in nanny.

It was more costly than my previous arrangement outside of the home, but it was the only solution that removed the need for drop-offs and pick-ups. However, all good things come with a cost. In this case, it was our privacy.

We settled on Lotta, a twenty-something, intelligent girl from Sweden who we met only on paper. Lotta would start her life in Canada with us as Danielle's nanny, and in return, she would receive a paycheck and a sponsorship for her immigration to Canada.

Anxious for her arrival, we counted down the days for her to accept our offer, pass her medical, and book her flight across the pond.

Lotta was kind, conscientious, and remarkably shy. We welcomed her into our home and did our absolute best to make her feel comfortable by releasing her of all duties not directly attributable to Danielle's wellbeing. However, she seemed immediately overwhelmed by her caregiver role.

What was she expecting? I feared if I asked her to attempt any of the light household chores detailed in the job description, she would surely blow a gasket, and six weeks later, *she did*.

This was not the job, the life, nor the country for her. Whether it was immaturity, homesickness, the language barrier, or the not-so-simple job of caring for my infant, we were not a fit for her. She caught the next flight back to Sweden on her parents' dime. We never saw nor heard from her again.

More nanny interviews, more agency fees, more unsuccessful attempts to find a caregiver. Over the ensuing weeks and months, in fits and starts, nannies came and left us for no apparent reason. We were frantic to find a caregiver, and Danielle was not yet a year old.

I asked for nothing more than to look after our daughter, and still they would find a reason we were not a good fit. What exactly was the problem? Was I to blame for this upheaval and, if so, what had I done? We repeatedly paid finder's fees to access more resumes and recruit other caregivers. 'We only have one child and there is nothing more you need to do. You can live in or live out. What can we say to help you decide "yes?"'

I was so desperate to make things easy for our latest nanny, I'd jump out of bed early to prepare anything and everything I could think of for Danielle's ensuing day. If the nanny drank tea, I would make it for her. If she wanted breakfast, I would show her the fridge.

'Help yourself. Is there anything else you need before I leave?' I was going insane.

Then a miracle happened. We found Genie, a stout, forty-seven-year-old Filipino woman whose smile lit up a room. She was grateful to have a job, and it showed. She was conscientious, her manner pleasant and positive. She worked hard, surprising me with completing household tasks I hadn't asked of her and didn't expect her to do. And still, she had endless energy to spend with Danielle, playing with her, teaching her, and reading to her. She seemed to meet her every need. She kept to herself when she wasn't working and was quiet and respectful of our privacy. She wasn't only Danielle's nanny... she was mine!

With Genie so perfect, you would think this would make my morning departure easy and lessen those nagging pangs of mom guilt, right?

Wrong.

Every morning, I put on a brave face, especially when Danielle started her tantrum. Standing at my front door, my briefcase in hand, she hugged my calves with all her might.

'Why do you have to leave me, Mommy? Why? Why do you have to work, Mommy? Don't you want to stay home with me? Please! Don't leave.' Turn the knife while it's stabbing my heart.

Genie assured me Danielle stopped crying and moved onto something else before I had reached the bottom of the driveway. Even if she was telling me a lie, I needed to hear Danielle would be alright. Still, as I turned the ignition and waited for my car to warm up, I searched for a radio station playing a song I liked, one that I knew the words to so I could sing the lyrics. Singing took my mind off the separation anxiety, but all that kept me going was the constant thought, *In nine hours, I will see her again.*

In the evening, when I burst through the door, I couldn't tell who was more excited: our high-strung poodle, or our excited toddler. The welcoming committee didn't wait for me to put down my briefcase or discard my high heels. As I knelt and outstretched my arms to embrace Danielle with my biggest hug, Tasha barked and leapt around us saying, 'Wait, it's my turn! What about me?'

I attempted to counter lost hours during the day by spending evenings at Danielle's disposal. In order to be *present* for her, to leave my work behind, I perfected my super mom powers. Before, during, and after dinner was a non-stop playdate. We had a lot of ground to cover.

At night, John and I took turns tucking Danielle into bed, reading her any number of Mercer Mayer and *Berenstain Bears* books, her ritual concluding with singing a French lullaby, *Fais dodo*. The routine was consistent, but exhausting. When we (accidently-on-purpose) missed a page or skipped over lines, we were chastised, 'Hey! Wait, you forgot this part... go back.'

When Danielle was tucked in bed and dozing off to sleep, I tiptoed out of her room to find my briefcase. *I must put a dent in my outstanding to-do list before morning*. And so began my night shift.

I'm not the first nor the last working parent to go through these motions. At times, you think you'll go crazy with your lack of sleep, and you marvel at the sheer will it takes to read that same ABC's book yet again, pointing out the letters and their associated apple, banana, and cat pictures. But you do it because you love them, and if you miss a night for whatever reason, you actually truly regret it.

There is an irony there, and I think it's both beautiful and difficult to navigate. No one said parenting would be easy, but no one said it would be that wonderful either.

Learning to troubleshoot, juggle, and survive

Prior to motherhood, my priorities were simple: maintain my health, advance my career, and be a supportive spouse. As I suspect, evolution and the survival of our species has a hand in influencing us, because having a baby immediately shifts your priorities. My daughter moved firmly into position 'A', having melted my heart before she could even say, 'Mama.'

I wish I could report that settling into motherhood was easy, but it was far from it. It began with my difficult delivery of her into the world and continued with my utter ineptness as a mom. I learned to cope, like most parents do, through trial and error, bouts of tears, and the rollercoaster ride of stress, anxiety, and guilt—it's just how parenting operates. While I experimented, learned, and established a routine that fit us both best, I promised to fulfill a non-negotiable piece of the bargain—to raise a brave, beautiful, and independent young woman.

Just so there is no misunderstanding, let me make two things perfectly clear:

1. *I thank the heavens and stars above for the miracle of birth.*
2. *I am eternally grateful for my perfectly imperfect experience as a mom.*

There, had to get that off my chest.

Lessons I learned as a spouse and a new mom:

- The best part about dating a friend or a colleague is the ability to be yourself from the word 'dolmodakia.' Should you choose to marry your best friend, *what they see is what they get*—there are no false pretenses to hide behind. With any luck, thirty-six years later, you will still prefer to spend your days together versus apart, share private jokes, have joint and separate hobbies, strong family ties, and everlasting memories.

- Parenting is really hard. Ask for help. Don't expect to get it right the first time or every time and don't be too hard on yourself when you mess up. Because you're going to.

- There will always be guilt felt when sacrifices are made. Learn to live without regrets. How? Pick your battles and keep in mind there are certain milestones, no matter the consequences or the costs, that cannot be missed. Someone or something can always wait; there is no meeting that cannot be rescheduled (even when you have to tell a little white lie about what you are really doing).

- Be *present* to support your daughter; encourage her and inspire her. Be a role model. Bring the best version of yourself to her. Demonstrate through your actions that she can be anything she sets her mind to—brave, beautiful, strong, smart, and loved. The sky's the limit. Tell her she can be an independent, successful woman, like you.

Reflection Questions

1. How do you deal with and acknowledge the guilt arising from sacrifices you make to yourself and others closest to you? How do you keep these feelings from negatively impacting your wellbeing?

2. What actions can you take to achieve a work/life balance on your terms? What if these actions don't produce the results you hoped? Do you have a Plan B?

3. How do you identify and apply the resources and support systems available to help you solve complex problems? (i.e., dealing with change, sourcing reliable childcare, returning to work after an extended absence, leaving a job you love, or finding meaning in a new career.)

Part IV: Learning to Expect the Unexpected

'Storms make the oak grow deeper roots.' — George Herbert

When I was in grade school, Aesop was my go-to moralist. His stories entertained, influenced, and foreshadowed mistakes to avoid. I learned *perseverance* from 'The Tortoise and the Hare', the trouble with *false alarms* from 'The Boy who Cried Wolf', and *kindness* from the 'Lion and the Mouse.2019

In adulthood, however, life's lessons—the worthiest ones—are more bashful. They don't reveal themselves in the moment but wait to present themselves when and where you least expect to find them. They seem to prefer a reserved entrance, appearing as 'aha!' moments.

Do your life lessons hit you over the head with a sledgehammer or simmer quietly on the stove waiting for you to take notice? Mine seem to perpetually simmer.

In the following chapters, I want you to understand something important. Many of the teachings, the things I learned, were not obvious to me, because I was either preoccupied with inconsequential thoughts, or I was not looking in their direction.

It was only later, upon deeper reflection that my 'aha!' moments appeared, and many of these significant moments were made possible not from my own initiative but through the selfless acts of others who looked out for my best interests. With the help of others, I discovered the importance of developing connections, building resilience, creating solutions to live life your way, accepting what you cannot change, listening to your gut, and the incredible ROI you get from volunteering. I hope you find the treasures buried in these next chapters useful.

You will also read about a shattering life event thrust upon me without warning or time to react. This is a fragile story that began with emotional pain and despair and took me on a rollercoaster of panic and fear, even today when I think about it. But I urge you, please don't stop reading when the going gets tough, or you will miss the main point—how I discovered a message of gratitude and hope, of restored purpose and changed perspective. It is a grown-up's tale of 'A Mother and a Boy' with a larger-than-life lesson that answers the question, '*What matters most?*'

I'd argue it is proof that we are given only as much as we can handle.

To quote Audrey Hepburn, 'Anyone who does not believe in miracles is not a realist.'

10

Saying 'Yes' to Stretch

Shortly after I returned from maternity leave, the partner-in-charge of the Mississauga office, Ian, was asked to join a not-for-profit board, the Mississauga Arts Council (MAC). It didn't take him long to decide it wasn't a fit for him, so he marched straight into my office to ask if I would be interested in taking 'his' place on this board.

Juggling my new reality with a child, I had my hands full between work and home. But rather than saying 'no' immediately, I asked a few more questions. Volunteering in the arts, with my background in drama and dance, was intriguing. So, when Ian told MAC he had found someone else in the firm interested in their board, they decided to give me a look.

Joining the board was not as simple as saying, 'Yes, I'm in!' I had to be elected by the membership and this required me to give a speech at their Annual General Meeting on why the membership should vote for me. I was quick to learn that this wasn't a slam dunk either. I was up against qualified artists, businessmen, and well-known leaders in the community, and I was just some nobody auditor.

This was my first attempt at being involved in my community, and as I stood at the podium, I explained how I was an accountant and an auditor with PwC by day, but deep down a lover of the arts as a former dancer and drama student. I held my nerves in check as best I could while I shared my personal background to a packed audience of complete strangers: artists, politicians, retirees, volunteers, and businessmen. There wasn't an auditor or accountant for miles.

I did get elected that night and started my journey into the interesting world of volunteering. It was an ego boost. I had my accounting expertise to share with the board but didn't have to be the Treasurer, and I was glad they could accept this deviation from the norm.

I was asked to chair the Grants Committee for the Council, which reviewed the applications for city funding for arts organizations—the original reason MAC was formed. I had much to share, and my opinion was valued. Within a few months, I was asked to be Vice-Chair of the Council and take on more responsibility.

While volunteering, I learned how to run an effective and efficient meeting, and more importantly, how to get volunteer board members to put their hand up to do something while holding them accountable in the nicest way possible. If you want to learn how to encourage, negotiate, and influence others, sit on a volunteer board!

When the chair, my mentor, decided her time was up, I was offered her place. This meant time spent in the evenings and weekends at ribbon-cutting ceremonies expressing my best wishes on behalf of the MAC.

At first, I would meticulously draft every word that I intended to say so I wouldn't make a fool of myself. But I found this way of delivering my message impersonal and ineffective. I would stand at the podium clutching my speech in my hands, reading it while barely lifting my head to look at the audience. I felt so ridiculous and amateurish. What happened to the drama grad? Where was she hiding these days?

However, after I got a bunch of speeches and presentations under my belt, I realized the notes were a crutch I no longer needed. With experience, I developed the courage to leave my notes on the podium and look up at my audience. It was liberating. I could say what I wanted to say, and actually string my words together sensibly. Imagine that! People sat up and listened and laughed *with* me not *at* me. My message was making an impact!

During meetings, I learned to take control while chairing, cutting people off like the polite Canadian I am if they went on for too long or were off topic. Many skills I learned in the not-for-profit world helped me in my for-profit business world. It translated to more presence, more confidence, and best of all, speaking without notes.

These were unexpected, tangible rewards I received beyond the thrill and energy this work gave me! While I was helping fund artists, increasing awareness of the arts, and enriching the lives of fellow Mississauga citizens, I was developing essential life and business skills in a non-threatening, low-risk setting with people that appreciated my value. I received immense gratitude for my effort and skills. I found a fit with my fellow volunteers who were from more diverse backgrounds than my fellow accountants—including their ethnicity, profession, age, gender, and culture—and this gave me firsthand experience with the value of diversity of thought.

Who could have predicted that filling in for my male PwC colleague, the man originally requested for this role, would place me in line for pivotal career opportunities in the decades to come?

This is what happens when you're not afraid to accept an opportunity, even if you don't know where it might lead.

As I piled on the experience volunteering, I was learning, in the months since my promotion, that being a new manager in a high-stakes environment was difficult. And while the growth I experienced at PwC was stretching me, my personal life was challenging me in even more meaningful ways. Over the past twelve months, I filed for my own divorce, got pregnant, remarried, became a new mother, and purchased a new home.

Dealing with this degree of change was enough to take me off balance. I had to constantly remind myself to hold on and consider how fortunate I was to live a life I only could have dreamed of as a teenager. I had come so far already.

In retrospect, my most important task amidst the swirling tornado of change was learning how to keep these unfamiliar balls in the air, then figure out which ones were worth juggling and which ones I could let drop. Most importantly, when those least important balls dropped, I had to remember to show empathy to myself. I couldn't be all things to all people.

What I hadn't learned yet was how to say 'no' more often and be okay with disappointing others. Easier said than done, isn't it? At that time, I wish I had realized that the person I was letting down most was myself. When I finally had the courage to say 'no', a huge burden was lifted off my shoulders. I was proud to have set and stuck to my boundaries.

I put Danielle, work, and John first. I placed myself, my needs, and my wants *dead last*. With a 60-hour workweek, there was no time left to recharge my batteries doing activities that could have helped me physically or mentally. I forgot the important lessons dance taught me, the way exercise made me feel, the endorphins and energy I felt afterwards. Exercise, sleep, reflection, connecting with family and friends, reading, or simply doing nothing at all moved to my lowest priority for many years.

Compartmentalizing work and home was a challenge for me. I always had impending deadlines I couldn't ignore, or I'd stay awake thinking about staff who were relying on my review to approve their work. It became even worse when, later in my career, I received my first Blackberry phone with its countless emails I couldn't possibly address. Yet, my eyes insisted I read every single one of them. The 'always on' society that was brought about by technology was no friend of mine.

After I made it through another grueling week, John would often say, 'If I worked as hard as you, I would be dead by now.' That was particularly troubling to hear. I, too, was surprised I could keep up this pace. I worried I was doing some major unknown damage to myself—something that would show up in my later years... *a silent killer*. But I put those dark thoughts aside and kept going, like the Energizer Bunny. *Tomorrow is another day. I will get through this.*

Still, amidst the chaos of being a mother, a wife, and a rising businesswoman, I fantasised about the day I would wake up and find that the train had left the station *without me*. I wanted it to leave me behind. I longed for my life to slow down long enough to take it all in properly—my daughter, my surroundings, and even the food in front of me. I would imagine my life, sleeping in as late as I liked, stretching in my comfy king-sized bed, rising slowly, effortlessly.

But that fantasy wasn't who I was. I knew, at this stage in my life, I would be miserable with a slower pace. I was learning to thrive in the chaos, and that train was *mine* to conduct. I wasn't about to let it leave the station without me on board, and it just so happened that my train was about to switch tracks and take me down a path that was to be my destiny.

Mike, an experienced, well-respected Toronto partner, was up next on a journey that took me beyond the walls of my Mississauga connections. Early on in my time with PwC, I had the pleasure of meeting Mike on the dance floor at my Seniors' Conference—my comfort zone and a place I could shine. He was a man with good rhythm, making it effortless for me to build a rapport, then strike up a meaningful conversation while we tripped the light fantastic to Wham's 'Wake Me Up Before You Go-Go'.

Mike, who I thought of as an approachable colleague more than as a partner or a boss, would play an important role in my future. With him, I shared my original wish to be a teacher, as well as the roundabout way I landed a career with PwC. What I didn't know was that he tucked away our conversation for later.

Teaching had always been a passion of mine. Explaining difficult concepts, breaking them down into manageable chunks, and seeing a student's confidence brighten the room with new comprehension, gives and always has given me purpose.

As it happens, PwC had a training department: National Continuing Education (NCE). The firm's in-house CPAs serve as the department's course developers, teachers, and trainers, and every couple of years, a few high-performing managers with a knack for teaching, and a desire to develop course material, were invited to join NCE for a two- or three-year stint in the department.

It was marketed to the few uniquely qualified individuals who didn't mind taking a break from chargeable audit work. Over the duration of their secondment, these managers honed their subject-matter expertise and presentation skills and developed deep relationships with partners and managers across the country and internationally. Their experience at NCE helped further their careers.

This opportunity was destined to collide with my north star. My friend, Mike, was the leader of this department, and he remembered our discussion years prior about how I switched my path from teaching to auditing. He had waited for the right place and time in my career, and with an upcoming opening in his department, *he made me an offer I couldn't refuse.*

I was enjoying my current responsibilities in audit, but a secondment in NCE to teach, develop courses, and train the trainers? That was attractive.

Who would have thought that, to fulfill my dream of teaching, I would have to give it up, become a CPA, rise to manager in a public accounting firm, and randomly meet a guy at a conference who would offer it to me? Even today I marvel at how my career took another jog in its atypical, non-linear path.

The secondment in NCE was a significant change in role and scenery. It required me to leave the safe haven of my friends, colleagues, and clients in Mississauga, and take an hour-long commute each way into downtown Toronto. This seemed a small sacrifice for the exceptional opportunity Mike was offering.

The timing was also nothing short of a miracle. With a toddler at home, this opportunity gave me the flexibility and hours I craved with less demanding, non-client-based deadlines. It was a change from my last five years in the audit practice, yet I was still technically in audit, trying on something new, challenging, and exciting. Awesome!

In this role, PwC staff were my 'clients'. As long as I set my priorities to meet the firm's deadlines for course materials and delivered them on time, I could plan my days and my weeks without the unpredictability an external client load demanded. Moreover, even though I would be working hard, I escaped my audit busy season. Another bonus!

I loved how creative I could be, using my experience with prior clients to develop practical, real cases. I tackled concepts that were at one time difficult for me, and I invited others to ask questions to avoid the mistakes I had once made. It was easy to come up with all kinds of relevant material, given where I had come from with zero accounting background and everything to learn.

One prerequisite of my role, as the creator of the course material, was to teach the instructors for the course, which meant...

Drum roll please···

I had to travel to the Caribbean PwC firms!

Wait, what? I am *required* to teach my courses in Barbados and Trinidad? Pity.

I didn't think I could love anything more than auditing, but NCE was my newfound love. So, after my first term, I asked Mike if I could extend my secondment by another year. With gratitude, he accepted my request.

Over time, I was given more responsibility managing the review and supervision of course development while coaching the new managers rotating into NCE. In the back of my mind, a little voice was coaxing me to stay here longer. Maybe my permanent place was here?

Not only did I love the work, but I also got my first taste of travelling for business with NCE. Meeting staff from other parts of the world demonstrated how small and connected our world was. I saw firsthand how diverse our firm was, and I witnessed how we were more similar than different in our values, ambitions, behaviours, culture, and work ethic. Little did I know how this experience would come in handy.

My time in NCE did not slow my progression in the firm, unlike the rumours I had heard. The powers that be saw it fit to promote me to Senior Manager as my third year in NCE was coming to its conclusion, even though I was pregnant (again) and would be taking another extended six-month maternity leave.

I couldn't have been happier; my heart was full. My career was progressing. I was expecting my second child, and my due date had been timed to coincide with the conclusion of my NCE secondment (not *totally* on purpose).

Moreover, looking ahead to the future, after my second was born, I couldn't wait to return to Mississauga as an experienced, confident mother *and* a newly promoted Audit Senior Manager. Career was finding its place next to family, and together, we were firing on all cylinders.

But when it seems too good to be true, *it usually is.*

11

How Priorities Are Set (What Matters Most)

We are naïve to think life is straightforward. Dreams don't come true because we wish them to. Life is going to throw us curveballs whether we are ready to catch them or not.

A tragedy or death in the family, a sudden divorce, a market crash, a global pandemic, or even a natural disaster—these are just a few of the things that can catch you off-guard, resulting in a paradigm shift for you and those you love. When they do happen, because they inevitably will, we can let these things break us, or we can become stronger, wiser, and more compassionate people.

After three fantastic years with Danielle, I had a new baby on the way, and one of these paradigm-shifting curveballs was thrown in my direction as I rounded second base. It was thrown hard, catching me in the chest, leaving me breathless as it passed straight through to my heart. The strength of my marriage, the conviction of my life's ambitions, and the capacity of my heart to keep from breaking was my next test.

We planned for our second child this time, and my timing was perfect. I would give birth to a little brother or sister for Danielle and enjoy an intentional break with both of my children before transitioning back to audit in the Mississauga office. Another six-month maternity leave, a live-in nanny for two kids, a return to full-time work as a newly-promoted senior manager, and Bob's your uncle.

Danielle turned three as I was preparing to deliver our second—the perfect age gap for besties. Genie, our live-in nanny, was doing a great job taking care of Danielle while I worked full time, and I expected to continue this routine until my kids no longer needed nannies.

As with Danielle, my second pregnancy was easy breezy; no morning sickness and minimal discomfort other than sleeping with a progressively protruding belly for the last trimester. I worked my typically long hours up to my last possible workday. It was the delivery that was no picnic—I was meant to *have* children, not *deliver* them.

My unborn baby was ten days past its due date. My family doctor set an inducement day, and as this day approached, John and I arrived at the Mississauga Hospital for my scheduled admission at 8:00am. To my surprise, John drove the speed limit, stopping at every red traffic light he encountered. He may very well have brought his all-important coach's lunch, but I don't really remember—I wasn't having heavy contractions while he was preparing it!

My admission to the hospital started out simple enough. After being hooked up to the oxytocin drip, I waited for my body to do its thing with the help of the inducing drugs. I played cards with John for hours, while the contractions began softly, ever-so-slowly. More hours passed, nothing much changed. Lunch and then dinner came and went. Still nothing but the faintest fluttering of contractions, which I, the scaredy cat, was completely at peace with. The nurses were not concerned, which meant neither were we.

The on-call gynecologist came in to check on me around 8:00pm, disappointed and frustrated I had been left so long with so little result. This was not right; not enough was happening to do anything meaningful. So, she upped my dosage immediately.

Within minutes, the contractions came like a tidal wave I couldn't stop. No more light flutters, just heavy, debilitating contractions that felt like my insides were whirling around. They came on intense and strong, and without warning, my pain threshold went from 0-60, too fast for my pain sensors or my brain to amicably tolerate. Everything I learned about breathing deeply or taking it slow and easy went soaring out the window.

My mind recalled my suffering through the hours and hours of pain and contractions I experienced with Danielle. Three years ago felt like three minutes ago—I was not ready to relive that again, ever. My tolerance for pain was sinking faster than the *Titanic*; I was drowning, no lifeboat in sight.

I swallowed my pride and begged for the epidural to make the pain go away. *Now.*

Several hours flew by until my cervix was dilated the prescribed ten centimeters and it was time to push. Now, the timing of my deliveries is not my forte. A few moments earlier, I was given a top-up of the epidural medication and, just like my first pregnancy, I was totally frozen from the waist down. The similarity to Danielle's delivery was like watching a bad B movie. I could no more push this watermelon out of my uterus than wiggle my toes.

Doctors had no choice but to grip that baby by the head with their trusty forceps and yank it out. So, at 12:19am on April 20th, I heard, 'It's a boy!' What a relief… I had one of each!

I whispered to John with a mix of despair and happiness, 'Thank God I don't have to go through this pain… *ever* again.'

The doctors wiped this little gem of a boy clean and put him on my chest for us to bond. He weighed in at 8.5lbs and had a cute, little, scrunched-up, red face and a pointy head. I could see the indents from the force of the forceps against his crown. He had the *Star Trek* look of alien descent, but of course, he was beautiful to me. He was called 'Baby Allen' as was hospital protocol until we came up with a name, which, as two tired, happy parents, we were unconcerned with.

Baby Allen was just as tired. He cried and cried the entire time he lay on my chest. Try as I might to comfort him, I couldn't, but I just attributed this to my basic inability to soothe or calm any baby under two. That seems to be my way.

Still, for several minutes I tried. I must have looked desperate, because the nurses took pity on me and whisked him away to their calmer, experienced arms. Then, he was taken out of the birthing room altogether. I didn't ask where he was going or why he was leaving us, because, honestly, I was too tired to care.

I was in desperate need of a good night's sleep. John was asked to go home, to leave me to sleep, and as excited as we both were, we were just as happy to hear it was time for us to get some rest. He kissed me goodbye, added a loving, warm embrace for good measure, and promised to return first thing in the morning.

That night, instead of getting the restful sleep I longed for, I was left in the same room I had delivered Baby Allen. *What kind of recovery room is this? Why do I have to endure an overhead light shining so brightly on my face that I can barely sleep?* It was infuriating. No one came by to check on me for what seemed like an eternity.

Finally, at 7:00am, a nurse shuttled me off to the maternity ward, where I thought I should have been sent hours ago, and presented me with a large, sun-drenched, private room. *Halleluiah!* Someone had the decency to treat me special; a respectable private room all to myself to share with my newborn. Now we were getting somewhere!

I couldn't wait to see my baby. Despite having had all of fifteen minutes of sleep that night, I was anxious to see him. *He must be hungry by now. Maybe this meeting will go better than our first encounter since I have something he wants: milk!*

But instead of seeing my baby, I was graced with an early morning visit by my family doctor, Dr Thorneloe, and the hospital's on-call pediatrician, Dr Adleman. They came in, each wearing a somber face, and sat down on either side of my bed.

'Could you get John on the phone for us?' asked Dr Thorneloe.

My heart sank. My chest started to palpitate. I thought I was going to throw up. What could these two doctors possibly want with both of us? And why are there *two* of them?

Somehow, I composed myself enough to dial my home number, fingers and hands shaking. Hearing a sleepy hello from John, I passed the receiver over to Dr Adleman. He needed us to hear and absorb every word he was about to say, so he held the phone receiver up to his mouth as he looked at still and silent me. Dr Thorneloe sat down beside me and held my hand. His sad eyes told me I was about to hear something no mother would ever want to.

Dr Adleman began, 'I have some news to share about your son. He has a life-threatening congenital heart defect. I am a pediatric cardiologist, and I have been working through the night to determine exactly what is wrong. I believe your son has transposition of the great arteries and two holes in his heart. The two holes are keeping him alive right now, but we need to get your son to the Hospital for Sick Children ('Sick Kids') in Toronto immediately for further tests to confirm my diagnosis. Once there, I will arrange exploratory surgery to determine if he is strong enough to tolerate open-heart surgery to save his life.

'This exploratory surgery is risky. There is a chance, a significant one, that he could have a stroke while we are performing this procedure. However, if we do nothing, he has 48 hours to live. This procedure will help us determine the best course of action for his survival. We are preparing the helicopter to take him to Sick Kids, now. Susan, as his mother, do we have your consent to do this exploratory surgery?'

My mind had caught up to my racing heart; both were spinning out of control.

How did my little perfect world just turn upside down in a blink of an eye? My eyes welled up in tears. I didn't know what to think or what to say.

'Of course you have my consent,' I whimpered in total shock. What did they expect me to say?

With the flick of a switch, I felt suddenly alone in this world. I felt the warmth of Dr Thorneloe's touch; his eyes were fighting back tears himself. He had been our doctor since Danielle was born, and I had selected him, among the seven doctors at our clinic, because of his reputable and empathetic bedside manner. He was my age, someone I could relate to, and he was more than my family doctor; he was a trusted medical advisor and friend. Dr Adleman, who I had only just met, was equally credible and compassionate.

The doctors left me alone in my thoughts, my worst fears and uncontrollable tears rising to the surface. It is impossible to understand or even share the dark thoughts one has in a moment like this. We spend hours of our time, days even, imagining a future that we think we have complete control over, and then when we are torn down off our podium of self-determination, we are left without answers. They are replaced by fear, anger, despair, and, if you let it, a dash of courage and hope.

Moments after the news, a nurse came in to tell me I could leave the hospital whenever I felt up to it. That was when it hit me.

This is why I was given a private room… there's no babies coming here.

In the nurse's wisdom and compassion, she thought she would save me the anguish of lying next to other new mothers. I should have been appreciative.

But my private room was no longer a sign of privilege, privacy, space, or light. This was a room full of darkness, a chamber for my living hell. I hated everything it about it, what it meant for me, my son, and my circumstance. My mind longed to get dressed and get the hell out of there, but my body would not reciprocate.

I was so tired, so sore, and so stiff from the sleepless night and the painful delivery. I could barely lift my torso or move my trembling legs. I ached to hold my son, to hug him, and to let him know everything was going to be okay, even though I was not convinced of that myself.

Baby Allen was stabilized, wrapped, and bundled into a helicopter on the hospital's own landing pad. Doctors and nurses joined him for the journey to Sick Kids, 36 kms away. John followed the helicopter by car, taking the highway to downtown Toronto, arriving shortly after the medical team. He promised to return to pick me up from the hospital as soon as he could. All I could do now was wait… and cry.

Within hours, and way before I should have been released, I was driven to the children's hospital. I was a hormonal mess—exhausted, achy, emotional, and unable to walk on my own. When I arrived, I looked for a wheelchair to plunk myself into. But as this was a children's hospital, it only had child-sized wheelchairs. So, I swallowed my pride and squeezed my massive hips, uncomfortably, into the biggest chair on wheels available.

A life that had grown inside me for nine months had been stripped from my arms and my body, given to fate, faith, and doctors to choose whether my newborn would live or die. I was losing control. There was nothing anyone could have done to prepare us for this eventuality. We had no concept of what to expect or how to react.

By the time I reached the hospital, and only fifteen hours after my baby was born, his first surgery had been performed without complication. For Baby Allen, weighing in at 8.5 lbs was noticeably to his benefit. He was considered a strong and stable candidate for this latest and greatest type of open-heart procedure.

He would be the 50th baby in the hospital, and in the world, to undergo this innovative corrective heart surgery. The surgical correction was developed by doctors at Toronto's Hospital for Sick Children, a world-renowned teaching and research facility we were fortunate to have in our own backyard.

But there was a catch. There was labour unrest at the hospital and a nurses' 'Work to Rule' strike was happening for better hours, wages, or benefits. This, unfortunately, left a frequent shortage of nurses available to tend to the sick children in need of their care *post-surgery*. My baby would need a nurse on constant standby both during and after his surgery. I felt completely helpless while we waited for our allocation of nurses to be available for Baby Allen's

24/7 care. It felt like the whole world was crashing down around me with every passing day.

It was time to give Baby Allen a name; Andrew Robert was my choice. I liked Andrew combined with my family's connection to Robert (my dad's and stepdad's middle names), but in truth, John would have accepted 'Sam McGillicutty' if I had asked. He just wanted to ease my suffering and emotional pain.

Within hours of Andrew starting his tenuous life outside the womb, I entered the Neonatal Intensive Care Unit (NICU) to see him post-exploratory surgery. I heard his heart monitor beeping—his heart was beating so fast. He lay still like a doll in a small, plastic bassinet with a hinged top that acted as a roof to keep out unwanted germs. There were two sleeve openings in the front where adults could fit their arms through soft plastic to adjust his monitors and carefully caress his tiny body. The nurse motioned me to come closer.

Andrew had become bloated overnight; his eyes now swollen shut, the skin on his tiny limbs taut, his flesh bursting from its invisible seams like sausages. This heart defect had caused significant fluid retention. Andrew, unable to see anyone or anything, lay there motionless. So, I bent over, closer so he could hear me. 'Hello, my sweet boy, it's your mom. Do you know I love you?' My voice cracked as I choked on my words, tears welling up in my eyes. I was not prepared for the sight I was beholding. He was an innocent little baby who did not deserve this. No one deserved this.

However, if you take the time to notice, life is filled with magical moments. Many happen when we least expect them to... sometimes when our hearts need them most.

Beautifully juxtaposed alongside this moment, my lowest since his birth, was one of the most tender, profound connections I would ever share with my young son. As I listened to the steady, rapid beeping of his heart on the monitor beside me, I noticed the pace was slowing. The NICU nurse touched my arm that hung limp beside my trembling body and whispered, 'Andrew knows you're his mom; he's happy you're here.' I was *not* stroking him with my fingers through the long, plastic arm holes. I was simply standing there, speaking softly, gazing in disbelief at my newborn, whose two puffy eyes were blinded, clamped shut.

Was this voice the familiar sound he had listened to for nine months in the womb? Nurses spoke all day long in this room, but they didn't affect the monitors. Andrew preferred the sound of *my* voice. Mine was a special voice; the voice that told him his mom was here. It calmed him.

I longed to hold Andrew in my embrace, smell his new baby smell, kiss him, tell him I would never leave and always keep him safe. But, of course, I could not. Instead, Andrew chose to tell me, in the only way he could, that he knew I was there, and I was comforting him. That was all I needed to start the waterworks flowing.

I get teary-eyed remembering the magic of this moment. I can't recite this story without my emotions taking over, my eyes welling up again at my son's precious way of expressing, 'Thank you for being here, Mom. I need you and I love you.'

As each day passed in NICU, John and I watched our infant progressively deteriorate. Andrew became puffier and more bloated. His body was retaining fluids so much he could have passed for an over-inflated balloon about to burst.

Every day, we visited his NICU corner and sat with him for as long as we both could. We were conflicted with the need to go home to our toddler, who was missing us and needed our attention and love. John agreed to take more shifts at home with Danielle, but my maternal hormones were raging like a momma bear with her injured bear cub.

For the next four days, which seemed an eternity, we suited up in our hospital scrubs, sat by his side, and caressed his stiff body through the plastic incubator arms. The sound of beeping machines surrounded us, ever present, lest we forget his uncertain future. Could he last one more day and still be strong enough to endure open heart surgery? I spoke softly to him every waking hour of my day, 'Mom is here, I love you. You are such a strong boy.'

On the third day of our waiting game, I stepped outside his room to take a few, deep breaths, stretch, and regain my composure. In the hallway, I was welcomed by a young, soft-spoken priest with empathy oozing from every pore on his slight frame.

'Hello there. Is there anything I can do for you?' I was startled by this kind, gentle man wearing a white collar, who seemed to step out of the shadows. We spoke about nothing important at first, but as I wiped my tears with my sleeve, I found I was unable to express what I was really feeling. *How did I get here in this moment in time? What is to become of my son?*

'Do you believe in God? Do you have faith?' the priest asked in earnest.

'My husband is Catholic, but I'm not,' I said, embarrassed to admit I was not a person of faith. I believe his disposition would have convinced even die-hard agnostics to consider the benefits of faith, hope, and charity.

He offered, 'If you'd like, I can baptise your son, here and now.'

'Right here in the hospital, in his incubator, before his surgery?' I may not be Catholic, nor religious, but I wasn't born yesterday. I knew why he was asking me this.

Did I want him baptised... *just in case?*

I gathered my strength to answer, 'No, sir. That won't be necessary. But thank you. I appreciate your offer.'

A baptism was not required... *at this time.* My son was going to live. There was plenty of time for a baptism when he was older. He could go with his sister who, ironically, was yet to be baptised.

Five terrifying days passed in NICU before a collection of nurses could be scheduled to tend to our newborn in critical condition for his post-surgical stay in the Intensive Care Unit. It was scheduled for Tuesday, April 25, 1989. An arterial switch procedure, with Dacron mesh closing his two holes, would be performed by the hospital's head pediatric cardiologist, Dr Williams.

We arrived at the hospital at 8:00am on the morning of his surgery and were met by both of our extended families in a show of support. We didn't see Andrew that morning—he had been whisked away to be prepped in the operating room.

Instead, we waited and waited and waited some more. For ten hours we waited to hear news, any news. We walked, talked, paced, sat, stood, drank coffee, and tried to comfort each other.

Over the course of the day, we noticed an increasing number of vacancies in the waiting room left by departing families whose children's surgeries were complete. We watched as doctors came out of operating rooms to give anxious parents their child's status as well as instructions for their speedy recovery. Smiles, hugs, weeping, nervous laughter, and 'Thank you, Doctor!' were the themes of the day.

By 6:00pm, we were the last remaining family in the once-crowded, now spacious and foreboding, waiting area. At last, Dr Williams emerged from the operating room, still wearing his blue scrubs and surgeon's cap. True to his word, he came to the waiting area to give us the results of the surgery and Andrew's prognosis as fast as he possibly could.

Dr Williams had grown dark circles under his eyes since we last saw him. His head lowered as he slowly stepped towards us. He considered how best to say what he was about to say in a thoughtful, professional way.

'Good evening, I'm sorry to keep you waiting for so long. I've come to let you know the surgery is done and it went...' There was a long pause. '... *okay*.' He looked down at his clasped hands and glanced back towards the operating room. He did not sound overly concerned, just serious. I had the impression, however, that he had seen better days. Then, without another word, he disappeared into the abyss as quickly as he had appeared, assuring us he would return later.

I couldn't shake the feeling there was more to this than we were being told. Did I detect something cautionary in his voice and demeanour? We all felt it. 'It went *okay*,' hung in the air like the stench of engine exhaust. I was looking for reassurance that my son was safely out of the woods, but all I had to hang my hat on was a reserved, 'Okay.'

Could this be Dr Williams' typical communication style with parents? After all, we had just met the man. Maybe we were overreacting? How should we interpret this? We dissected his choice of words and demeanour and developed unhelpful theories of what he meant.

Hours passed, it was getting late, and our family had done all they could to support us. We thanked them and ensured them we would let them know as soon as we heard anything. We bid them farewell with tearful hugs.

Meanwhile, John and I waited alone, anxious for a second update—something positive to ease our growing concern that our son and his future was in jeopardy. Two more hours passed like watching a snail cross a highway, before Dr Williams emerged once more from the operating room. This time, however, the doctor was expressive.

He admitted he was unable to give us the full update during his first visit. When he returned to the operating room to wrap up the surgery, something was concerning him. Something wasn't quite right.

There was a complication. 'Andrew had a bleeder,' he said, explaining that our son was bleeding somewhere internally. *Somewhere* being the operative word. Dr Williams and his team acted fast to determine exactly where it was and what could be done to stem it. Masterfully, when he reopened his fresh incision, which spanned the entire length of Andrew's baby chest, he located the haemorrhage, patched it, and stitched him back up again. *C'est fini*.

The doctor explained this unexpected hurdle as if it was something he had dealt with before, but I translated his look of concern as something he was not always successful repairing. In this case, however, he was genuinely optimistic and relieved, and he reassured us he really *was* done with the surgery and Andrew was not just *okay*, he was going to be *fine*.

I would have preferred he used a more dramatic term like *great*, or *like new*, or *perfect*, but Dr Williams was more conservative than an auditor.

Andrew spent the second week of his life in the post-surgical wing of the hospital's ICU, attached to a respirator and a pacemaker. In due time, he would graduate from the respirator and have his pacemaker wires removed, but only when his doctors were certain his little heart was strong enough to beat consistently on its own. In the meantime, the monitoring equipment, and those two inconspicuous pacemaker wires protruding from the side of his abdomen, were his lifeline.

We were invited to visit Andrew in ICU the following day. He lay there motionless, eyes still forced shut. He was covered with medical interventions, his lifelines, from head to toe. It was devastating to see. The thought of such a tiny person starting life this way was beyond imaginable. I started to sob. I cried at anything and everything now, never knowing what might set me off. While his heart was repaired and healing, mine was breaking over and over.

The nurse, trying to provide comfort to me in my weak state, said, 'Go ahead, you can touch him.'

'Where?' I asked. 'There's no place on this body that isn't covered. There is no place on my son left to touch him!' She wasn't helping my agony.

After Andrew's birth, word spread through PwC of our frail, ailing child, his heart condition, and the grueling surgery he would undergo. My colleagues at NCE sent a gorgeous, oversized fruit basket to my home, with a card inscribed, 'We are thinking of you.' I was deeply touched. Similarly, the Mississauga office of PwC, where I was to meant to return as a Senior Manager after my extended maternity leave in six months, sent bunches of flowers and cards with kind wishes.

My friends and family filled my home with food and hope and well wishes. Genie and my mother took turns looking after Danielle. Our support network, which I had taken for granted, was a tremendous boost to our wellbeing as we learned to navigate through our toughest, darkest days. I never realized how important they would be when called upon to step in.

To my surprise, David (the reason I joined PwC) called the hospital and asked to speak to me in ICU. He wanted to check in on me, John, and Andrew, and asked, with his characteristic compassion, how *I* was doing. He wanted to reassure me that all I needed to do was ask if I needed anything at all; he and PwC was there for me. The lines of life and work had blurred together into one.

I wasn't ready to speak to anyone outside of my family yet, least of all David. I started to cry while listening to his voice and his genuine concern for Andrew's health and full recovery. I couldn't speak and swiftly hurled the nurse's station phone at John to save me from myself and my state. He gave David an update on Andrew's prognosis and thanked him for his kind words and thoughtfulness.

My experience with Andrew's traumatic birth was a blessing in disguise. John and I never, ever blamed each other or our family genetics for his defect. We accepted this as no one's fault, and if a cruel act of nature had dealt us a bad hand, our experience with his birth bonded us as husband and wife, stronger forever more. I witnessed John's anguish as he did mine; we both hurt so much. I never want to see my husband hurt again the way he hurt during this period, and I know John feels the same for my pain.

This moment gave me pause to consider my life and my priorities, again. I would never take my health, the precious health of my children, or my husband's health for granted.

If I thought I had been down this road before when I inserted Danielle into my already hectic life, fate was requiring I double down. I asked myself:

What is most important in life? What matters most?

My career may have been the driving force for the better part of my first three decades on this planet, but this experience made me feel different. I was changed.

As if my love for Danielle wasn't a firm punch in my gut, Andrew's birth was a blunt knife forcibly stabbing my wounded, bleeding heart. I decided that my career couldn't define the person I wanted to be. Time spent with loved ones matters! Dah.

This experience was destiny straightening my north star, signaling me to stop, to not take the love and lives of my children, or my husband, for granted.

My son's birthday is April 20. However, he was given his new lease on life thanks to the skillful hands of the doctors and nurses at Sick Kids five days later, on April 25. I celebrate both dates, giving the second date the prominence it deserves.

12

Bring Him Home

'Bring him peace, bring him joy, he is young, he is only a boy,
You can take, you can give, let him be, let him live,
If I die, let me die, let him live. Bring him home.'
— Jean Valjean, *Les Misérables*

It was time for a reset of our previously well-functioning home.

We were now responsible for caring for a sick infant, monitoring him, and reporting anything unusual. (What exactly is unusual?) Was he thriving or merely surviving? We were instructed to feed him thick, extra-strength formula to help him gain weight with the least amount of sucking effort.

To add to our anxiety as second-time parents (are we having fun yet?), we were tasked with administering his medications twice daily. We filled a baby-size syringe of liquid Lasik, a diuretic to help with his fluid retention, and a much less tasty syringe of Digoxin to support his irregular, weak heartbeat, and lessen the potential for heart failure.

We administered his drugs at the same time each morning and evening. We were made acutely aware that Digoxin was a dangerous drug to be giving anyone, never mind a newborn, and an accidental overdose could be fatal. That put the fear of God in us.

A foolproof plan was created to make sure a medical error would never happen. When one parent gave Andrew his medications, be it morning or evening, that parent would dutifully initial the AM or PM box on the appropriate day on our fridge calendar. We decided that a nanny would not be given this task, ever. Two CPAs? We've got this... *don't we?*

Danielle's loving nanny, Genie, was still working for us while I was dealing with Andrew's birth and hospital stay. But now that I was home, I found it difficult to navigate our new life with a newborn, a toddler, and Genie at my heels. She was in her late forties, I was 32. She reported to me. I was supposed to tell her what to do, yet, she was more mature, more experienced, and much calmer than I. She sported a perma-smile with a high-pitched, kind laugh that was getting on my nerves. I think it was becoming a nervous laugh—she was on shaky ground.

Why couldn't I accept the help she was more than willing to provide? This wasn't working out as I imagined.

I think it was our age gap, combined with our experience gap, that stressed me out. I didn't have the energy to instruct someone on how I wanted something done, and I selfishly expected her to read my mind and do things I needed done *my way*. That was unfair to her, as I was still figuring out how and what I needed done for myself.

As expected, Danielle preferred to be with her mom over her nanny. Try as Genie might to run around after our active toddler, Danielle ran to me while I was learning to care for our recovering, fragile newborn. My two arms were never enough. I loved the challenge and change it posed from the stressful workday I was used to, but it was exhausting being a mom. Still, I told myself to *enjoy* it. I knew my time at home would be gone again in a flash.

Next on my Super Mom agenda was to prep and cook all meals. I rarely had time to do this while I was working outside the home, so I learned how to cook from my Italian mother-in-law and came a long way since my first *Roast Chicken à la Sue* disaster with John.

As the days and weeks progressed, I longed to be the sole caregiver for *both* of my children. I feared I would not get a chance like this again, just me and the kids bonding all day long. So, I did what any mother would do in my position: I demoted Genie to tedious household chores I could care less about.

Somehow, her sunny disposition never faded. She was just too good.

But this was a classic case of inadequate delegation. The near-perfect nanny arrangement while I was working fell apart while I stayed home. And its demise? My failing.

Genie was a caregiver turned maid who, in her new role, was mostly unnecessary and too expensive on one income. Bless her soul, I would catch her leaning into our sparkling-clean bathtub giving it her once-over scrubbing, in spite of the fact that it never got used. Who has time for a relaxing bubble bath?

Ultimately, I couldn't live in the employer/employee relationship I created for Genie. It wasn't practical for me, nor fair for Genie, to find somewhere else to live and work while I was home, then expect her to come running back to me in five months when I returned to work. So, I did the unthinkable: I asked her to look for another family to sponsor her. I was letting her go.

Thankfully, this story has a happy ending. By coincidence, Andrew's pediatric cardiologist, Dr Adleman, hired Genie to care for his family. I can't recall whether I referred Genie to him during one of Andrew's monthly baby checkups, or if fate brought them together. In any case, I was glad they found each other, and to learn that Genie was employed by him for many years thereafter. Undeniably, she was a find.

So, there I was again, counting on finding another nanny for my kids closer to my return-to-work date. Even though I was a seasoned veteran in this department, it was risky. But what was one more nanny search to save my sanity for the next five months?

As I neared the end of my second maternity leave, I began the critical search for a new, live-in nanny. I sought referrals from nannies I met at the playground, and within no time, I was introduced to a friend of a friend.

A thirty-something Filipino named Mina needed a family to sponsor her immigration to Canada and was looking for work as a nanny. Trained as a nurse, I was drawn to her empathy, positive attitude, energy, friendly disposition, and intelligence. Being younger than me was also a drawing card; I wouldn't feel awkward teaching her how I wanted my children raised (even if I was learning the ropes myself).

John worked full-time while I stayed home, but he was no slouch. He spent his weekends and nights during my maternity leave finishing our 1500 square-feet of basement space, fitting it with a separate bedroom, a four-piece bath, and a sitting area for our new caregiver. It was a win-win, providing us and our nanny the privacy we craved at the end of the day.

All was neatly falling into place for my eventual return to work. Mina was bonding seamlessly with my children. She worshipped them as Danielle and Andrew happily spent more and more of their day with her.

I should have been relieved and proud of my succession planning efforts. Instead, I felt torn and anxious. I was secretly jealous of the routine Mina was creating, and the fun experiences I would not take part in. Sacrifices were never easy to accept. My return to work in a few weeks didn't feel right. Andrew was not out of the woods from a health perspective, and I adored providing answers to Danielle's innocent questions. She was a curious, intelligent little girl; Mom's little helper. I've always thought children should pop out of the womb at three—they are so much more fun to be with, and you can reason with them at that age!

My return to work as a new senior manager entailed more responsibility and a learning curve to master. I was to receive a new portfolio of clients, unfamiliar teams to coach and train, and there was, of course, the swift reinstatement of my audit busy season. Oh joy.

Still, in my heart, I know I wanted to return to work.

No, I *needed* to return to work, for the same reasons I gave when Danielle was born. My career was part of what made me happy. I knew, however, I didn't want to work *that much*. I was positive this mother of two would be content with less, and with the lessons I learned after Andrew's complicated birth, I had to find a way to dedicate more time to what mattered most.

Because my work was never restricted to 9 to 5. I wish it was, but meeting client deadlines, and unforeseen requests in a client service business, spilled into my nights and weekends. It would not be any different returning to work this time. I would be fighting a constant battle with myself and spending more time with my family would draw the short straw. I had to design a solution where I worked less and had less on my plate.

I decided that it was time for another flexible work arrangement. I *demanded* it. But I also realized I needed to be sensitive to the firm's business needs. So, what was my creative proposal?

Work four days a week in the fall, three days a week in the summer, and a full-time five+ days in the winter during busy season. I would be home more often when the weather was best and work was slower, and I would be working harder, longer hours in the winter when the firm needed me most. It was my creative 80% solution.

There were no other part-time female senior managers in the PwC Toronto offices, which meant there were no tried-and-true, cookie-cutter options to base my part-time program on. I had no one to confer with or coach me on whether this would be acceptable to the firm, so I took my shot, hoping for the best. *I had to be true to myself.* I had to be there for my family.

Because, despite the doctors telling me everything would be alright, I had yet to come to grips with how long Andrew would be on this earth. How many more surgeries would he need? Would his new, reconstructed heart grow properly into his little boy's body? Would he be a strapping, athletic teen who could play baseball, soccer, and hockey like other Canadian boys? Or would he always be as frail as he was when we first brought him home? These aspects of his future the doctors could not confirm, despite their positivity around his successful reconstructive heart surgery. What precious time he had now, I would make the most of, within my established parameters of a mom who wanted to keep working.

I discussed my solution to John to ensure he was on board, but I had no Plan B should PwC deny my proposal. This was a huge risk, but it was my *only* path forward. Andrew's terrifying birth and uncertain future, as well as my emotional trauma since, delivered the profound inner-strength I needed to ask for this, no matter the consequences. Kids will do that to you.

It was, truthfully, a ludicrous ask at this time in the world of business, but this wasn't the first time I would have to blaze my own trail.

If the firm wanted to retain me, if I was worth keeping, if they saw me as future partner material, then this was how it was going to be. This was the pint of blood I was willing to give. Full stop.

You might think my all-male complement of Mississauga partners with stay-at-home wives wouldn't get it. But you'd be wrong. Similar to releasing me for three years to NCE, once again, they had my back. In my opinion, this arrangement was sensible and fair—some of me is better than none of me.

I will never know how hard the partners argued for or against my flexible work arrangement behind closed doors. What I do know is it was unconditionally granted. John and I were thrilled.

So, as Labour Day arrived, I blissfully began the first tranche of my flexible work arrangement, starting with every Friday off. But it was by no means perfect; I would be lying if I told you otherwise.

I was asked to work on my days off. I seemed to be more flexible than my clients or PwC were, and I accumulated nearly as much (unpaid) overtime as I would have on a full-time basis.

Life at home was not easy either. Mom guilt reared its ugly head during busy season, and I counted the days until it was over. But what I found almost as hard was having to defend my decision to remain part-time with John. His constant criticism stung. I had poor answers to why I hadn't stood my ground. 'This is just terrific, Sue. Now you're getting paid *part-time* to work *full-time*. Why are you doing this? Why don't you say something? This isn't working for me.'

The truth was, I wasn't completely at odds with it. I savoured my days off when I took them, imagining I was playing hooky with my kids. So what if I had to put in a few hours of work here and there? This was better than the full-time alternative.

But I was desperate to make this really work. I had managed to gain PwC's full support, and I needed to demonstrate to myself (and the women that would follow me) that a flexible work program was possible. We *could* have it all.

There were growing pains and compromises on both sides throughout my arrangement. Partners needed to show greater respect for my 80% work schedule and my scheduled days off, while I needed to monitor my overtime more closely and speak up before it got unreasonably high. But, most of all, I needed the courage to say 'no' to unplanned requests that thwarted my days off.

One noteworthy struggle I dealt with during this time came from Don: my trusted mentor who was pushing me to become a partner in the firm. I felt honoured to have such a reputable, respected leader advocating for me, which made his request of me even more difficult to turn down.

He asked me about my interest in taking the lead on a new, high-profile client. His pitch was tempting; considered a stretch assignment for any senior manager. The job was managing a high-risk, challenging first-time audit fraught with potential litigation upon its conclusion. It came with his warning: my work and that of my team would be heavily scrutinized by third parties looking to fault our professional judgement. But Don assured me he would be integrally involved and would support me at every step. I believed him. He was a straight shooter who I could count on to give me a heaping dose of direct, honest, practical feedback, whether I had asked for it or not.

Today, I can acknowledge he was my *sponsor*. At the time, however, a relationship such as this was not codified in HR terms or programs. They had yet to be created for influential men to put their reputations on the line for rising professional women like me, who were in need of support beyond mentoring.

If I took this on, plans I had made to manage my overtime during busy season would have blown up in my face. However, this type of assignment didn't come along every day. How could I say no to someone who believed in my leadership and technical abilities with such conviction?

On January 15, at 5am, I watched snow falling as I stood freezing in the shadow of a grey brick building, waiting for people I had never met to let me in.

'Surprise! I'm from PwC, and I'm here to observe your inventory count.'

This assignment *was* everything Don said it would be, and then some. It was a pivotal, developmental audit experience that defined me for many years to come, and the project was cited by others as something to be proud of. I knocked it out of the park, and I felt privileged, not sorry, that I said 'yes' to this one, because I was given the option, and *I* made the decision to take this client on. Your gut rarely leads you astray.

My unique work arrangement had its flaws, but I stayed on it for three years and returned to full time when both my kids were attending either half- or full-time school. The compromise allowed me to stay in the profession and the firm at a time when I could have called it quits.

I admired that PwC was willing to try my experimental work arrangement and help me achieve a more seamless career/parenting balance. Together, we learned to be open and flexible, to give and take, and when I accepted the high-profile stretch assignment, it shattered misconceptions of what happened to women on the *mommy track*. I learned some of the critical success factors that made part-time arrangements work and drew upon this knowledge when I was asked to help other part-time moms.

The atypical work arrangements I have disclosed to you—my work-sharing arrangement as a Cashier at UTM, two extended maternity leaves, and my 80% part-time work arrangement—were designed by me, for me. They served their purpose, fitting my unique circumstances at the time.

I hope these examples give you the courage to try something bold when you face competing priorities, a change in circumstances (like becoming a mother!), or you need a change in pace to breathe. I want you to take a stand for yourself, your wellbeing, and your happiness. You may just find your employer is more willing than you think to say 'yes' to a well-reasoned, fair request. You'll never know until you ask!

REFLECTION

How to prepare yourself to Expect the Unexpected

I've demonstrated how our childhood experiences aren't the *only* ones that shape our worldview, the people we become, and the values we espouse. Similarly, difficult and painful experiences in adulthood can leave an imprint on our soul, defining our character.

The traumatic birth of my son is the most challenging life experience I have to share with you. The stamp it left on my soul pushed me beyond the outer limits of emotional pain, but this same experience intensified my resolve on the importance of my work/life balance and strengthened the bond of my marriage. Then, it presented me with one of life's small, remarkable miracles, teaching me the lesson of *what matters most.* I still can't comprehend how, more than thirty years later, I tear up without warning when I am asked to recount the story of Andrew's birth. I can be such an emotional trainwreck; the story had a happy ending!

I don't share my experience to make you feel sad or sorry for me. I share it to prepare you in some way for the unavoidable, senseless, unexpected life-changing event that you, too, will someday experience out of nowhere (if you haven't already).

When one of these events do happen, can you, will you, be strong enough to take appropriate action? Moreover, will you be kind to yourself, take the time to heal emotionally and physically, lean heavily on your support systems, and get professional help if you need it? That is the wise counsel of my trauma I wish to impart upon you.

I have come to learn that everyone has their cross to bear. We really don't know what a passerby or a co-worker has endured in the past or is dealing with today, do we? Despite the positive attitude, kind eyes, and friendly smiles, I think these are often the masks they have chosen to cover their pain. So, how can we help them?

Be an empathetic listener. Be a sensitive co-worker. Be a true friend!

Here are some other lessons from this part to reflect upon:

- There is value in volunteering your time. The tangible skills you learn in a non-threatening, low-risk environment translate seamlessly into the workplace. You will learn skills such as how to encourage, negotiate, gently nudge, manage and influence others, how to set and achieve budgets, and how to run an effective meeting.

- Deal with competing priorities by figuring out which balls are worth juggling in the air, and which ones can be dropped with little consequence. You can't be all things to all people!

- It's okay to say 'no' to opportunities, particularly when they don't align with your terms or your circumstances. Set and stick to your boundaries.

Reflection Questions

1. How do you stay in the present for the things that matter most?

2. How do you assess whether to say ‘yes’ or ’no’ to a work opportunity that presents itself?

3. How do you decide which priorities are worth juggling and which ones are not?

4. Have you considered volunteering your time to build or apply your skills to a cause that is meaningful for you?

Part V: Taking a Risk or Staying Comfortable?

When you have the courage to let your biggest dreams be heard with your outside voice, you may just find that they'll come true.

Do you have role models that you aspire to be like? Do you see yourself as a role model for others? And if so, how does this impact how you project yourself and how you lead others?

Early in my career, as a female in a male-dominated industry, I sensed junior women observing me. They watched how I communicated, how I carried myself, and how I managed and led teams. I always wondered: did they accept my feminine style, my open 'ask me anything' personality, how I wore my heart on my sleeve, and the passion they heard in my voice, or did this detract from my impact and influence as a leader?

I watched for unfiltered reactions and wondered, *What do others think of me?* I set high standards for myself and expected the same of my teams. But I also showed empathy and patience, especially with junior staff, because I found it easy to slip back into their shoes. I never forgot where I came from. No matter how stressful the situation, my outside voice said, 'Don't sweat it. There must be a lighter side to this. Where's the learning, the fun, and the humour? We are auditors, we aren't saving lives!'

When I reviewed a staff's name attached to a working paper, I wanted to know the person behind this work, their story, and how they came to be here. To be relatable, I let them know my story, and how I came to be here, too. I wanted them to know me on a personal level.

Would my behaviour and character leave a positive impression on others? My goal was to portray my authentic self, to be engaging and personal, and to inspire a high-performing culture of respect for all. I believe the most effective way to lead with impact is not to *select* a 'masculine' or a 'feminine' approach, but to develop a style that suits you.

But this didn't happen overnight either. My leadership style developed over time, until it became second nature for me. Eventually, I felt comfortable that I was uniquely me, just as your style will develop to be uniquely you.

Still, the weight of my responsibility as a female leader was constant throughout my career, but never as much as when I was being considered for partnership at my firm. This brings me to the next part of my journey where I grappled with my future and the most important milestone of my working life. Would I measure up as a leader in the eyes of the PwC partners? Should I stay or leave the firm? Did I even want to be a partner?

There may be similar questions many of you will need to reflect upon over the course of your careers. Do you accept the risk, anxiety, and growth that comes with a new challenge, or do you stay in the comfort of what you know and love?

13

Daring to Say It Out Loud

There are people who dream big from an early age and then build the necessary skills that eventually translate into their profession. When inherent passion complements the required skillset, we have a recipe for success!

And then there are others, like me, who wonder what each new day will bring. We're content to execute our current portfolio of tasks with commitment, expertise, and enthusiasm. The more we love our job, the easier it is to accept the passing of our workdays without focusing on our future and charting our direction. Sure, we expect to get promoted and handed stretch opportunities, but we take for granted that *someone else* will recognize us when we are ready. *Someone else* will present new opportunities to us, like a waiter pouring a glass of Dom Perignon, asking, 'Is this is to your liking?' How naïve.

Without a long-term plan in place, I continued to follow the path that others presented to me. It started with my father coaching me to attend university, then Mike offering me a secondment in the NCE department, and finally with Don encouraging me to return to the Mississauga office to set myself up for partner.

When would I learn to put my hand up and *ask* for a promotion, a leadership role, or a stretch opportunity? When would I demand a role I was passionate about and ready to leap into? I needed to grow some balls. *Tell me I didn't just write that.*

Many managers at PwC have the goal of one day becoming a partner. This promotion is the pinnacle of their career, their *big hairy audacious goal* as coined by authors Jim Collins and Jerry Porras, in their bestselling book, *Built to Last: Successful Habits of Visionary Companies.* Partnership is recognition of the long, hard road it takes to get there. It also marks a milestone—you are a respected, credible, and valued professional in the long-term view of the firm.

Naturally, a public accounting firm is selective at each stage of a professional's journey on the path to partnership—from recruiting the brightest and best recruits from a pool of exceptional candidates, to seeking foundational technical qualities, decision-making abilities, and supervisory skills. The path becomes more selective the further up the managerial ladder the professional climbs. The competition becomes more intense as each outstanding hopeful is compared to their equally distinguished and qualified colleagues. It's a funnel that comes to a pin-point opening.

Early on in my day, professional firms employed an 'up or out' mentality at each rung of the promotion ladder. Everything changed in the late 1990's, when the war for talent raised the stakes, and the high cost of recruiting, hiring, and training was weighed against the cheaper cost of retaining experienced specialists who were trained in-house. The 'up or out' mentality became 'hire and stay' as firms made the conscious move to retain valuable 'non-partner' talent by placing them in permanent senior positions. This also provided an option to those career senior managers and directors who didn't *want* to be partners.

But what exactly is a partner you ask? Right off the bat, forgive me for oversimplifying.

A partner is an owner in the firm's (i.e., PwC's) business. This means they share in the profits and are responsible for paying the liabilities. In effect, they are the 'CEO' of a portfolio of clients, many of which the partner brought into the firm on the strength of his/her personal relationships, or technical, industry, and subject-matter expertise.

In my line of work, it is argued companies don't hire the firm but, rather, the partner, for they trust this person to help them solve their most important problems. The buck stops with him/her. They must respect the rules and laws of accounting and make the hard calls, since it's *their name* that appears alongside the firm's signature on the audit opinion.

So, how does this added risk and responsibility get rewarded? A partner shares in distributions of the net earnings of the firm with a big, fat paycheck. *Boom.*

Once admitted, partners are an integral member of the broader, global PwC family. They are the future leaders of the firm, the role models staff look up to, and the architects of the firm's culture. There is a high hurdle to clear before being admitted into the PwC partnership/family, and while one can be aligned with the foundation level attributes and skills required to qualify for promotion, there is also a 'je ne sais quoi' skillset that is less easy to define.

If I was forced to put it into words, I'd say it's an irresistible sense of intrinsic qualities an individual possesses which leaves you thinking, *This person is partner material; he has the 'it' factor.*

So, what are the revered qualities of this swagger? Is it the confident, market-driven connections in his rolodex, or is it his decisiveness? Are these intangibles more typically aligned with masculine or feminine traits?

It is always hard to tell when you're in the thick of it, but as my career progressed, I would come to better understand the unconscious bias that pervaded business culture up and down almost every organization I came into contact with. When I understood it, I was then able to expose it with PwC's full backing.

But, at this time, I was focused on playing the game, putting my nose to the grindstone, and achieving that big hairy audacious goal: partnership.

As an experienced Senior Manager in my thirteenth year with the firm, I had taken a few jogs down the non-linear labyrinth known as my career path. My three-year secondment in NCE required me to transition back into audit and rebuild my client base. Then there was the two six-month maternity leaves and my 80% work program, and I knew there were few, if any, examples of women achieving partner status in this timeframe with internal roles, time off, and part-time work like me.

To add to this uncertainty, the firm wasn't particularly good at informing partner candidates when or if they were on the partner track. So, I just assumed I wasn't until someone told me differently.

Upon returning to work after my second maternity leave, I was required to complete my annual personal plan. When I got to the section asking what my long-term goals were, I left it *blank*.

Here I was, coming into my thirteenth year with the firm, being asked to state my long-term goals, and I was hesitant to put down anything courageous on paper. I wanted to be a partner, but I was afraid to commit to a goal I had no control over. So, I caved and eventually drafted a lame administrative goal to fill the empty space: 'I will keep current on my technical training and submit my time and expense reports on time'. I don't know if it was my lack of maturity, or my lack of belief in myself, but I hid behind the safety of my indecisiveness.

The managing partner of the office, Ian, was my partner coach. As he read my personal plan, he was confused by my meaningless goal with no long-term commitment, and he called me out on it. I'm grateful he did, because how many other women, with my seniority, were leaving that goal blank?

Ian walked into my office with a silly grin on his face. He couldn't believe the conversation he was about to have. At point-blank range, he asked, 'Susan, do you want to be a partner?'

I looked at him with the eyes of a child that said, 'Tell me what I should say.'

'Do you?' he repeated, to which I replied my uncertain, 'I suppose so.'

'Then you need to say that somewhere, so we know your intention. Here, under your long-term goals section, write, "I want to be a partner!"' His fingers were pointing—no, *stabbing*—at the plan on the page. He was dumbfounded.

How embarrassing. Here was my coach helping me with one of my most impactful career goals, saving me from myself. I edited the document and resubmitted my plan.

This got me to thinking. Once I had actually said it out loud, I wondered if maybe this *was* what I wanted to be when I grew up? Maybe this is what I have spent the last thirteen years of my life striving towards? And just maybe I am worthy.

I loved my work, the people, and the clients, and I was good at my job. So, after letting this thought simmer, I convinced myself that *yes, I do want to be a partner in PwC!*

Why did it take Ian stabbing at the page with his finger to ignite the fire inside of me? Why were others constantly directing me versus me taking centre stage in my own career? This is a very complex question for me to answer, and perhaps a difficult one for so many reasons.

I'm not alone in my behaviour. This is a common theme that plays out for women in the workplace, and frankly, it's bigger than me. Women aren't groomed from childhood to be leaders; we are praised for playing 'nice' in the sandbox and scorned for demonstrating leadership qualities that don't conform to societal gender norms. Instead of appearing assertive, decisive, and strong when we act in a typically male fashion, we are seen as bossy, pushy, and arrogant, and many men (and women!) use the 'B word' to describe us when we step out of line. So, we learn to play it safe, happily collaborating with our teams, while receding into the quiet shadows just outside of the limelight.

Women use their emotional intelligence to read the mood or unrest in a room, but we are also challenged to use our voices and female frames to take our rightful place and speak our minds in front of men. We find reasons to give credit to others for the outstanding work we have performed, but in doing so, we understate our potential to our superiors and can be overlooked for assignments which could propel our careers forward. And, as I've noted from my own experience, we don't think we need to share our desire or readiness for stretch opportunities, so, we wait for someone else to notice us. We need others to tell us 'It's okay to strive higher, be something more. You're ready, you've got this.'

Thinking back to that day with Ian, I believe I was afraid to ask for something that wasn't meant for me. It was Rexdale Sue bubbling to the surface, reminding me of where I had come from, and that people like me couldn't possibly attain such an audacious goal. I was listening to that inner voice I had silenced for many years.

Could I, Sue Allen, really have that 'je ne sais quoi' quality of a PwC partner?

I am forever indebted to the PwC partners who valued the woman I had become. They looked beyond my self-imposed limitations, my persistent self-doubt, and my second guessing that had me seriously doubting there was space in *their* world for someone like me. These selfless leaders viewed me as the capable, conscientious professional I was, rather than as a female, a working mom, or a fraud from the other side of the tracks.

Once I accepted the challenge Ian presented me with, to tell PwC I was interested in becoming a partner, I decided I needed to give it my best shot. How could I make this happen?

However, just when I had wrapped my mind around the idea of becoming a PwC Partner, a new opportunity was thrust upon me, and it was one that deserved a second look.

Isn't it remarkable how timing works?

I was working at a client that was even closer to my home than the PwC Mississauga office. This company was engaged in an industry I was excited to be a part of—one I could relate to, had firsthand knowledge of and experience with. The company was a decent size, $50 million in sales, and profitable, with a famous, high-profile leader at its helm and a reputable, inclusive culture. The company's head office was in Mississauga. Its parent, a global, private US company, was the sixth largest of its kind in the world.

As the experienced senior manager on the audit of this client for several years, I had developed a strong, professional rapport with the company's President and Chief Financial Officer (CFO), both of whom were men approaching retirement.

Unexpectedly, while I was visiting him one day, the CFO asked if I was interested in applying for his position. It took me by surprise but did not shock me. Many managers are offered positions at their clients'. Frankly, I wondered why it had taken this long for me to finally be offered one.

So, why not? I was perfect for the role, a senior female in a women's industry, and I was experienced, young, and ambitious. I fit in, knew and loved the management team, and they knew me. I was a low-risk hire. He mentioned how much he made with bonuses, and, at the time, I was making significantly less than his base salary with no bonuses.

Timing is everything. Three months later, it was entirely possible I could be promoted to partner. I didn't know what to expect with a salary increase at PwC—there was no internet to google questions such as these—nor did I know of my likelihood of getting promoted. There were so many what-ifs in my immediate horizon, and so much I was not *supposed* to ask about, speak up or inquire into.

I thanked the CFO for his unofficial offer and said I would think about it. Then he sweetened the pot.

He wanted to fly me to their US head office to meet with the President to hear what else the company had to offer. Apparently, I had already passed through the interview process in his mind, and he was moving straight to the US company for approval. He was looking for a succession plan not only for himself, but also for the Canadian President. After getting my feet wet and proving myself as the

Canadian CFO, he thought I would be next in line for the President's job.

Wow. That was a lot to take in for an unscheduled walk by his office. I thanked him warmly for his openness, confidence, and support in me, and asked for a few days to think it over. I didn't want to waste their time, or mine, if my mind wasn't open to a career change.

It was time to discuss this opportunity with John. He was a good litmus test, first having worked at PwC, and now having worked as an executive in industry. He knew whether this would be a fit.

I started making a list of pros and cons.

Under the 'Stay at PwC' list:

- It's challenging work that I love
- There is a potential partner opportunity in the future (but not guaranteed)
- Good pay (but unknown long-term upside)
- It's the devil I know

Under the 'Leave PwC and go to this Industry Job':

- There is opportunity for growth and change
- A better work life balance (this was a 9-5 job)
- A great culture and work environment
- Better initial pay and significant short-term upside
- The potential opportunity for promotion to company President

One look at the list and it was smack-me-in-the-face obvious that I should leave PwC. There were so many incredible, tangible rewards to do so, and I was struggling to find the downside. After taking a look at the list, John strongly encouraged me to consider this opportunity, because it would free up time to spend at home, and I would have been less stressed at work. I would earn more money doing a job that was easy to learn and excel at.

It was so tempting—'yes' was at the tip of my tongue—but I needed to stress test it further. So, I decided to share my unofficial offer with my esteemed friend and mentor, Don. I admired and respected him deeply and appreciated his sound guidance. Most beneficial, however, was that he was the Audit Partner for this client, which meant he could give me his insider's view. I was nervous to tell him, but thought if I was going to leave, I wanted his advice first.

His reaction was unforgettable. 'Sue, this sounds like a wonderful opportunity, and I know you would do an amazing job as CFO for them, but you will be bored within a month.'

Damnit, he was right. Don told me what I needed to hear, and what I was thinking but was too afraid to put into words. This was a great company, but a simple one. I could do the CFO role in my sleep. Even if I did become the company President, I didn't think I would be offered the same challenges I was faced with every day at PwC.

I looked at my list of pros and cons again. It was a logical, well-constructed list, and everything my head was telling me. But what was missing was what my heart was saying. Bored in a month? Don's advice stung. It was ringing in my ears. I couldn't bear unsatisfying work; I'd left that environment thirteen years ago when I resigned from the Cashier position. I promised I would not do that again. *Ever.*

I didn't know if I was going to make partner at PwC, but if I left now, I would never know. And, if I didn't make partner, these types of jobs would always be out there with my name on them. My heart was telling me, *PwC is part of my family, my friends, my home away from home. I am proud to work here. I earned my CPA here. I would be proud to say,* 'I am a PwC partner.'

My job was not just a job. It was a career I woke up to every morning and was excited to start my day. It was more than the paycheck I earned.

The hardest thing to say no to was the work/life balance that this CFO job would have provided me, but I decided my lack of balance was *my* doing, not PwC's, and it wasn't beyond my control. I was comfortable with the career I had built, and I believed John and my kids were too.

Five months later, in May of 1994, only six new partners were admitted to the Canadian partnership. That was a tiny fraction of the number of senior managers in the firm, but guess what? My name was among them!

I was the only female on the list, and the first female partner promoted in the Mississauga office. One of several firsts to come!

I received the news of my promotion the day prior, likely because Ian couldn't keep it to himself for one minute longer. On the morning of the big day, Tom, PwC's CEO, welcomed the new partners in a touching announcement to all staff and partners. He went one step further and offered me his congratulations person-to-person. I felt privileged. Tom's warm smile, eye contact, and tight handshake were signs that he was genuinely thrilled to have me on his team. And here I thought he barely knew me.

One by one, the Mississauga partners, as well as my mentors, friends, and sponsors, visited my office to congratulate me and welcome me to the club. My phone rang constantly, with clients, staff, and partners from across the globe sending me their well wishes. My office looked like a florist shop. I felt lighter than air and sported a perma-smile all day.

At the end of the day, the office staff and partners took me to a nearby bar to celebrate (on my credit card, as is the tradition). John attended this celebration, bringing my two biggest fans to run around and cause mayhem. Andrew showed off his new light-up sneakers, while Danielle, the ringleader, got them both into repeated bouts of mischief.

A few weeks later, I would meet 400 other new partners recently promoted at PwC's inaugural Global New Partners Conference. The location selected for this elaborate affair was… Sydney… no, Amsterdam… no, New York!

Nope!

The conference was held in Mississauga! Whoop-de-freakin-doo! I couldn't believe my luck. I could have thrown a stone at the hotel from my bedroom window.

When I shared my disappointment with the conference coordinator, he asked, 'Would you rather wait till next year for your promotion, so you can attend a more exotic location?'

Okay, he had a good point, so I stopped my bellyaching and decided to network and make as many future contacts as the time allowed.

I didn't think it was possible—the elation, the high, the joy I felt at becoming a partner. It somehow exceeded the emotions I felt passing the CPA exam. Partnership, and all that the future could hold, was a true milestone and pinnacle moment in my career. Thirteen years and two degrees later, I had finally figured out what I wanted to be when I grew up.

A PwC Partner. Duh!

14

Accepting the Challenge

In the late 90's, PwC formalized the importance of developing one's industry specialization. It was seen as an essential differentiator—the key to understanding a company and its business. Thus, the sooner partners and staff developed expertise by industry, the more likely they were to offer relevant, sage advice for a client's most important problems. If we could stand in their shoes and listen carefully to the unique issues they faced, we would be better prepared to develop appropriate, tailored solutions. Without specialization, we were just another uninspiring professional services firm with boilerplate answers.

By virtue of joining the Mississauga office, I served clients in the manufacturing, distribution, and retail sectors, which meant I was a member of the Consumer, Industrial Products, and Services (CIPS) industry group. Although it was more coincidental than planned, I was proud to belong to CIPS after almost two decades in its fold. It was my safe harbour; all I ever knew.

Allan, a leader in the CIPS industry group, poked his head into my office. 'May I come in?' Allan asked as he made himself comfortable in one of my standard-issue office chairs. He dismissed the look of my messy desk.

He had a straightforward, simple proposition. 'How do you feel about changing industry groups?' I stared back at him, speechless, but he continued without missing a beat, 'Would you consider transferring to TICE?'

TICE stood for Technology, Information, Communications, and Entertainment. I assumed, rightly, that he meant Technology and was using the generic TICE acronym for short.

Is he really asking me to move to the technology sector? This came straight out of left field. It was such an innocent question, but I knew my answer would change everything.

There was a lot to consider. The year was 1998. The emergence of technology and tech-related companies of every size, shape, and profile in every field imaginable, were beginning the ride of their young lives. Private companies, termed 'start-ups', were popping up everywhere, marketing their innovative solutions and new business models in the fields of software, telecommunications, mobile phones, music, the internet, social media, online anything, and the list went on.

Networking companies were formed by engineers inventing new ways to connect more devices with never-before-seen features and functionalities. Faster and faster ways of seamlessly communicating across different platforms became the name of the game. The need for bandwidth increased as personal computers became the norm for every home and office alike. As technology advanced, users demanded more and more speed to operate their computers, their phones, and their connected lives.

We were witnessing a bold, innovative episode in history, and if we followed the path, it was set to enrich the lives of every single person in ways previously unimaginable.

Beam me up Scottie! We're boldly going where no *man* has gone before!

'Go into technology?' I replied. 'Are there any women in tech?' Evidently, I used my outside voice to pose this question, and once it was out, I couldn't take it back.

'I don't know... I think so...?' was Allan's confused response. The curious look on his face told me he was baffled why I would even ask this. His head cocked to one side, as if to say, 'What difference does that make?' As a privileged, middle-aged, Caucasian man, assessing gender balance in technology was not on his radar.

Could I blame him? He didn't understand my hesitation to enter a field where I might be the only woman in a male-dominated industry, where it would be rare to find trusted, female peers to confide in or learn the ropes with. Where would I find role models, coaches, and sponsors who looked like *me*?

This was a considerable ask to switch industry sectors. I had spent almost two decades in CIPS, and I was comfortable with it. - There's that *comfortable* word again.

But why the hell would I consider a leap into the unknown, where few women worked? What was in it for me?

Few women entered the field of technology in the 1990's, because very few women graduated with 'STEM' degrees, including computer science: a new field of specialization that men flocked to. The few women who jumped headfirst into this field were brave trailblazers that paved the way for women choosing engineering and computer science degrees in the 2000's.

But even today, men still outnumber women graduates from these programs by three to one, and men outnumber women in higher paying, more senior STEM jobs after graduation by more than four to one. (This is according to Catalyst.org research, August 4, 2020, "Women in Stem" for Canada.) There are some STEM Programs that entice young women to enter the science disciplines in high school and university, and to support them entering the workforce upon graduation. But as the numbers bear out, we have a long way to go.

So, it would stand to reason that, in 1998, the vast majority of technology CEOs were engineers, founders, and male. Their networks were predominantly comprised of—you guessed it—other men. The entire industry was a big pool of mini-mes, and those who were promoted to executive positions generally walked, talked, and thought like their boss. It was hard for women to break in.

Unfortunately, I didn't fully appreciate these statistics or potential biases when I asked my loaded gender question, 'Are there any women in technology?' Why couldn't I have been more aware of what was I getting myself into? Years later, when I discovered the gender disparity, I decided it was time to change it.

I wasn't convinced by Allan, nor was I excited about the opportunity. However, saying 'no' was still foreign to me. I didn't want to show I wasn't flexible or ready for a stretch assignment in *the* up-and-coming tech industry. Perhaps Allan was counting on this.

He was waiting for a response, right then and there, and a tentative 'I guess so?' exited my lips. Allan stood up, thanked me for being willing to do this, and got up to leave. My timid response was taken as a definitive yes, and that was all he needed to hear; he had found his sacrificial CIPS lamb. His job was done.

What the hell had I done? Why couldn't I just learn to say 'no'? I knew so many women like me who struggled with this. Why did we always let others tell us what we wanted? We needed to start *owning* our decisions, not be swayed or dragged into something others wanted from us.

But I had yet to learn this lesson. I was stuck in my people pleaser reality, blindly accepting what got thrown in my direction.

Before I could say, 'Wait, what, who, me?' my transfer to TICE was set in motion and there was no turning back. News spread of my decision, and, with that, I received a friendly, warm welcome from my fellow partners.

There was also the expectation that I would transfer to the Toronto office, to sit beside other TICE partners and staff. But this was where I put my foot down. 'Not so fast,' I argued. 'Why would I part with my fifteen-minute commute to the Mississauga office only to sit for an hour and fifteen-minutes in a car commuting downtown each way? I didn't sign up for this.'

The national TICE leader, Laurie, who happened to work in the Toronto office himself, cautioned this wasn't an ideal way to immerse myself in a new industry, build my practice, and get to know my colleagues. He was firm on this and reluctant to acquiesce, partly, I assume, because he feared opening the floodgates and being forced to deal with a tidal wave of similar requests. Why should I be given special treatment?

I'm happy to report that today's 'work-from-home' and hybrid working models offer greater flexibility and mobility to employees. But they were foreign concepts back then. As I am sure you are painfully aware, the catalyst for the swift adoption and acceptance of this trend, flipping our traditional way of working on its head, was the global pandemic and the demands of the great resignation of staff that followed.

But at the time, Laurie had a valid point. Close proximity to the core group was useful and would help me in the long run, but I had two school-aged kids with sports and other after-school activities, my volunteer board work on two not-for-profits, and a working spouse carrying a full load himself in his executive position. We were a two-career couple, living full-time lives outside of work.

Achieving work/life balance was never easy. However, one thing was *critical* to me. I had to achieve this balance (or lack of one) on my terms. I never quarreled or put up a fuss over my need to work long days to meet client deadlines and audit partner and staff responsibilities, but spending two and a half hours a day in rush hour traffic, so I could feel the tech vibe beside my colleagues? Nope, not my first priority.

I stood my ground, unconcerned about the consequences. I stated my position passionately and persuasively, and Laurie heard me loud and clear. This was a dealbreaker for me, and I prevailed. I said 'no', and it felt damn good too.

We agreed to a TICE satellite office concept in Mississauga with three team members: me, myself, and I. With his surrender, Laurie earned my deepest respect. He'd conceded on something he was clearly not a fan of by gaining an understanding and appreciation of how integral this was to me.

As a partner, I had more flexibility in my career than ever. Computers in the workplace were commonplace, allowing work to be reviewed and questions asked of my team members whenever it was convenient for me—after hours included. As long as I met my client deadlines and the firm's expectations, no one asked when or how I got my work done. I could leave the office by 6:00pm, have dinner with the family, and pull out my work again sometime after 8:00pm, having tucked Danielle and Andrew into their beds after reading their favourite books and singing their favourite song. You know the drill.

By adhering to this nightly routine, my kids and I spent special time together, and afterwards I was left with three solid hours of uninterrupted time to attempt to complete my outstanding list—reviewing audit files, answering emails, administrative tasks like time and expense reports, and prioritising my to-dos for the next day.

I often collapsed into bed by eleven, finding myself bleary-eyed after being at my computer accomplishing nothing in particular. I constantly, and foolishly, kept telling myself *this needs to get done!* but it was often the case that my late weeknights placed more stress on my professional career than anything else. John never could understand how I did it, night after night. Frankly, neither do I. The pace was exhausting.

Despite this endless running on the treadmill (I wish I was doing *that* kind of exercise), when I awoke each morning, I was ready to give my best for another day. I pushed repeat and off I ran.

Mornings were more hectic than my evenings. There was a finite amount of time for me to get myself, my kids, my dog, and anything else I deemed necessary, ready. *I must leave for work at some reasonable time in the morning! I can't be late again!* My kids were always a part of my equation, because spending a few minutes of happy time with them—feeding them, dressing them, getting them ready for school—gave me the drive and incentive to get through another long day without them.

But mornings were chaos, and never more so than this single moment John and I would never forget.

When Andrew was less than a year old, and still on his daily heart medication, I carried him downstairs to administer his morning dose of Digoxin and Lasik, in that order, as we always did. Afterwards, I swooped him up in the air and passed him over to our nanny so I could get ready for work. I had a lot on my mind as I galloped up and down the stairs, running late for work, as usual. I turned to say goodbye and was horrified to see Andrew in John's arms, receiving his medications... again! Doctors warned us a double dose of Digoxin could be fatal, so we had a system to make sure this never happened. *Or so we thought.*

I screamed, 'STOP! I already gave them to him!'

'What?' John cried, his eyes nearly popping from their sockets. 'It's not marked on the calendar!'

'Oh God, I forgot! I'm so, so sorry!' I was tearing up. It was my fault, multi-tasking with too many things on my mind. But *none* were as important as this. How could I have been so careless? 'What are we going to do?' I asked, briefcase dropping to the floor.

John looked puzzled and in shock. Then he looked at the baby-sized syringe in his hand. 'I just gave him his Lasik. I didn't give him the Digoxin, yet.'

'Oh, thank God. We need to call the hospital, emergency, poison control, or Dr Adleman's office. Who should I call to find out what we should do?' My fingers trembled as I pressed the hospital's poison control line and bawled.

I explained the chain of events that had transpired. An empathic nurse explained, 'You've dodged a bullet. Lasik is a diuretic. You'll go through a few extra diapers today, but your son will be fine.'

'John,' I sighed in relief as I hung up the phone. 'Why did you give Andrew the Lasik first today? That isn't the order we do this.'

'I don't know... I really don't know,' John confessed, his arms around Andrew hugging him as tightly as he could.

This moment still gives me goosebumps. To think that a single instant of my careless, unfocussed attention and haste could have had devastating, unbearable consequences.

I must be present.

At that moment, I knew I had to get off the treadmill, slow down, and get to bed earlier so I could get up earlier. I had to better plan for interruptions throughout the day. I had to be more realistic about what I could and could not physically (and emotionally) accomplish in twenty-four hours. My days would never fall neatly into place, but I told myself I had to do better—for my family, my firm, and my sanity.

This was a difficult lesson to apply. Over the following months and years, I dabbled around the edges of my promises to plan better, to slow down, and to be more realistic with what I crammed into my day, but I never achieved the change in behaviour I was gunning for. I concluded that some traits—including my always on, high-energy, multi-tasking, Type A personality—were hardwired. No matter how hard I tried to modify them, I never got to the place I would have liked.

I gave myself credit for trying. I didn't pass harsh judgment on my occasional misses, and that made it easier to accept my slipups. Good thing too. I had a few more imperfections to unpack and lessons to learn in the days and months and years that followed.

So, as a partner in my fourth year, even though I was still constantly juggling the time I spent at home and work, I was no longer the new kid on the block. More was expected of me. My personal goal as a partner was to increase my revenue base, but with my fresh assignment to the tech industry, I was building a new portfolio of clients from scratch. How would I do this exactly?

As a start, my fellow TICE partners kindly handed me a few of their friendliest clients in technology, just as I had transferred my beloved CIPS clients to new CIPS partners. This would give me firsthand knowledge of the typical accounting and technical issues they faced, all of which I needed in my toolkit.

Laurie also supported me with leads. Sometimes I would win the work, but more often I would get the familiar, 'Thanks for your proposal; we have chosen to go with another firm.' I was disappointed but not terribly surprised. I was not the cheapest alternative nor the most experienced. I was falling short of my competition and didn't have a compelling reason for why they should pick *me*. I needed a more targeted, winning approach to fulfill my revenue goals.

I decided to concentrate my selling efforts on developing connections with veteran bankers, venture capitalists (VCs), and lawyers working in the technology industry, with a goal of adding them to my TICE rolodex. The most influential among them would have referrals that I could potentially tap as 'warm' leads, while also assuming these referrals were reputable companies with integrity who were worthy of my time, effort, and attention.

I then asked my technology industry colleagues for assistance on leads and invited myself to the anything-but-sexy 'speed dating' events, where CEOs share their elevator pitch (explaining what they do and why they need money) to technology associations. Soon I was invited to other networking events, some held by bankers, lawyers, and VCs—the very guys I was itching to meet.

A personal connection was key. I was quite capable of starting a conversation with other professionals at these events—that part was easy for an extrovert like myself—but I was unimpressive once the conversation progressed to something deeper. I did more listening than talking, which is not at all a bad thing for an auditor or a consultant to do, but when it came to sharing a similar story or offering my solutions, I seriously lacked depth and insight into their issues.

Most days I felt like I was being interrogated with a bright, white light shining directly on my face. Instead of being asked, 'Where were you on the night of the fourteenth?' I imagined someone announcing, 'How dare you parade around here like you belong? You are nothing but a fraud!' Indeed.

How could I avoid showing my ignorance to the industry experts? When they got technical, my head exploded. I could barely follow the language never mind the issue they were trying to solve. They were speaking in Klingon, and sentences like, 'Yes, I can see how that would be a concern,' came stammering out of me with no authenticity. I was the imposter of all imposters, adding no value to the conversations I tried desperately to belong to.

I asked myself some difficult questions.

Am I feeling like an imposter because I lack confidence in myself and my abilities against the backdrop of the men I compare myself to? Or do I feel this way because I am working in a world that I wasn't meant to be a part of?

I was the only woman in a vast ocean of qualified, confident men. I knew when I signed up for this gig I would be working outside my comfort zone, but I didn't realize just how *far* outside. I had so much learning to do.

As I came to discover, Canadian start-ups needed help raising capital, growing revenues, and hiring talented software engineers. Could I confidently and authentically help these companies with their pain points? My inner voice screamed, 'No, no, and no!'

So, I continued to slog on, trying to get noticed by those that mattered, while praying I wouldn't do anything to embarrass myself or bomb my reputation beyond repair.

Then, something happened that I thought would sink me with TICE, and perhaps even with the firm.

If my meagre networking efforts weren't humbling enough, I soon learned there was another catch to joining this burgeoning industry group. TICE partners and staff were *strongly encouraged* to obtain their US CPA designation, which really meant we *had* to get it.

I had some serious studying to do. Believing I would never have to write another exam in my life, fifteen years later my worst nightmare had come true. The US CPA exam was a 150-question multiple choice exam with the passing grade set at 75%.

To help staff and partners studying for the US CPA exam, the firm recommended and paid for a prep course. I signed up and tried to make my studying as productive and painless as possible.

I listened and learned, remembered and applied what they taught. It was tough slugging with two kids and my heavy partner workload. My CPA exam fifteen years earlier was worlds away from me, and as hard as that was, it seemed far easier than what I was preparing for this time around.

In the end, I did what I thought was sufficient to pass the exam, and always weighed that against the demands of hectic workdays and lost weekends to studying and parenting. I wrote the exam and left feeling the same way I did the first time I wrote the CPA exam: not great.

The results were sent out by mail eight weeks later. I nervously ripped open the envelop to read the contents. It was a brief paragraph from the Board of Examiners starting with, 'You received a mark of 74%.'

One... fricking... percent...

The news was shattering, and it was made infinitely worse because I was a partner in a major accounting firm. I had a reputation to uphold, but now my ego was shot, left for dead, and there was no picking it up or dusting it off.

I had let my firm down, and more to the point, I had let myself down. It was as devastating as it was embarrassing. How could I show my face at the office? What were my staff, my peers, and my leaders going to think? Could I recover from my shame? What happens to my transfer to TICE if I can't pass the required US CPA?

Questions were swirling around in my head faster than I could squash them. It was hard to breathe. Imaginary walls were closing all around me, and the sunny fall days felt noticeably colder and darker. I had no idea what to do next.

First, I knew I had to let my nerves settle. Positive talk followed.

'I have to be strong; I am better than this. I can't let this define me. I am better than the mark I received on this stupid, irrelevant exam!'

Then, the next day in Mississauga, I walked into Rick's office to disclose my fate. I needed his advice. Rick was my personal coach, but more than this, he was a friend with whom I regularly went out to lunch and felt comfortable telling my troubles to (regardless of whether he was ready to hear them!).

But, as I suspected would happen, the waterworks came first. I was blubbering uncontrollably before anything sensible was uttered. There were so many emotions I was feeling, and I needed a shoulder to cry on. I know he felt uncomfortable, yet he remained calm, professional, and collected. He seemed genuinely surprised by my news and offered his support.

'Sue, you only missed it by one mark,' he reasoned. 'It could happen to anyone. Don't beat yourself up. It doesn't matter. Really, it'll be okay.'

I lifted my head from my lap where it was bowed in shame. I listened to his words of encouragement, wiping the tears that flowed down my cheeks, ignoring the smudging of my mascara and the resulting raccoon eyes. 'What should I do?' I asked in desperation.

He continued, 'You know, you could try again. But that's totally up to you. You came so close. You can do this but believe me when I say it's no big deal either way. You mustn't feel like it is.'

He waited for his words to sink in, then carried on, 'Take your time. Think about it. It's your decision. Either way I will support you.' He was reassuring, empathetic and patient. Exactly what I needed to hear.

I left his office feeling like I just might make it through another day. I had been given a lifeline by someone I respected. He'd instilled in me a renewed sense of worth.

I knew I had overreacted. I had jumped to false conclusions. I saw my glass half-empty. I promised myself I would stop thinking this way.

Still, I didn't advertise my failure to anyone. If asked, I told them the minimum, then moved on to change the subject. I accepted their explanation for this travesty: an unmanageable workload must be to blame. That may have had something to do with it, but it was not the whole truth. I had to face facts.

I convinced myself that, had I spent the necessary time to study, I would have passed. I hadn't applied myself. I had lost the study habits and determination that got me through the first set of CPA exams fifteen years earlier. Using work/life imbalance as a crutch did, however, seem the least offensive way to save face in the moment. But the truth was simple: I could have passed that exam if I'd given it the attention it deserved.

And how maturity changes your perspective! This was immensely worse than not making the cheerleading squad in high school. How inconsequential it was to think I wasn't pretty enough because this was infinitely worse. Now I wasn't smart enough. *Ouch.*

Over the weeks that followed, I analysed my failure. What lessons could I learn from this experience, and how could I avoid repeating the same mistakes next time? It was time to *own* my grade and learn from it.

I concluded there was much more to learn, and I needed to tweak my approach. I swallowed my pride, put this setback behind me, and committed to trying this exam with deliberate course corrections. *I can do this!*

I made studying my first priority, even put it ahead of my family for twelve long weeks. My children, my husband, and to some extent, my firm, had to understand. My study plan included solid, uninterrupted hours several nights a week on both weekdays and weekends leading up to the exam. That took personal commitment I hadn't attempted since writing my Canadian CPA. Thankfully, my understanding spouse stood beside me as my faithful co-pilot, taking on more than his share of duties at home, supporting me, the kids, the chores, and everything in between. I was left to focus exclusively on my end goal: to pass this sucker exam.

The weight of my vow manifested itself into my becoming a more stressed-out and anxious woman than usual. I snapped easier, smiled less, and was wearing an invisible 'Do not disturb' necklace. I told myself repeatedly, *This will be over soon. I* can't *fail. I know it will be worth it.*

What I didn't know was how to explain this new, short-term arrangement, or my resting bitch face, to my kids. I worried they would learn to live in my new reality and accept their mom wasn't going to be there for them. I tried to ignore the lyrics to, 'Cats in the Cradle' which seemed to constantly pop into my head at times like these.

The plan included memorizing, and I mean *really* memorizing, the nasty personal and corporate US tax returns. It was a stupid waste of brain space, but I did it anyway. I reread the binders of technical material provided by the professors and made my own notes. I knew from the Canadian CPA exams that was the way I learned best.

I got plenty of sleep and exercised when I could. I took distinct breaks from studying to enjoy time with my family. I took a natural supplement, ginkgo biloba, to improve brain clarity and memory recall. I was pulling out all the stops.

I took the exam for the second time in September 1999. Upon finishing, I felt as good as anyone could. I had done all that I could do; it was no longer in my hands.

Eight weeks later, I received the letter I was waiting for. It read, 'Congratulations, Susan, the Board of Examiners is pleased to report you have successfully passed the US CPA exam. You obtained a mark of 89%.'

Bam!

And that, my friends, is how it's done. It was time to celebrate with some well-deserved, much overdue family time!

REFLECTION

Knowing when and how to take centre stage

The jury vote is in. And it's not looking great for us.

Women need to get over themselves! Enough hiding our desire for stretch opportunities and waiting for someone else to notice us. Enough giving credit to others for the outstanding work *we* have performed. Enough self-sabotaging! By doing these things, we understate our potential, and we're overlooked for opportunities to propel our careers forward.

When we *dare to say it out loud*, we are forced to accept the risk, anxiety, and growth that comes with a new challenge, and admit to ourselves (and others!) what we truly want. This was a reckoning for me. It was finally my time to come to grips with and believe in the future I wanted.

If it wasn't for my male heroes, a suite of determined bosses with my best interests in mind, I would not have anything further to report, nothing to say. This time, I was saved by Ian who *forced* me to face the risk (and my fear) of putting pen to paper on the big hairy audacious goal of becoming a partner. Asking for what we deserve is not supposed to be that hard!

So, my friends, your choice is simple. Tell your boss, your partner, your friends, and your colleagues about your dreams and develop goals to achieve them. Say these goals out loud, write them down, take action on them. Hell, shout them from the rooftops if it helps! Or humbly stay in the comfort of what you know and love and let the chips fall as they may... or may not.

Here are the lessons to consider as you take control over your future:

- Assess and consider emulating the qualities of managers for whom you do your best work. Adopt the attributes of those individuals who inspire you, encourage you, support you, and those you have learned the most from.

- Even if its uncomfortable, risky, or downright scary, when you need advice from a trusted superior, have that conversation. Staying silent robs you of that wisdom and guidance. Listen to what they have to say and weigh it against your views. You can still make up your own mind, but you have the added benefit of their insider's perspective.

- Developing a truthful, complete list of the pros and cons is helpful when you are dealing with a weighty decision. Don't forget to listen to what your head and your heart are saying. Then, do what is right for you.

- Be realistic on what you can and cannot physically (and emotionally) accomplish in twenty-four hours. Stand your ground and state your position for your dealbreakers. If you need to slow down and get off the treadmill, start by getting to bed earlier and rising later. You need that rejuvenating sleep you (and most of us) are sorely deprived of. It is nature's best medicine.

Reflection Questions

1. Do you accept the risk, anxiety, and growth that comes with a new challenge, or do you stay in the comfort of what you know and love?

2. What manager qualities inspire you? How will you adopt these attributes in your leadership style and remain authentic when dealing with others?

3. Are you leaving your long-term goals 'blank'? What will you do to change this?

4. Are you considering a field or industry where you are in the minority? If so, where will you find trusted peers to confide in or learn the ropes with?

Part VI: The Transformation

Become the subject-matter expert you know you can be, provide value to others, and watch your imposter syndrome melt away.

Since the early days and weeks of my first job as the UTM Cashier, I promised to never be bored in a job again. I kept that promise.

When I joined PwC, I stoked my love-of-learning gene by accepting new challenges, new clients, new teams, new roles, new surroundings, and more recently, an entirely new industry.

By welcoming change as a regular feature of my workday, boredom was kicked to the curb. As I progressed with PwC, I learned to view change with a growth mindset, using my passion for trying something new to keep me engaged. Never settling for the same old routine had its challenges to be sure—it took effort to make work and life co-exist on reasonable terms—but the benefits always outweighed the costs. Just because it's hard doesn't mean it's not worth doing.

Although the pace of change energized me, I had more than the occasional day where I was, admittedly, terrified. There was intense pressure to stay current in accounting and to keep up with the technical aspects of my job, all while keeping the independent watchdogs holding powerful scrutiny over my work, and my profession, at bay. Moreover, during this time, I had trusted relationships with new tech clients to secure and build. I needed to become an expert.

I have yet to comprehend the rush one gets, or, shall I say, *I get*, from the sink or swim environment I repeatedly placed myself in. While I complained outwardly about how chaotic life was, I thrived in the madness of it. I think most high achievers who complain do, and if you're one of those people who don't thrive in the madness, I might suggest taking a step back and re-evaluating your current path. Your mental (and physical!) health should always come first.

I say this to prepare you for the lightning-fast pace of change that came next in my career. My transformation from nervous novice to savvy subject-matter expert was the result of choices I made, the support I received, the leadership roles I accepted, the clients I served, and the people I met. I developed more sales, marketing, negotiating, leadership, and business skills in two years than I had acquired in my previous nineteen years of work experience! In short, I became confident, and this propelled my career into overdrive.

How did this happen? The overwhelming difficulties and pressures I faced were precursors to the expertise I gained. They were inseparable during the storm. But, when the rain stopped and the sun peeked through the clouds, a surprise awaited: the gift of *earned* experience. The challenges I endured were eclipsed by the gifts delivered in return. I had a better understanding of the tech industry for certain, but the bow that wrapped around this gift was my proficiency in the practice of humility, tenacity, compassion, and teamwork. Like the friendships I made, these traits were more precious than fleeting industry knowledge. They would last a lifetime.

Growth happens when you are lost, scared, and alone in the thickest part of the forest. Transformation occurs when you are forced to draw upon inner-strength and courage to plan and pursue the path that enables your escape. Don't be afraid to enter the forest.

15

Do you know the way to… Silicon Valley?

At the conclusion of a conference tailored to Canadian TICE managers and partners, Laurie announced an interesting, *self-sacrificing* opportunity.

'I have been asked by Global TICE leadership to let you know the US firm is in dire need of TICE staff. They are looking for managers, partners, and seniors to join their San Jose, California office for a minimum period of six months… preferably for the next two years. Folks, come see me if this is something you are interested in pursuing, and I can give you more details.'

It was 1999, and San Jose, California, part of the larger Silicon Valley region, was one of the fastest-growing technology regions in the world. The San Jose office was unable to keep pace with the ever-increasing volume of new work and demands placed on their staff and partners. New companies surfaced daily in need of our services. From 1999 to 2000, over one-thousand of these start-ups asked for auditors like PwC to help them go public (Initial Public Offering or 'IPO') on the US stock exchanges. Auditors were exhausted.

If we wanted to step into this new frontier (or warzone!), all we needed to do was tell Laurie and we'd be packing our bags and headed to the Valley of the Sun's Delight pronto.

It sounded fascinating, but I was not even close to considering such an absurd proposal. I was barely acclimatizing to the technology scene in Mississauga. How would I cope with the pace of change in the Valley? And, if I couldn't accept working twenty miles away from home in downtown Toronto, how could I possibly agree to traveling 2600 miles from home to work in California? I was far from a subject-matter expert in the technology industry and this move would expose my significant limitations. Could my ego handle this?

Yet, the thought wouldn't go away. My penchant for pain was acting up again.

If I was immersed in Silicon Valley—a booming technology hub at the centre of the industry—I knew I would have no other choice but to soak up everything this experience offered. I could learn to float with water wings in a pool of sharks and, over time, become the competent swimmer I wanted to be.

If I remained a TICE partner in Mississauga, my progression among my fellow partners would stall. My satellite office experiment hadn't worked as I had hoped. I was struggling to learn the industry, build a client base, and fit in. If I shifted to San Jose, I would get the experience I needed, and then return as a seasoned, subject-matter expert in the tech industry.

As I drove home from work that evening, I contemplated the pros of a compelling stretch assignment for myself, as well as an exciting new adventure for my family. But there were also many cons.

There was the risk of failure and the ramifications of that on my career. Moreover, I would be faced with increasing demands on my work/life balance, there would be a stall for John's leadership position as Assistant General Manager and CFO with his employer, we had no support system in San Jose, and my kids would have to adapt to a new school in a foreign country.

No, no, no.

There were too many hurdles to overcome. I could never in a million years accept this. I was dead set against it.

Over dinner and light conversation, I mentioned the invitation to John. I kept eating, not even looking up from my plate. It was something I mentioned in passing, for fun.

John swallowed his mouthful of pasta and put down his knife and fork. He startled me with his conviction. 'What are you waiting for? That is an amazing opportunity for you. We need to go!'

Danielle, half listening to our conversation, perked up and asked, 'What would be an amazing opportunity?'

Turning to both Danielle and Andrew, John asked, 'How would you kids like to move to California? Let Mom work there for a few years?'

'Wow, that would be really cool! When can we go?'

Those are not the droids I'm looking for.

John and I thought more seriously about the possibility of a move to California over the coming days. Working in technology in the Bay Area would be a once-in-a-lifetime opportunity for me and my career. Besides, I wasn't going to argue with sunshine and warm winters, as well as the unique challenges and opportunities for not only myself, but for each of us to experience change and growth together. If John's employer was supportive of him having someone else steer the ship while he was away for two years—and John was willing to put his career on hold—there was nothing holding us back. Time to pack our bags!

The moment I put my hand up, the ball was set in motion. US TICE leadership in New York gave me the green light, and the San Jose office leadership were eager to hand off as many clients as I could handle. Five public company audits were passed to me on my first day!

Yikes! Wait till the US firm realizes what they signed up for: a recycled CIPS partner...

We started looking for a place to live, but in 2000, there were no apartments, homes, condos, tents, or shacks to rent during the height of the technology boom. We looked everywhere for something to own or rent, but they were gone before you could say 'Silicon Valley.' Housing prices were ugly expensive, with increasing demand from entrepreneurs flush with excess 'cash' moving into the bustling tech area, outstripping supply. The longer we waited, the worse it got. We resolved to take whatever we could find, but there was a distinct chance we'd be living in a rental car hiding out in a Denny's parking lot.

I mentioned my frustration to my long-time secretary in Mississauga, whose surprising answer saved the day. 'Sue, let me ask my sister. She has a place in Mountainview that she hasn't put on the market yet. I think she's getting it ready to rent now.'

BINGO! What amazing luck that, at the last possible minute, we rented a place exactly where we needed to live from my *Canadian* secretary's sister! We rushed to sign a two-year lease with her, regardless of price, sight unseen. I crossed my fingers, hoping it would serve us well.

Next on the agenda was schooling. This was no easy task. Like the housing boom, there were very few openings for kids entering the area from out of town. When schools made space for one or two more, they were selective, because they could be.

My kids completed their applications, wrote aptitude tests, submitted essays and reference letters, and if they passed the initial screening, they still had to get lucky enough to receive a phone interview from the school's headmaster.

But Andrew and Danielle were stars. They passed the admission screening and got into the schools of their choice. Everything was falling into place!

Movers packed up our furniture and belongings and began the southwest trek across North America to beautiful Mountainview, California. We flew direct, moving into our lovely five-bedroom bungalow in an established residential neighbourhood. We arrived in July 2000, and by the start of school in September, the kids were settling into their classes, and making new, lifelong friends. As for me, I settled into my office and jam-packed client load working fifty-, sixty-, or seventy-hour weeks from the word 'go.'

I learned there were plenty of high-paying jobs for John's sought-after skills as an experienced CPA, and I was frequently asked if he was interested in working part-time, full-time, or anytime. My answer was always, 'Thanks, but no thanks.' The kids needed their dad, and I needed my co-pilot to support our chaotic new lives at school, work, and home. John was the family lifeline.

From day one, I was well aware of the enormous sacrifice John was making to suspend his career while I advanced mine. John's days involved puttering around the house, parading as Mr. Fixit doing this and that, building and checking off his list of to-do's—a million little *five- minute* jobs for our forty-year-old rental that needed love.

As time passed, however, John tired of his insignificant work demands and looked to fill his free time in the land of sunshine and warmth. With what else? Golf! To save money on the increasing number of games he would squeeze in between kid drop-offs and pickups, he volunteered at the golf course as the Tuesday afternoon starter. When my San Jose colleagues, the male partners who were working just as hard as I was, learned how John spent his days, they couldn't believe it. Envious and wishful, they aspired to be him. 'What the hell did I do wrong? Your husband is living my dream!'

John took on his role as professional golfer, homemaker, fixer of all things, master chef, and primary childcare provider with passion and enthusiasm. I was jealous he was the one who knew the kids' friends, their parents, the teachers, the sports coaches, and our neighbours better than I. He was first to hear what made the kids angry, sad, or happy each day during their drive home from school. I would hear about their lives without the passion they shared with him. Their stories would be recounted only when I asked, or when they remembered to tell me in passing. It was hard to take a back seat to my children's lives on account of work and the everyday pressures of my career. I constantly had to remind myself to leave it at the office, come home, *forget about it*, and be present for my family.

But no matter how hard I tried, my work/life balance was put to its ultimate test. As a partner, I found I had more control over my day, but my day was tripped up with last-minute client emergencies, *all the damn time.*

I longed to attend as many soccer, basketball, baseball, water polo games, and track meets as I could. It was my intention to be more than a parent watching their lives from the sidelines, but to do this, I had to see them during my workday, in secret. I assumed this wasn't accepted practice because it wasn't a topic discussed amongst the partners. I always wondered if other partners and managers wanted to attend their kids' daytime events. If so, how did they do it? Why wasn't anyone talking about this?

Taking matters into my own hands, I blocked time off in my calendar. As far as anyone at PwC knew, I had a *work* commitment. Clients and staff could reach me after hours if it was an emergency, but rarely was it so important that their 'emergency' couldn't wait till the next morning. Disconnecting from work to see my kids playing their favourite sports, on my terms, was my elixir when the days were too long and too stressful to bear. An hour or two in the middle of my workday was my personal win-win.

My secret approach gave me permission to be a happier mom, which in turn, made me a more engaged PwC partner. I should have shared what I was doing to give others permission to do the same, but I was in denial that this would be accepted without scorn. *One day,* I thought, *when I am a more established partner and more secure in my skin, I will tell others... and maybe that will give them tacit permission to do the same.*

That day never arrived. Not until much later in my career.

Landing in San Jose in the height of the tech boom with no industry experience required me to learn at the speed of light. It also required me to rely heavily on my fellow partners and managers for guidance and support. I had to suck it up and plead ignorance to my colleagues daily, which reminded me of my first weeks at PwC straight out of my cashier job. Oh, the circle of life! Long hours and stressful times defined my existence. If I didn't learn fast, I knew clients would catch on pretty quick that I had no clue what I was talking about.

Innovation in the networking and communications (N&C) industry subsector of technology was where my quest for industry experience began. I was assigned to this sector for no other reason than that's where the greatest need for a partner was that month, that week. I was given a full portfolio of work from a retiring partner: five public clients, dozens of private start-ups, and as many new opportunities to draft an audit proposal for as I could handle.

As one of three women partners in an office of forty-seven male partners, I felt outnumbered and not my usual excited and outgoing self. This entire experience had me *way* outside my comfort zone, again.

I spent the first few weeks getting my bearings, learning how to work with and delegate to my new executive assistant, and collaborating with fellow N&C staff and fellow partners. Everyone was eager to have me on board, and they welcomed me instantly. Once I was introduced to my clients, however, that welcoming attitude shifted, because I became fair game for a barrage of questions. They assumed I was an expert.

My clients were excited to start their relationship with their new partner and to pick my brain for advice on their issue of the day. The only problem with this approach was *there was nothing in my brain for them to pick*. They would have had as much success asking my dog.

But I couldn't give them nothing. My response to their urgent technical question was always, 'Let me get this straight...' after which I would repeat the issue I heard, then I would politely reply with, 'I see. Can I get back to you on this?' I was so lame.

The next step was to find the manager assigned to this client, ask them what their question meant, and get their advice. Nine times out of ten, they knew the answer. This made matters worse for me, as I realized how much I had to quickly learn. If I needed more help, or a second opinion on a more contentious issue, I walked into my friendly neighbourhood partners' offices, begged for forgiveness, and got their recommendation on the correct answer. So humbling. I learned to grovel.

My neighbouring partners, all men, did their best to answer my questions or point me in the right direction. I couldn't have survived my first year in San Jose without their mentoring and coaching; they were my heroes, my teachers, my lifelines, my buddies.

To be fair, when I reflect on how I handled the difficult technical questions posed by my clients, my approach had its merits. I shared what I knew and what I didn't, and I was honest about this. I worked on the best solution in tandem with CFOs, digging deep into the specific facts and circumstances of their issues. I shared whatever guidance I could find in the technical literature that existed. Then, as a team, we developed solutions that worked both for them and PwC. I was not seen as the 'know-it-all,' but I was respected for how I did my best to help them solve their most important problems. I believe an authentic 'what you see is what you get' style builds deeper trust. This is what is called building 'relationship capital.' And that is definitely not lame.

In between putting my clients' fires out, I boldly asked a couple of the male partners I engaged with the most, 'Hey, what are you doing for lunch today?' Rob and Dave were my usual targets; sitting in offices next to mine, they were easy pickins. However, in the beginning, too often, I looked up from my desk with the sound of chatter outside my door. Then, at noon each day, I watched them leave the office without me, without so much as a peek inside my office. *Hey, I'm in here! Come ask me to lunch!*

My mind cast me back to those horrific first two weeks of training at PwC, left to eat alone every day while the guys went to the men's only bar. I couldn't go through that again. Not here, not now, and not for the next two years.

I was somewhat more confident and mature now. *I am a partner for god's sakes!* With nothing to lose and everything to gain, every day after that, I burst into one of their offices like *Seinfeld's* Kramer at ten minutes to noon, and asked, 'Hey, where are you going for lunch today?'

After that, I rarely took my lunch alone. I wasn't a burden; I was a colleague and a friend who they seemed happy to spend time with. That's my story and I'm sticking to it.

16

My Rise and the Tech Collapse

As one of only three women partners in the San Jose office, I was asked to participate in the office recruiting efforts. It was something I had done in the Canadian firm for years, and as this was a break from the weight of my technical accounting day, I was pleased to help out.

Women were graduating from university at an unprecedented rate, and I knew I had a relevant story to share with the would-be CPAs—one that was even more unusual in the US than it was in Canada. I'd attained an atypical degree, received a timely promotion to partner after two six-month maternity leaves, and I'd worked out a flexible, part-time work arrangement while parenting two children. How did I do it?

A working spouse with children was an anomaly in the office. Maternity leaves longer than six weeks? Unheard of. Working part-time? That's one way to sideline your career until further notice.

There were too few senior women partners with my career path. Successful career women had stay-at-home husbands to look after the kids, or a two-career household with no children.

The female graduates I interviewed expressed their relief and delight in hearing my story, and in their eyes, it propelled PwC up in the ranks. Many suddenly saw that a future with the firm was possible because they saw it could be done. It was a classic case of looking up the ladder at someone like you and being inspired to try it too. Today, this has not only been proven to work with gender, but also with BiPoC, LGBTQ+, religion, and culture.

Mine was the career path these young women longed to emulate. They wanted it all, *on their terms*. They wanted the option to have a career and be mothers and spouses with outside lives. This was sadly not the story they heard from other women leaders in the profession who had 'made it,' and they confided in me they were finding their place in the accounting world hard to imagine.

During one of my in-office interviews, I was given a resume and background with a pleasant surprise. It was a female graduate with an accounting major, of course. But, more importantly, she was also a dance major from Santa Clara University. A woman after my own heart! I couldn't wait to meet her and learn all about her dance experience. I was definitely going off script for this interview.

I found my doppelganger. I instantly connected with her and her background, although I suspect she thought I was a little *too* excited to talk more about dance than of PwC and the thrilling life she would enjoy as an auditor. Our conversation steered in the direction of how much I would love to still be dancing.

'You can!' she responded. 'The head of dance at Santa Clara University has her own studio with classes for people like you.' Wait for it... 'You know, women that have significant dance experience from their youth, and are now, uh... *your age*.'

Ouch. Dagger to the heart, get out of my office (kidding!).

Still captivated, I wrote down the name of the studio, and it wasn't long before I'd signed up for back-to-back adult jazz and tap classes for *old* women like me. Soon it became three glorious hours every Tuesday evening, where I could relive my childhood and move my body in ways I had not moved in decades. It hurt, but it was worth it, because it was also refreshing and rejuvenating—a wonderful stress relief for my days in the office.

I hadn't really exercised like this since having children. My thought had always been that it would take me away from time I needed to spend with my family. I was clearly working too many hours away from them, so I couldn't possibly take time to do something for myself, right?

Nonsense!

Upon my return to Canada, I promised not to lose this incredible feeling of purpose, energy, worth, and health that dance provided. Besides the aerobic exercise, increased flexibility, strength, and rebirth of dead leg muscles, losing myself in dance cleared my thoughts. I felt relaxed and better able to take on whatever the rest of the week might bring.

I was a better partner, wife, and mother because I had taken time to do something for myself. It didn't make me feel guilty either. It gave me the energy I needed to get myself through another day. It was my runner's high.

By the end of my time pitching PwC to female graduates, we saw a rise in our share of the brightest and best women our competitors were vying for! My hope was that they'd been inspired enough to stay, get their CPA, and remain in the profession in whatever capacity they'd always dreamed of.

Eighteen months into my secondment, I was summoned to meet with Marshall, the Managing Partner of the San Jose office. My first thought, of course, was, *What have I done now?*

It was not at all *that* kind of meeting. Marshall was letting me know he had recommended me for Linkage Inc's Corporate Fellow Award. Linkage, a consulting firm focused on purposeful leadership development, advancing women leaders, and creating diverse and inclusive workplaces, was honouring me for the impact I was making as a woman in leadership.

Whaaaat?

I was flattered and surprised to learn that he felt I had made an important impact on my staff, my clients, and my partners since coming to the US. I had earned his respect and personal recognition. This alone was more relevant to me than any outside award.

With this honour came my invitation to attend an educational, inspirational three-day Leadership Summit with like-minded women in various stages of their leadership journey. My heart was racing, and my mind was jumping for joy.

The catch to receiving this award was I had to give an acceptance speech at the conference in front of an impressive list of confident females—the 'who's who' of Corporate America.

I had to make my time on stage count. I wanted to make a lasting impression with my message. But how? What topic could I speak about that would resonate with them, influence their thinking, and change their behaviour in an impactful way? I'm a boring auditor, not a Mount Everest climber! I procrastinated, sat on it for far too long, then my clock ran out.

The conference started on Friday afternoon. It was Thursday night, and I had yet to put pen to paper. I usually worked better under pressure, but this was too much! With less than 24 hours before the big event, a blank Word document stared back at me, mocking my every attempt. My intense fear of humiliation took a firm grip on my fingers.

Then, out of nowhere, words started flowing and I started typing effortlessly onto the page. Before I knew it, my speech was written, and it was exactly what I was looking for. Sometimes, somehow, from somewhere, I pull a rabbit out of a hat, and it all falls into place. This was one of those times.

The sheer size and calibre of this networking, educational experience was like nothing I had ever experienced in my life. Eight-hundred senior executive women, and the next layer of high-performing female leaders in every profession and industry imaginable, were in attendance from across the US. Standing in front of the largest crowd I'd ever spoken to, I had ten crucial minutes to make a difference.

My time on stage was sandwiched between a keynote address by the late Madeline Albright, the US Secretary of State at the time, and Cokie Roberts, a well-known TV anchor, personality, author, and journalist. I sat beside Cokie in the front row of the grand ballroom, waiting, both terrified and excited to share my prepared remarks. I tried to remain calm, and busied myself by convincing myself, *Sue, this is a friendly crowd; they want you to succeed!* Nonetheless, I couldn't help but reflect upon the fact that I was representing PwC and winning a *leadership* award for my impact on women, while speaking between two heavyweight, inspirational household names. Butterflies were finding a permanent home in my stomach. My mouth was dry.

I have absolutely no idea what Madeline Albright spoke about for the hour leading up to my ten minutes of fame. I'm sure she was globally significant and insightful, but try as I might, I didn't hear one word. I was in the front row, losing my mind!

As I made my way onto the steps of the long stage, walking towards the podium, the MC revealed to me and the audience that I was the Leadership Summit's *first* international winner of the Corporate Fellow Award. Great, thanks for the news. Raise the expectations.

In response to the inflated announcement, to shake my own nerves, I joked, 'Hey, I'm just a girl from Toronto trying to figure out how to say "out", "about", and "roof" correctly.' Soft chuckles filled the room, the audience reacting to my Canadian mispronunciations. It was enough to shed a good portion of my nerves.

After thanking Linkage Inc and PwC for bestowing this honour upon me, my remarks turned to the winding road that landed me here.

I proudly revealed how I had been promoted to partner in thirteen years, the same length of time it took my male counterparts *with undergraduate accounting degrees*. I had done all this despite my two longer-than-average maternity leaves, and my three years in a flexible part-time arrangement. I smiled at eight-hundred faces in the grand ballroom, and said, 'How cool is that?' and they answered with heartfelt applause.

I was getting warmed up. The meat of my speech was not about me.

I told them that, like many other women leaders in the room, I climbed the corporate ladder, doing it my way as a businesswoman, a wife, and a mother. Charting my course was unknown territory at every turn.

'This conference is asking us to think about vision, balance, strength, resilience, and courage.' It was time to broach my main topic: the role of ethics in business and life. Sounds like a sleeper, right? Wrong.

Corporate America was in shambles. In the remaining minutes I had on the podium, I was going to try my darndest to stand up for my profession—the role accountants play in capital markets to ensure companies *do the right thing*. It was my duty as a CPA and an auditor. The following is verbatim from my speech:

'We make decisions every day that set us apart as individuals and leaders. And we have options. I am talking about the critical path we forge when we use principles to guide our decisions, when we apply ethics and integrity in our companies and in our lives.

'We are living in a highly competitive, global economy with increasing pressure on companies to perform, to do more with less, to make their numbers, to manage their earnings, and to meet Wall Street's expectations. Put this pressure on the backdrop of a country in a recession (it was 2002), exacerbated by the (still very raw) terrorist attacks of September 11, and now what is being termed the largest business failure in corporate history… Enron.'

Enron needed no explanation. They'd eroded the country's trust in Corporate America and dragged my profession through the coals.

But if I was to make a real difference with these women, I needed to speak to them on a deep, personal level.

'When I was thirteen, my grandfather gave me a book that had been given to him by his mother on his tenth birthday, and in it he inscribed, "To my first and only granddaughter, *may she always be true to herself.*" Pretty deep thoughts for a man who never passed grade five,' I said. 'I didn't appreciate the strength of his words or the magnitude of his message until several decades later.'

Then, I asked them to consider something closer to home, that each one of us has experienced at some point.

'When you are checking out at Safeway and the cashier mistakenly gives you an extra twenty dollars back in change, what do you do? Do you slip the bill in your pocket and walk away or give it back to her and explain her mistake?

'Would your answer be different if your son or daughter was standing beside you? You can choose to make it a teaching moment for your kids, or you can rationalize why you deserve this extra cash and say nothing. It's up to you.

'Know that what you decide to do at that moment impacts you, your kids, the cashier, and anyone who may be watching. This simple act of returning the change that doesn't belong to you—what effect does that have on others? On you? Think about it. What pressures do *you* face on a daily basis?'

Then a thought came to me; I was going off script. This was something I *never* would have tried in a million lightyears prior to my volunteer board experience. But my term as President of the Mississauga Arts Council prepared me for this very moment. I wanted to dream bigger.

It was February 2002, and the Winter Olympics were underway in Salt Lake City, Utah. The pairs skating competition had finished a few days earlier with a pair of Canadian skaters, Sale and Pelletier, who were taking home a respectable silver medal for their performance. Nonetheless, the public was outraged at their standing behind a pair of less-competent Russian skaters.

A swing vote to seal the fate of the Canadians came from a French judge who, under pressure, admitted to cheating in exchange for favourable ice dancing judging from the Russians.

This was *the* sports scandal of the day, and Americans, including those women in my audience, had taken up the cause for the Canadian skaters whose gold medal was stolen from them.

'Have you seen the look on someone's face when you tell them they gave you too much change? At first it is a look of disbelief. Then, their whole face warms up and it's as if the "Star-Spangled Banner" starts playing in their mind.

'Yes, I am Canadian. But I have a confession to make. I am a big fan of your American national anthem. It is *so* patriotic; *so* inspiring. When I sing "O' Canada" it just doesn't give me the same goose-bumps.' Then I paused for effect. 'But we *CAN* skate!'

My knowing smile, tongue-in-cheek, was enough. Everyone recognized what I was driving at, and they went wild, clapping and cheering. I'd hit a chord and maybe a good ole' American home run. If I thought they weren't listening to me before, now I knew they were hanging on every word. I glimpsed down at my *prepared* remarks.

'In these difficult times, auditors, more often than we'd like to admit, have to deliver bad news to our clients. We have to make tough judgment calls, ones that do not win popularity contests.'

I described the critical role that auditors play for shareholders, the investing public, and the capital markets. I acknowledged it was my responsibility, and the responsibility of my fellow CPAs, to restore their trust. We could not let a few bad actors (i.e., Arthur Andersen's boys in Texas) tarnish the reputation and value we brought to the table.

I shared a few business situations I experienced to give weight to my responsibility as an independent professional who had dealt with ethics in business before.

I explained the dreaded 'going concern' opinion I had given to companies on many occasions, stating my doubts about the company's ability to continue, which typically sends their stock on a downward tumble.

'Believe me, these are not easy discussions to have with CEOs and CFOs whose bonuses may depend on making their numbers. It is easy to deliver good news. It is an experienced, empathetic, supportive leader that delivers bad news well.

'On my bad news days, I am comforted by the support of my partners, my firm's values, and especially by my grandfather's words: to always be true to myself.'

In striving to give a more balanced, less doom and gloom perspective, I shared the next true story.

'And then there are the good days. The unexpected, positive findings of an audit, because I really do love my job! Like, for example, when I recently identified my client made an error whereby they paid a million-dollar invoice to a supplier twice… which was obviously well-received! But why didn't the supplier identify this error first? I wonder how my client feels about doing business with them going forward?'

Next, I talked about the time my Canadian client was about to pay too little (in millions of dollars) for an acquisition, because of an error in the purchase price equation the seller made. I knew the seller would not be any the wiser for his error, but I couldn't keep it to myself. My CPA code of conduct wouldn't allow it any more than my conscience would.

I was, in typical Canadian fashion, *apologetic* for finding such a costly error.

Without missing a beat, the CFO concluded, 'This is unfortunate, but we have to do the right thing.' They paid millions more for the acquisition because of me.

'Sometimes, it's not my call to make, only my duty to inform. When companies like my client choose to do the right thing when they have no monetary gain from exposing the issue, only a personal and corporate loss, I am encouraged. It is companies such as these who have laid the foundation for the highest ethical standards, whose executives "walk the talk" and expect no less of their employees, that have the most successful track record for performance and longevity.'

I invited my audience of leaders to join me in a call to action:

'Have you drawn your line in the sand? Have you shown your children where that line is, so that they will draw their own line someday? And what about your employees? Will they draw it where you would like it to be drawn? Will your children and your employees have the confidence to confide in you on the moral dilemmas they will inevitably face?

'These are sobering questions to consider, and as role models and leaders you have an important role to play. You set the "tone at the top". Your standards permeate through your entire organization. Your employees follow your lead, and so do your children.

'I know that you are made of the right stuff. Let's make sure we all do the right thing, every day, in business and at home. And I hope that you will always be true to yourself.'

I left the podium to the sound of loud applause. As I sat there listening to Cokie Roberts, a respected influencer, refer to my remarks during her address, I knew I had made a difference. I had inspired her! That felt incredible.

The conference came to an end, and I spent the next few months in auditor bliss, riding the confidence I'd gained from the conference as well as from my increasing base of knowledge. I'd hit my stride, and it felt like nothing could get in my way.

And then it happened; something no one wished for, some were expecting, and still others were loath to consider... the technology bubble burst.

The free ride had dried up, as did the entrepreneurial dream and the spirit of Silicon Valley. Private companies were the first to dissolve. Public companies, both large and small, were next, as market confidence was shaken and spooked.

As the market imploded, public company share prices dropped like bricks from the lavish, multi-storey glass buildings they'd erected two years earlier. Technology executives and their employees could do nothing more than watch their fortunes erode day after day. Millionaires were a magic act, disappearing as fast as they were made. Dreams of a cozy retirement faded as jobs losses swelled.

During this time, I audited a public company who developed a web-enabled, wireless mobile touchscreen service to integrate Google's search engine with speed and functionality. It was so advanced there was only one mobile device in the market capable of taking advantage of their functionality. They went public within eighteen months of their inception and fell violently, with $2 million in revenues and $40 million in losses. They peaked five years too early. In my opinion, this company failed for no other reason than their concept was not ready for primetime.

Another public company I audited developed a standalone device strikingly similar to Apple's yet-to-be-invented iPad. Their device had a QWERTY keyboard attached to a flip-top screen. It was, for all intents and purposes, a portable, dumb computer equipped with only one feature: the ability to read, write, and send emails. Their target customer? Grandparents living across state lines who, they assumed, would pay a monthly fee for regular, easy-peasy communication channels to their children and grandchildren.

However, this company, like many others, failed because their business model was flawed. The flaw was in its limitations. First, the demographic they were seeking to attract, *grandparents,* were not known for early adopting technology of any kind. Revenues were a slow grind from inception, and in the end, grandma and grandpa preferred to stick to the lower cost, familiar alternative: the land line.

A company's negative cash flows, mounting losses, declining share price, and spiraling revenue were chronic themes of the week. My signed, 'qualified' PwC audit opinion describing doubt about the company's ability to continue as a 'going concern' was essentially the final nail in the coffin of a company on unstable ground. Did I precipitate their bankruptcy, or was their failure a fait accompli notwithstanding? I will never know. But this was not an easy time for me.

What I do remember was a particular difficult conversation I had with one company's middle-aged, white male CEO and CFO. As I spoke, I witnessed my once mutually respectful relationship melt away. They didn't buy my arguments. I was being over-dramatic (i.e., too emotional, too erratic, too female). Why couldn't I accept what they knew to be true? They *will* get themselves out of this bad quarter. Just wait, you will see.

They didn't trust me, so I resorted to my secret weapon: the second partner on the audit who was also a seasoned, older, white male. The second partner is normally kept in the background for support and for risk management purposes for the team, and they are almost *never* introduced to the client. However, in this case, I was in need of help. I needed him to plead my case and help me stand my ground.

Sadly, but as I expected, they accepted *his* words of wisdom, which were essentially mine repeated through the mouth of a man.

I asked myself for years after that incident: 'What could I have done differently other than change my gender?' That moment hurt. I had established myself as an expert, but no amount of experience seemed to matter to them.

The pain kept coming. One by one, I found myself handing clients from PwC's audit department to the firm's insolvency group. It was heart-wrenching watching my clients collapse and fade away. Many were business colleagues who accepted my guidance and whose growth and vision I supported. These weren't bad companies. They were victims of an apocalyptic collapse that no one saw coming.

The meltdown impacted the PwC office as well. Staff were idle, with no scheduled audit work and clients dissolving daily. Seen as an empathetic female partner, the firm's leadership asked me to inform affected staff, and even managers in my group, that they were being laid off... ON THREE SEPARATE OCCASIONS. Once is hard enough, but three times? I was reliving my notorious Black Friday on steroids. Devastated staff wondered, *Am I next?* It was emotionally draining on me. These were people I worked with and cared about.

By the third round of layoffs, we were terminating our 'better than average' dare I say, 'high performing' CPAs on international secondments (like myself!), who had been transferred here in 2000 to help the San Jose office during their desperate time of need. This action was not taken lightly. The firm knew that shooting themselves in the foot today would haunt them later when the market turned itself around and the demand for staff outstripped local supply. Everyone assumed it would, but today was today, and tough decisions needed to be made.

Somehow, I survived the purge, and my two years had come and gone in a flash. The kids were settled in their American schools, had developed close friendships, and were thriving in sports, academics, and whatever else they put their minds to. We had each overcome personal challenges, but we battled through them, and as a family we were stronger, closer, and wiser for it.

The rewards this secondment offered Danielle and Andrew were enormous. Life in a new country gave them the skills to adapt to change, and they became closer, best friends even, and their sibling relationship was in greater shape than ever before. I couldn't have been prouder of them.

As for me, I experienced the best and worst Silicon Valley had to offer—the ups and downs of this fickle industry—and developed the subject-matter expertise I came here to obtain.

But now there was a new wrinkle to consider. Despite the downturn, I was being asked to consider partnership in the US firm. They wanted me to stay in San Jose. It was a tough call, but there was more than just me to consider.

Though John excelled as the primary caregiver and was sharpening up his golf game, he was growing bored with his lack of mental stimulation. As we approached our two-year time commitment and were considering a permanent move here, his employer got nervous. It was time to share their succession plan. They offered to sell him their company if he returned... *now*.

We sat down and had a family meeting. Do we pack up our life in San Jose and move back home as we originally planned? John had an opportunity that was hard to walk away from. The kids were ready to return to their old friends and their new or former schools.

My family had sacrificed so much for me, and I had done what I came here to do. I would return to Mississauga with an unparalleled level of confidence and industry expertise to build new networks, sell services, share my experience, and be ready to take on new roles and new challenges. I had acquired a shiny, new set of tools for my toolbox, and I was itching to show them off. It was time to go home.

I wouldn't have traded this experience for any other time or any other job in the world. This secondment was the true tipping point of my career and propelled me to new and unforeseen heights.

17

Canadian, eh?

My family's return to Canada was déjà vu. We moved back into the same home in Mississauga we left two years earlier. Our home didn't look much different on the outside, but each of us, holding our personal experiences and lessons learned, were very different on the inside.

The kids settled into their new and former schools quickly, and John returned to work at Omni Floorcoverings, the company he had joined fifteen years earlier as CFO, to take on his greatest challenge yet. It was time for him to acquire the company and take over the helm as its new owner and president.

One matter I hadn't contemplated upon my return to Mississauga was the vanishing act of my husband as my beloved Mr. Mom. We crossed the border and, somehow, John forgot how to cook! Thankfully, John remained true to his handyman predisposition, but his enthusiasm for running errands, and playing chief cook and bottle washer, took time to gain the traction it had for two blissful years in California.

Our household had fallen out of balance. The kids no longer needed a nanny, but with John working full time in an expanded role, I needed one. He had barely settled into his CEO position when I called a family meeting.

How were we going to help our teenagers in their new surroundings and balance this with reigniting our careers? Danielle needed our support as she settled into boarding at her unfamiliar second high school in as many years. Every weekend she came home was a homecoming for us, and we spent as much time with her as she would permit us, peppering her with questions of how she was faring in her independent life away from home.

Thankfully, with no cajoling whatsoever, my mom and her new husband came to our rescue for Andrew, who needed daily transport-ation from school. They offered to drive him home, take him out for treats, and generally spoil him with their attention, while John and I took turns dropping him off. I personally never tired of hearing what he was up to with his friends or asking what he was learning or finding interesting in class, so I often raised my hand to be the one to drive him in the morning, regardless of how that may impact the rest of my day. At least I was starting off on a great foot in Mississauga.

We hired a housekeeper to come several times a week to do our laundry and clean the house, so John and I would have the quality time we craved in our new situation. I reasoned that the cost of hiring outside help was a small price to pay in return for spending more time with my kids. John dutifully completed my 'honey-do' lists, including meal prep and repairs on a house that had been without his watchful eye and attention for two years. I chose to apply flexible hours to my chaotic workday, reducing a long commute by starting my day later in the morning. The consequence of this, however, was that I often returned home later in the evening, after the kids had eaten dinner.

Other than dreading the Canadian winters I had escaped for the past two years, my return to PwC Canada was seamless. Sure, there were a few leadership changes, but my PwC felt like the same PwC of two years ago.

I once left this place for my three-year secondment in National Continuing Education, and on two more occasions for maternity leaves. So, this time my return was a slight bend in the road. It was easy to pick up where I left off and rejoin my colleagues, and I was thrilled to share my experiences from Silicon Valley.

What I didn't count on was the pressure I would face to relocate my home office. My new partner coach, Paul, was kind, persuasive, and reasonable in his ask of me. 'You have so much to share of your experiences in the Valley. Your colleagues in Toronto could learn so much from you, Sue.' Flattery will get you far. He put the thought in my brain to consider, and I couldn't stop thinking about it.

So much for the satellite office concept I had worked so hard to negotiate only two short years ago. Working with technology clients, alone and isolated in the suburbs of Mississauga with CIPS partners, was never going to work. He was right.

My secondment, and the valuable experience I gained, would have been a missed opportunity if I stayed in Mississauga. Every rational bone in my body was telling me I should be working alongside the TICE team members in the downtown core, so I surrendered to the personal inconvenience I would face in my work/life balance, because it was the right thing to do. I *should* be sharing my lessons learned. I had a unique perspective with valuable lessons to impart.

I knew it, and everyone else knew it too: I could not have picked a better time to be in Silicon Valley if I'd had a crystal ball. I witnessed business models fail because they were as fragile as the napkins they were written on. I witnessed the implosion of giants like Enron, Worldcom, Tyco, and most shocking for me: the collapse of our competitor, Arthur Andersen.

To witness the boom and the bust, and the rise and the fall of the greatest technology phenomenon of our time, was unprecedented. I learned more in two years than others saw in ten. This timing made my perspective even more valuable. I was no longer the auditor reciting a technical accounting solution. I was retelling how I stood in the shoes of my US clients, how I lived their woes and learned how to overcome challenges in their industry and markets. I helped them solve their most important business problems, and when they needed me most, I was there to help them land softly on the ledge of bankruptcy.

I was more confident than I had ever been. Instead of calling in the older, white male partner to negotiate my stance through a difficult conversation, I was now in my new skin, negotiating for myself. I recall what could have been an intense, combative meeting with one of my new clients—the founder and CEO of a technology start-up.

My manager had identified a thorny issue. Software revenue recognition accounting rules were complex, evolving, typically punitive, and thus, annoying. In this company's case, these rules required a deferral of seventy-five percent of their annual sales. It was ugly, no doubt, and the company's CFO had chosen to record his revenue upfront, reasonably assuming that he could book the revenue when the customer paid the invoice. *Not.*

The rules dictated that sales could not be recorded until every last detail of work the customer was promised in their contract had been performed. For sales contracts with recurring maintenance support and services, and system upgrades when they were available, this meant revenue would have to be recognized over a five-year period—a slap in the face of the CEO who was eager to show his investors how successful his company was, because it *was* growing by leaps and bounds with new, long-term customer contracts.

I tried to avoid mansplaining the complex accounting rules, walking a tightrope between spewing technical jargon and sounding condescending, while acknowledging how devastating this was for his current year's earnings. I offered to guide him in drafting language for future contracts that could provide more palatable accounting results for investors. I showed empathy and understanding in his extreme disappointment. When I was done, he acknowledged my position and recognized it wasn't my fault. 'I see you are passionate about this. Frankly, if it means this much to you, you must be onto something. Make the correction, carry on.'

I believe my feminine style and my passion played to my favour. I felt as good as the day I had managed to snatch my grandpop's family secret sausage recipe out from under his very eyes!

This isn't the only or the *correct* way to navigate tough conversations, but speaking with confidence, being passionate in your position, providing solutions for the future, and listening with empathy and understanding, in this case, won the day, and it would continue to do so until my retirement many years later.

In the evenings, when I attended networking events with VCs, bankers, lawyers, and CEOs, I was a relevant, passionate, engaging professional. I was eager to offer my advice and share my stories of the Valley, describe their US counterparts, the proverbial 'funding on the back of a napkin' stories from clients I came to know and love, and how Canadian tech companies compared to the American landscape.

Fortunately, I had a keen audience of influencers and CEOs at my disposal, for it was time to build my practice from scratch, once again.

But as the days and weeks rolled along, I found out that PwC was keen to use what I had learned in the past two years to their advantage. Upon my return and transfer to the Toronto office, Dave, the new Greater Toronto Area (GTA) TICE leader, asked me to lead the Emerging Company Practice for the GTA. What a welcome surprise! It made perfect sense to me to lead this practice area, which was aimed at helping high-potential, private start-ups with their growing pains. Moreover, it had its roots in Silicon Valley.

My task was to invent a *hook* for the TICE partners and managers to build stronger relationships with emerging companies. I had a generous budget, but I needed an idea to spend it on. There were plenty of 'best of' awards, speed dating opportunities matching investors with founders, and more general networking events designed as meet and greets. However, we didn't need another 'let's get together to sell you our services' event. We needed something new, unique, and different.

My first thought was to find a unique way to capitalize upon my extensive knowledge of public and private clients' issues in San Jose. For the past two years, I had a front-row seat to my clients' missteps and successes. Although new issues arose each quarter, I was struck by how often Toronto tech company issues were comparable to so many of the issues that had tripped up my clients in San Jose. It was uncanny how often I heard the same problems and themes discussed.

I weighed in on operational, strategic, and financial matters, and I was not shy to offer my educated suggestions while always being careful not to cross the line of client confidentiality. Sharing this knowledge cost me nothing. It was timely advice that added value to the board and the executives. How rewarding it was to feel useful in the Canadian tech industry!

I learned what kept CEOs up at night. I listened to their concerns, asked questions, and if I had something of value to share, I offered alternatives. I had a suite of dedicated specialist resources back at the office if they needed more. If it was beyond the scope of PwC's experts, I tapped into my growing rolodex of contacts in the broader business community. Knowledge is power, as the saying goes.

With my realization of PwC's extensive network, I thought, *Why don't I bring our clients, and would-be-nice-to-have clients with extra-ordinary growth potential, together in a collaborative, non-threatening way to help them help each other?* PwC, as their independent advisor, was the perfect catalyst for this. I wanted to provide a forum for CEOs to meet and mingle with other like-minded individuals, discuss common issues, and be intellectually stimulated.

What was in it for PwC? We showcased our thought leadership, and our leaders met or reconnected with the key decisionmakers in the tech business community. Furthermore, we used our influence and position to make a positive impact on the future of the Canadian technology industry.

I wanted this to be an exclusive event for CEOs—in particular, *emerging software company* CEOs. It was intended to be a day away from the pressures of the office, to share, to learn, and to discuss whatever they wished.

The 'Vision to Reality (V2R) Conference' was born.

The hook? The conference was free to attend *if* CEOs completed a PwC survey in advance. The value proposition was an hour of the

CEO's time in return for a day tailored to their needs, to network, learn, discover, and be inspired.

In order to have something of substance worth sharing with CEOs, however, first I would need to identify and understand what their issues were. Voila! This is where the survey came in. With my handpicked team of PwC partners and managers in all three lines of service, we developed a set of questions focussed on their pain points, their growth objectives and results, their target customers, their markets, economic outlook, reservations, successes, and lessons learned.

In the first year, we had over 150 CEOs complete PwC's survey. It was a tremendous response that gave me a wealth of information, analysis, and thought leadership to share. My colleagues helped me analyse the results and capture the themes driving the emerging technology sector, and we dove deep into the challenges and opportunities identified.

I was thrilled with the value created, the connections made, and the accolades received from those who participated. The V2R Conference was an inspiring success!

As my reputation as the face of PwC's V2R Conference grew, I was invited to share my insights on local and national TV, radio newscasts, and industry magazines. I had become a technology influencer and subject-matter expert on CEOs' perspectives, challenges, and opportunities. How did CEOs feel about the economy, revenue growth, and their ability to attract talent? How are they dealing with the industry challenges they face? What lessons had I learned from them? What lessons could I share to help them be more successful?

I was a guest on several morning TV shows during their business news segments. As terrifying as it was to answer the anchor's off-the-cuff questions, after a few interviews, the hardest part of this ordeal was getting to the station in one piece for their entirely unreasonable time in the morning—before the sun was up! Beyond this predicament, data, figures, trends, and analysis would spew out of my brain on cue. I was a trusted, informed voice, an authority on subjects I could only dream of covering a few years earlier. What a difference ten-thousand hours in tech, a dynamic San Jose experience, and a few hundred CEO interviews makes!

Imagine me, a thought leader?

My success spring-boarded me to the national role of Emerging Company Practice Leader for PwC Canada. The V2R Conference became my brand, and it significantly raised my profile on a national level. I can confidently admit I had hit my stride, and I believed I was making a difference for the CEOs and their companies, doing something I loved.

Who would have thought Allan's harmless question, 'How do you feel about moving to TICE?' would have such an impact on my career?

For five more years, I hosted and led the direction of the V2R Conference.

Each year, I developed new ways to garner CEO interest and get new participants for the survey by tweaking the themes and the questions. New perspectives brought new insight to the emerging complex issues and changes happening in the technology sector, and likewise, in the CEOs' priorities and challenges. My report highlighted the industry changes, trends, and the CEOs' most controversial and interesting quotes.

In year three, for example, I surveyed the emerging company CEOs and compared their answers to the more established, public company CEOs. This gave me the opportunity to identify and share big tech company best practices with the start-ups, and it opened the door to in-person interviews with large Canadian technology company CEOs, which introduced PwC to them, and allowed our firm to establish a deeper relationship with their company.

Admittedly, I knew how CEOs were going to answer the survey questions before they did. Their issues were so familiar and similar that it reminded me of my quarterly board meetings in San Jose. But I never tired of hearing their anecdotes, capturing their learnings, and using their insightful quotes for my report.

Out of my deep respect for leaders and what they had accomplished, I used to be nervous and oddly guarded around them, including my firm's partners. Similarly, I held my client CEOs in the highest regard, deciding that they must be superior beings to get to their position of power and influence. However, as I matured and got to know so many of them on a deeper, personal level, I came to realize partners and CEOs are more like you and I than you think. Visionary and inspirational perhaps, but they are not immortal beings! They have faults and personality, hopes and dreams, feel emotions and harbour insecurities, just like you and me. I came to understand how isolated leaders could be, the 'lonely at the top' analogy. Our conversations, leader to leader, were a welcome diversion from their day-to-day grind. Recognition and praise too often came sparingly, and in small doses. Who thinks to give it to the guy at the helm? Criticism, on the other hand, comes with blunt force. The moment they screw up they hear it from investors, employees, suppliers, and customers. The buck stopped with them. I could relate to that fear.

During the fourth year of the report, I returned to San Jose to survey emerging company CEOs from the United States with the intent of comparing the challenges and priorities American start-ups faced versus their Canadian counterparts. In truth, this was a great excuse to visit my Californian friends who I sorely missed.

San Jose partners identified up-and-coming tech darlings in their networks, and in no time, I had dozens of influential, serial CEOs willing to give me an hour or two of their time. They opened their doors and their hearts to me to share their knowledge, failings, and advice without reservation. I listened to their journey, and searched for differences in their pain points, their struggles, and their transformation. The most successful of them freely admitted to their mistakes too!

These visionaries accepted my invitation, believing it was their *duty* to help me help other Canadian CEOs in their journey. More than most, they knew how difficult the road they chose was, and related to the struggles a CEO faces raising capital, hiring and retaining talent, and growing revenues.

Regretfully, I had no meetings set up with women in my crammed agenda on either side of the country. I questioned why there were no female CEOs at the controls. Was it simply the case that my male partners' networks did not extend to women entrepreneurs, or that qualified women were not entering STEM careers from university? I suspected both.

Silicon Valley had changed since my departure in 2002. It seemed to bounce back from the crash and burn as quickly as it fell. Oodles of small and *giant* tech companies embraced the vacant lease spaces I witnessed when I left. From the embers of the crash new companies had emerged stronger and more resilient. But had they learned valuable lessons of survival?

I was moved and inspired to observe the birth of new players. I watched as their vision was created from the ground up. Their boundless optimism stirred my soul with excitement. There were a few Silicon Valley experiences I simply cannot forget.

While parking in the *campus* of my old stomping ground of Mountainview on my way to one of my first CEO interviews, I was bombarded by a vast collection of floor-to-ceiling glass buildings. There were colourful accents, bike stands, and signage decorated in primary colours to match a distinctive logo. I felt I had entered a small city. On the multi-storey, opaque glass walls of each building, the company's name, a fictional word, was conspicuously painted in large, sans-serif typeface. This building hadn't even existed in 2002.

Finding my CEO's building number among dozens of lookalike buildings, I entered through glass doors to climb a circular staircase where I was met by a gregarious entrepreneur on the third floor. His office was messy and cramped, not another soul in sight. I couldn't help but enquire as to how he ended up in this space at one end of this industrial city. Was he connected to this formidable giant in some way?

'Actually,' he clarified, 'My company was here first. We've been *Googled.*'

I didn't understand the full gravity of that statement then, but as the years went on and Google went on to dominate the web, I always looked back on this moment as one of the last before there was a shattering global shift toward a single online search engine.

I mean, there's a good chance you've already googled my name. Maybe that's even how you found this book! But I digress.

As one would expect, during my US tour of CEO interviews, I noted cultural, cross-border differences worth exploring and describing further in my report.

In Canada, proportionally there were only a handful of Canadian venture capitalists (VCs) handing out fewer dollars to fewer

Canadian start-ups. Was this because US VCs had a greater risk appetite for new ideas, or was there greater competition among US VCs to get in on the ground floor of the Next Big Thing? I wasn't sure.

Either way, US founders *were* getting funded without the fundamentals Canadian CEOs stressed about. Were US founders just considerably more convincing to the VCs when explaining the untapped market potential of their product? I found that, compared to Canadian VCs, the deep pockets in the US were excited to support innovative technology, as long as there was an experienced management team behind it that could execute on their proposed strategy. There was a high demand to back serial entrepreneurs who had 'been there and done that' before.

Which made me realize that I didn't know many legendary CEOs among my software start-ups in Canada. Where were they hiding? Did they exist?

My question was soon answered, partly, by a notable US executive I interviewed. He explained the US tech success story this way:

'Founders in the Valley aren't any smarter than Canadian CEOs. We don't have *more* brilliant ideas or *more* capable engineers solving tech problems. We just don't. What we *do* have is our cookie-cutter approach to funding and building a successful company. VCs and founders have been down this road so many times before in the Valley, we know what works and what doesn't. We've figured out the secret sauce, the proven steps to succeed—how much to fund, when to fund, when to pull the plug, who to hire when, how to scale, etc. We build successful companies this way.'

I was intrigued by the simplicity and logic of his insights. I wrote frantically, capturing his advice as best I could, knowing it would make for a great quote in my report. His office was busy with people milling about in open concept workspaces. I had never heard of this private company; it was a relative newcomer in tech that was working its way up the ladder. I decided I must remember to keep an eye on how this one fares. And I did. It was *Salesforce.com*.

Both Canada and the US resorted to hiring engineers overseas to supplement their routine development needs by 'offshoring' tasks to India or the Philippines for a fraction of the wages paid locally. I knew of at least one Silicon Valley start-up that even went so far as to buy a company, not for its intellectual property (IP), its customers, its revenue stream, or its profit, but for its pool of software engineers! The purchased IP was mothballed and 'stay' bonuses were offered to the newly acquired engineers who apparently walked on water. However, what surprised me most was even more concerning than the engineers being lured south with more lucrative pay and opportunity, or the higher levels of funding received by US start-up companies compared to their Canadian counterparts. This much I knew. But I noted another subtle and important cultural Canadian/ US difference I wasn't expecting.

I often heard how 'state of the art' US technology platforms and applications were compared to their competitors. I learned how they were solving their customers' pain points with unique, advanced features and functionalities. They told me, 'We have the best solution. We have eclipsed the competition because we provide what our customer needs.' The US CEOs were proud of what they were offering, and priced their product at a *premium*. Their attitude was that a customer should be willing to pay *more* for their product or solution because it was the best.

Canadian CEO/founders had also developed unique technology with superior features and functionalities, and they too argued they were 'best in class'. You didn't just cross the northern border of the States and shift to a land before time!

But herein lies the rub. Rather than *premium* pricing their products, Canadian start-ups were *discounting* their prices!

'How interesting,' I observed upon my return to Canada. 'So, let me get this straight. You are telling me you have developed a *superior* product with all the innovations, bells, and whistles your customer is demanding, no one else has it, and yet you have *purposely* chosen to price your products and services at a discount? Why?' I was perplexed.

The common defense was, 'We can't compete in the US market. We are a small fish in a big pond with no reputation to command a premium price. We must discount our product so we can play in this market.'

Ugh! It seemed Canadian start-ups and CEOs had something in common with a young Sue Allen.

They had an inferiority complex! They were deferential to America's dominance and size over Canada, and this was reflected in their attitude towards their product's worth on the market. I thought CEOs got to their station *because* of their drive, ambition, influence, leadership, egos, and their ability to take risks! Yet, here they were, reluctant to ask for a proper, acceptable price for their product and demand what it was worth.

As a woman, reflecting on how much courage it takes for us to ask for a stretch assignment, a promotion, or a raise, I was uncomfortably drawn to their way of thinking. But I didn't dare go there.

So, how could I convince these guys they were playing a game that sooner or later would bite them—competing with Americans who could confidently negotiate higher prices, while selling their customers on their product's superior capabilities? 'You get what you pay for' was ringing in my head.

I shared my survey findings at the V2R Conference and asked Canadian CEOs to consider the cultural flaw I felt needed addressing. Could they be bolder, more aggressive, more confident, and show belief in their product's worth by adjusting their pricing? If they truly were delivering value, why couldn't they stand up for themselves and overcome their fear of being less worthy than American competition?

Like any deep-seated cultural change, this was hard for them to hear, and even more difficult to implement and ingrain into their way of thinking. As a woman, I felt a kinship to their struggle, which had me thinking...

Could it be that I had two strikes against me? My Canadian heritage *and* my gender? Geez Louise! This was double jeopardy!

But I had grown, and they needed to do the same. So, I tried my darndest to convince Canadian CEOs to set aside their inferiority complex while I kept mine in check. But, despite the strong, rational arguments I gave to CEOs, it wasn't enough. *I* wasn't enough. In truth, a tsunami wouldn't have been enough to make the wholesale changes needed to their Canadian pricing strategy.

The survey and CEO conference survived in some form or another for the next decade. When the time had come to pass my baby on to a successor, I was ready to let go. I groomed another partner for this role and proudly watched from the sidelines as he put his stamp on the conference. I watched it evolve into a different, but still insightful and relevant, initiative with each passing year.

My success and reputation in the firm and the TICE industry raised my sights for greater responsibility. I had acquired a taste for leading others and, frankly, liked the feeling. Influencing decisions that could impact the firm's direction motivated me to want to do more. I wanted more responsibility. I had never been more confident, nor did I feel like I had given everything I had to give.

So, I had to ask myself: 'What's the next logical step for my development as a leader? How can I make a difference in PwC on a grander scale?'

And then I was attacked by another set of internal questions: 'Am I being arrogant and egotistical? Who am I to think I haven't reached the max of my potential? Maybe this is as good as it gets?'

Who was I to ask for more?

I'll tell you who.

I, Susan Allen, had a unique perspective. I came from a different place, and I had examples that proved I was making a positive contribution! It took me some time, but I dropkicked that familiar, negative inner voice back into obscurity.

PwC answered my doubting Thomas by offering me the GTA TICE Assurance leadership role; a timely and fortuitous promotion. They saw my ambition to do more, so they gave me a 'profit and loss' role managing the operations of a segment of the audit practice in Toronto, while also coaching the partner team.

From what I had seen until that point in my career, women led HR functions, not operations with business lines and income statements to manage. This represented a welcome step outside the typical leadership trailblazed by women! And the best part? It came with a seat at the leadership table for the largest office in Canada: PwC's Toronto practice.

The handful of leaders on this team were held accountable for delivering on the firm's strategy, budget, revenues, margin, cost-management, *and* people initiatives. With energy and enthusiasm, I accepted the challenge. I couldn't wait to develop deeper skills in operations, expand my influence in the region, and deliver on results.

The Transformation – from Novice to Expert

Just because it's hard doesn't mean it's not worth doing.

San Jose, California was a tipping point for my career. Working in Silicon Valley during recent history's most tumultuous tech boom and bust years was a sink or swim environment from the word 'go'. Who could have predicted I would be at the center of this turmoil?

The result was Sue 1.0 being replaced with a new and improved working model. I transformed from a self-conscious CIPS partner to a confident Emerging Software Company Leader and sought-after subject-matter expert. Though it wasn't easy, I proved I had the chops to handle this and more in the years that followed.

As the auditor in me freely admits, I have been known to deliver bad news after good. So, now I will burst the balloon I just inflated.

If I left you thinking all stretch assignments came packaged with cute puppies and double rainbows, you'd be more than a little wrong. They come with an encyclopedia set of personal sacrifices and demands which, if not managed, can leave you with negative consequences and regret. I don't want that for you.

As I have described, to make peace with my self-inflicted stress and out-of-control environment, I did two very positive things that flipped the script and gave me the breathing room I needed to recharge and prioritize what mattered most.

First, after that chance encounter with a PwC recruit, I attended weekly dance classes, connecting me with my younger self, which gave me the lift of endorphins I needed to solve my undiagnosed cry for aerobic exercise and creative expression.

Second, and equally important, I kept the strict promise I made to myself fifteen years earlier to never miss the big moments. The hardest part was following through on execution. I had to plan my escape; a random afternoon leaving early or stealing a couple of hours midday to attend my kids' sporting events or other school adventure I couldn't bear to miss. This kept me grounded, and I frequently returned to work with a spring in my step, re-energized and ready to tackle the next big thing.

My regret? I should have shared my secret with others, to help them. And that's precisely why this book is so important to me.

Here are some other lessons learned through transformation:

- Count yourself in for the risk/reward premiums you are offered in life. Give them your very best shot and watch the opportunities unfold before you.

- Give yourself permission to block off time in your calendar for 'personal' meetings, commitments with your family, your friends, and yourself. Disconnecting from work is your personal win-win. Treat these as you would work commitments. Rarely is it ever so important that your 'work emergency' can't wait until tomorrow. Then, go one step further: tell your colleagues and subordinates, so they have tacit permission to do the same.

- Acknowledge you are going to miss some things in your life that you wish you didn't have to. Conflicting demands will make this inevitable, but it becomes easier when you admit that you are making personal sacrifices and this as a conscious choice. However, do not miss the milestones and events that matter the most. You can never get those back.

- When you are required to solve a complex problem, share what you know and be honest about what you don't. Deeper trust is built when your style is authentic, and relationship capital is built when you roll up your sleeves to solve the problem alongside those affected.

- There is an intensity to the pace of change, the chaos, the growing pains, and the stress endured in a high-risk, high-reward environment. Acknowledging this is the first step to preparing (and resigning) yourself to an impending storm. Identify potential issues and how you will solve them before they become unsurmountable regrets.

Reflection Questions

1. When you accept a stretch assignment, how do you reconcile that with the personal sacrifices you may have to make?

2. How do you maintain your health and wellness?

3. Are you confident you will act according to your moral compass when faced with difficult decisions? Do you live by your values consistently, even when no one is watching?

Part VII: Blazing a Trail to Pay it Forward

What are the characteristics of an effective leader?

Is your definition of an effective leader one who is assertive, decisive, independent, competitive, ambitious, a problem solver, and a risk-taker?

Or is she compassionate, understanding, loyal, tender, and sympathetic?

This answer drives at the heart of common gender differences in the workplace. The first set of traits are stereotypical masculine qualities, traditionally highly regarded in the workplace by societal norms. Since masculine traits were, at one time, more valued than emotional intelligence and empathy, men were seen as the ones to *take charge* and exert influence as leaders. (As per Catalyst.org research and article, Stereotyping of US Business Leaders Exposed, NY, 2005, titled "Women 'take care', men 'take charge.'")

The second list, as you may have guessed, are stereotypical qualities prescribed more often to women. These traits are typically regarded as weaknesses, or even tentative, gullible, and yielding behaviours. In the workplace, when less worth is ascribed to relationship-building, women who *take care* are not considered leadership material.

Differences between men and women go far beyond the workplace. In fact, they start in the playground, with socialisation from our family, peers, school, and the media. This shapes our behaviours, and over time, they become deeply ingrained. We conform to the expected norms and gender roles men and women should play, often without even realizing it.

Are you currently a leader, a leader-in-training, or a leader of the future? How do you stack up and envision yourself vis à vis masculine versus feminine traits? Reflect on this.

And then ask yourself why masculine and feminine qualities *have to be mutually exclusive.* Shouldn't the most effective leaders display some of both?

Traditional norms and societal influence, and their impact on gender in the workplace, helped me uncover new ways of thinking about my actions much later in my career. Particularly, it uncovered why I acted and thought the way I did, and perhaps the following chapters will shed light on some similar revelations for you earlier in your career.

By increasing your self-awareness, I hope you can avoid the common ways women miss opportunities and impede their advancement. I want you to circumvent and even put to rest common misconceptions about yourself as a woman in the workplace—many of which I carried for most of my career. Finally, I hope to leave you feeling armed with new strategies and greater understanding, so you may propel your career and life in the direction you wish to take it.

A note on generalizations:

Throughout this book, and in this next part especially, I share descriptions of gender differences found in the workplace and the typical ways women and men see themselves, act and behave. ***These are not hard truths.*** *They are broad patterns and aggregate level themes taken from research at a point in time. They do not universally define everyone, and you may not see yourself in these descriptions. I acknowledge this, as well as the fact that gender differences may have* *evolved since. We each uniquely experience our lives, and this shapes how we see ourselves in these generalizations in our own ways.*

Diversity, equity, and inclusion is a journey for which we as a society, and PwC, are on a continuum. We are not at the end of this journey, but what I share with you next is a critical step.

18

Putting Your Hand Up – Be All In!

In my first seventeen years with PwC, I did not apply for a single leadership position. *Ever.* Not a single one.

Every title I ever wore—Lead Recruiting Partner, Human Resources Partner, Operations and HR Partner (San Jose), Emerging Company Practice Leader, and my latest promotion to GTA TICE Assurance Leader—had been offered to me, and I thoughtfully accepted. Each promotion I'd largely *waited* for, fingers crossed, from the sidelines. *Maybe it will land in my lap...* That was my grand plan. But it wasn't really a plan at all.

Today, this strikes me as an extreme lack of initiative regarding my own future. It was odd and careless. Waiting to be asked for every role I was ever offered took me down a road someone else set, and not down a road I planned to navigate. Worse, waiting to be asked could have landed me nothing! What if no one saw me the way I wanted to be seen—as a *high-potential, high-performing leader?*

It was at this point in my career when I came to my senses. Why was I letting my boss decide whether I was applying my skills for my highest and best use for the firm? What if he decided status quo was my mode till retirement or 'firement', whichever came first?

Looking back, I'm frustrated that I was content to bide my time, waiting for the next promotion or the next opportunity for so long. What if my 'next' never came? Were my bosses mind readers? How were they supposed to know when I was ready for a change and what interested me unless I told them!

In my expanded role at the GTA leadership table, I was *okay* with what I was responsible for. I liken it to Dr Williams' 'okay' the first time he appeared from the operating room after Andrew's surgery.

What I was really thinking was, *'I can do better; I can do more.'*

The role of TICE Industry Leader for Canada (Laurie's role) was open due to a pending retirement. Firm leadership messaged partners to voice their interest in this role with a written submission. Interested candidates would be interviewed by the firm's second in command, the Managing Partner.

For the first time in my career, I threw caution to the wind and decided this position had my name written all over it. I was gonna go for it, come hell or high water.

But I felt vulnerable and exposed, even though in my heart I knew this was a normal progression, though perhaps more of a giant puddle jump than a small step. I was particularly drawn to the opportunity to have an elite seat at the Canadian leadership table, and to be among the executive leadership of the firm, which this position guaranteed. I could be part of something bigger, where the firm's most strategic, impactful decisions were made. My voice would be heard and counted.

As I rationalized this, I considered the facts. I was a thought leader, I had a personal brand, and I had a deep network of influence with CEOs from the emerging tech sector. More recently, I had gained experience in a smaller slice of this role as the GTA TICE Assurance Leader. My diverse perspective must have counted for something! So, I'd firmly decided it was time to tap into the full extent of my leadership potential and pursue this challenge *for myself.*

I submitted my paper supporting why I was perfect for the role. I described my prerequisite attributes and skills, how I planned to make a difference, what needed to be fixed, how I would collaborate, and explained my strategy for growing market share in the Canadian TICE sector. I knew the interview process would shine a light on my past achievements, and leadership would be looking at me under a microscope with my successes and failures rising to the surface.

Would I measure up? Was I ready for a role of this magnitude? I sincerely hoped so.

Because this was the big leagues, I would be managing and leading the firm's highest-profile proposals and directing and influencing our 'go to market' strategy. Internally, it included developing, managing, and prioritizing the firm's industry budget, coaching and mentoring other industry partners and leaders across Canada, and holding partners accountable for goals set for growth, staff retention, and quality.

My interview went as well as it could have. I answered the questions, no surprises, and searched for signs of senior leadership's approval. I felt supported, and my strategy was accepted with friendly nods and understanding smiles. My passion for the role was undeniable and very real. If my interviewer was unimpressed or hiding some fear of my readiness for the role, he did a damn good job of keeping it to himself. I was pumped, eager to bring my fresh ideas, insights, and value to the firm. It was meant to be—everything in my past had led me to this role, right here, right now.

Partners chosen for new leadership roles were announced in the firm's 'Leadership Update', a weekly email featuring topical, significant matters for partners only. However, as fate would have it, the announcement coincided with the annual partner's conference. Every partner in Canada was in attendance.

At a break during the partner's conference, my firm's CEO, Chris, asked to speak to me. He led me to a quiet, isolated corner of the conference hall and motioned for me to take a seat. I could tell he had done this before.

'Sue, thanks for applying. I appreciate your interest and the vision you shared on how you would shape TICE going forward.' *Pause for effect.* 'However, we have decided to give the role to Jennifer.' *Another pause to let this fully sink in.*

'I see.'

I was shocked. Dumbfounded. I could hardly believe my ears.

My inside voice begged me to ask, 'Who the *(fill in the expletive)* is Jennifer? How could I be overlooked and lose to someone I've never even heard of? What does she have to make her the better choice? And where in the *(fill in the blank again)* did she come from?'

The first stage of the Kübler-Ross model for grief and loss had become my modus operandi. Denial settled in.

My questions swirled silently, none of them making their way to my outside voice.

For the first time in my career, I'd put myself out there, leaned in like I was told, and BAM… face plant into a cement wall.

What possessed me to ask for a leadership role anyway? Where did this misplaced confidence come from? Who do I think I am? You knew you didn't do rejection well! That'll teach you to put your hand up. I should never assume I'm ready for something new.

I was too embarrassed to ask the decisionmaker what had gone so wrong. How did I not see this coming?

Instinctively, my arms crossed in front of my chest. My hands gripped my bare arms, squeezing tight, and, finding loose skin and flabby forearms, I wished I was more toned. *I must schedule my personal trainer to work on my bat wings next week.*

Damnit, Sue! Stop! I was just making matters worse.

My jaw was shut tight, teeth clenched. I glanced down at my lap, took a deep breath in, and buried my gaze. If I looked at him, it would have signaled my disillusionment with their process of recruiting a new leader.

I was squarely in stage two of my loss: *anger.*

My inner voice had taken over all rational thinking. *I am so disappointed. No, that's an understatement, I'm completely shocked. I have worked so hard for this. Haven't I earned it? Why couldn't this be given to me?*

I could feel my ears growing hot, my nostrils flaring. If I could have breathed flame, Chris would have been an accidental victim to a toasting.

But then I took a deep breath, calming myself as stage three of grief took over: *bargaining.*

I opened my mouth to speak but then snapped it shut like a Venus flytrap, refusing to take prisoners. None of my arguments were spoken out loud... of course. Because how could I sound so bold, so aggressive, so angry? That wasn't me. The 'B word' was never used to describe Susan Allen. So, I kept my angry child (and my angry, full-grown partner ego) to myself.

But I was still a competent partner. Wasn't I?

My internal rant was a pitiful case of sour grapes. I couldn't let anyone, especially the CEO, know how much his rejection had wounded my ego and my confidence.

Enter stage four: *depression.*

Stewing in my grief, I realized I barely knew Chris. What I did know was that he was intimidating to me. Maybe this was just a case of wrong CEO, wrong time?

Then I realized how quickly I had forgotten everything I learned as the Emerging Company Practice Leader, where I'd interviewed 150 freakin' CEOs.

Sue, CEOs are people too!

But I rationalized that this time it was different; I was dealing with *my* CEO—notably, the most influential person for my future at PwC.

As my mind raced through these stages of confusion and despair, I was having an out-of-body experience. Besides kicking myself for thinking I was good enough to apply for a leadership position, in nanoseconds, I was fourteen again, staring blankly at the list of names for the cheerleading squad, mine not among them. *I'm a loser. I'm so embarrassed. What was I thinking? How could I have put myself in this position?*

I expected his next comments to sting.

Instead, he was comforting, sincere and empathic. Of course he was.

'Sue, I know how disappointed you must be.' He paused again, waiting for my gaze to lift from my lap to meet his. He stared straight at me, through me, exactly how my father looked at me the day he told my sister, brother, and I he was leaving our family. *This is serious.* I stared back at him, heart bleeding, expecting the worst.

'I want you to take on another role, a very important one, a leadership role… for me.' Chris persevered, remaining on point. He embraced my piercing stare. 'As you know, we have been trying for years to get two initiatives off the ground: the 'Women in Leadership' mandate and the 'Retention of Women' initiative. We have made some progress with our current leaders, but it's moving too slowly.'

He continued, 'These initiatives would get more traction if they were combined under one leader.' *Pause.* Now he had my attention. 'I want *you* to be that leader; to champion these initiatives, reporting to me. We must make more meaningful progress on our retention of women. We must have more women promoted into partnership and into leadership positions. This is imperative for me as CEO if we are to be successful as a firm.'

Wow. I was not expecting that.

Instead of mulling over what had just been presented, I was thinking, *You know, you could have made me the National TICE XLOS Leader if you really cared about promoting more women into leadership positions?*

I was clearly overreacting and irrational. I subsequently learned that Jennifer was an experienced technology partner who had recently joined PwC from another global consulting firm. At her prior firm, she had built a significant consulting practice in the US and was seen as a high performer with a great future. She was obviously a good hire and choice, but so was I!

No, I had to stop already. Bargaining was futile at this point, and besides, the firm *was* promoting a woman into a leadership position: Jennifer, my ghost of Christmas future.

My head was spinning. Reacting to my stunned silence, Chris reflected on what he could say next to sway my decision. 'We must move the needle and make the step changes necessary for this critical initiative. This is important to me, and I think you are the right person to take this on. Will you consider this... for me?'

So, there it was: the rejection of my dream role, followed by an offer for a new role—two roles merged into one. Roles I had not the faintest idea of whether I wanted to tackle at this stage in my career. This was a lot to take in standing in a corridor at a conference.

'Of course I will consider it,' I uttered, wearing my characteristically positive people-pleaser hat.

This was unfamiliar territory—the CEO asking me to take on something meaningful, clearly of great significance to him. Yet, I was neither excited nor discouraged. Merely shattered, disappointed, and confused. I'd had my sight set on that role, and it was the first time I'd really stretched myself by taking the initiative.

As we made our way back to the conference hall, returning to five hundred of my closest friends and colleagues, I watched them chatting and laughing as they caught up with their work and family news while waiting for our conference to resume.

I stood back from the crowd, lost in thought. I put on a brave face when a colleague looked in my direction and smiled meekly. I glanced down at my feet to avoid further eye contact, to discourage conversation. No one knew what I had just learned. No one knew how broken I felt, how my balloon had burst. I was anxious for this conference to conclude so I could process what had transpired over the last fifteen minutes. My career at PwC had taken a turn for the worse. My stomach was churning. If I could have crawled into a hole to hide from humanity for the next thirty years, I would have. Give me a bag of rice, a pot, and some water—Sue is going full hermit until further notice.

Overnight, I weighed various aspects of the role. The combined Women in Leadership/Retention of Women (WIL/ROW) initiative was an *internal* leadership role, not the market-facing, external, strategic, industry role I'd applied for. Furthermore, I deemed it of low value to many partners outside of the CEO. It did not garner a seat at the Executive/Senior Leadership table, yet Chris was selling this role as one of great significance to the future success of the firm...

Red flag.

Furthermore, this role sounded like a *Human Resources* role, the all-too-common leadership position typically offered to women in business. My firm was following step with society and that irked me, because I had applied for a role with profit and loss responsibilities, as well as operational, strategy, sales, and senior coaching responsibilities. I wanted a position that would stretch me, push me in new directions, and allow me to rise through the executive ranks. But I was offered an internal role with no prospecting of new clients, growing firm revenues, or external industry initiatives involved.

Truthfully, the WIL/ROW role was lightyears away from what I perceived to be the more interesting role I had asked for. I saw it adding to my busy, finite day, compiling my overtime.

Moreover, I had seen this situation play out before. Sometimes, when a partner showed the courage to ask for a leadership role and the firm had someone else in mind, I saw the rejected partner rewarded with another role. Decisionmakers appreciated their initiative, and this was one way of saying, 'Thank you for asking.'

So, was this the firm's way of giving me a soft landing after the rejection? Or was leadership losing trust in me as a TICE partner and leader? I had a lot of thinking to do before I could respond to the CEO's request to, 'Consider this for me.'

But then I also understood why he thought I was right for this role. I was not like the other partners or CPAs. I was a female trail-blazer, married with kids from an atypical background. Wearing the

PwC partner title was proof that it could be done, that it was an achievable goal for girls like me, which meant it was achievable for non-BComms, for working moms, for two-career parents, and for those who grew up on the other side of the tracks.

The problem was I had *been* an HR leader, first in Mississauga, and later, for the three combined GTA offices. I had performed other HR roles, as a recruiting partner selling our firm on-campus, and in-office leading countless interviews in Toronto and San Jose. I was long in the tooth on HR roles, and at this stage in my career, they weighed me down.

Speaking to staff and potential recruits about how much I loved my job, and why I chose PwC, now felt insincere. Was I acting like a used car salesman to keep my positive energy flowing? It was starting to feel like a chore, and it was emotionally draining to speak about something that used to be so effortless, something I was so passionate about. What was happening to me? I still loved my job, but it was difficult to maintain that level of outward passion for something I'd repeatedly done for so many years.

Moreover, championing WIL/ROW had a multitude of embedded risks. Naturally, I felt more significant changes were needed for the women in my firm, but most alarming was how difficult it would be to influence others—the proverbial thankless job. If I failed to deliver, this would be a career-limiting move.

As I'd shown throughout my career, I wasn't one to shy away from difficult tasks or risks, but this time it felt different. I'd be leading an initiative that had stalled. I feared that I would be making more enemies than friends, walking a tightrope between what needed changing versus what realistically could be changed. I didn't want to become an enemy or adversary to my colleagues. I had a sneaking suspicion this was precisely why the initiative had so far failed.

To this day, I depend on my likeability factor as a woman in business. It gives me comfort and courage to think that, if I'm liked, I have a greater chance of being listened to. Once I'm heard, I know I can influence my peers, because my educated opinion does truly matter. But first, through no fault of my own, I have always had to overcome a nagging female predicament: the 'double bind.'

It goes without saying that men have historically been the dominant social group in Western society. As such, masculine attributes, traits, and behaviours are valued—particularly in areas such as sports, politics, and the workplace—more than feminine attributes, traits, and behaviours. Consequently, when women act in stereotypically feminine ways, they are disadvantaged to the extent that their behaviours are not valued—nor rewarded—in the workplace.

When women act assertively, decisively, ambitiously, or take a stand, they are met with resistance and perceived as unlikeable, unfeminine, too aggressive, or threatening. This is the 'double bind' dilemma women face. When we are too soft, our opinion is not respected. However, when we assert our authority, or voice a contrarian view, we overstep the imaginary boundary society has set for us. We are viewed as too tough, too bossy, or the other less flattering 'B words'. Women walk a tightrope between nasty and nice, competent and likeable, but never both. To be accepted, we must learn to behave in conflict with our feminine upbringing, speak with less authenticity, and land somewhere in the middle, like the temperature of Baby Bear's porridge: *just right.*

How good was I at navigating the double bind dilemma?

Case in point, when faced with this task, I was paralyzed by fear and my knowledge of the inherent risks and roadblocks I might face. Would my efforts be appreciated and rewarded?

Leadership role reporting to the CEO be damned! I needed a sign, a crystal ball—no, a lightning bolt!—to steer me to the answer and direct my future.

I needed to clear my head to reflect upon the red flags that blocked my vision. My gut instincts were telling me, 'Listen up! You haven't shied away from stretch opportunities in the past and just look at the fruits born from those choices!'

My inner voice was asking me to give this a closer look. Destiny was luring me into its orbit. Could this be another fork in my journey I was meant to take?

19

Risk and the Matter of Perspectives

Sleeping on matters that bother you and/or need reflection is a good way to clear your mind and focus your thoughts. And that's just what I did.

I woke up the next day thinking, *What if I could make a meaningful difference in the culture and careers for women at PwC? What if this role could serve as my legacy?*

This thought alone made me feel the WIL/ROW initiative was worthwhile. My truest test yet could be championing this initiative and putting my stamp on changing perceptions about the importance of diversity.

But, before I could take the plunge, I had questions.

Who were the naysayers, male or female, that would thwart my purpose? How could I influence others to see the big picture to rebuild momentum? What were my blind spots?

The Male Perspective

The perspectives of my male colleagues were important to me and critical to my success with this initiative. Could I ask men to jump on board the women retention, promotion, and leadership bus?

Moreover, why would men *want* to be displaced from their advantage? What if they disagreed with the premise that they start from a place of privilege? How would I ask my male bosses, colleagues, and friends—representing 85% of the partnership—to promote women into *their* sought-after leadership positions? Why would men support a concept that cannibalized their opportunities in the firm?

This was a sensitive negotiation.

I felt my male colleagues would argue they too faced work/life balance pressures, especially those with working spouses. It was 2008, not 1980, and men had taken on a greater share of the household chores and childrearing duties—certainly more than their fathers ever did. They worked just as hard to earn their promotion, even if they tooted their own horns more effectively than their female colleagues. They were not afraid to ask for plum assignments or speak to their boss about their readiness to take on more responsibility when they didn't have all the prerequisites for the job. I feared their attitude was, 'We didn't ask for special programs, or senior executive sponsors and mentors to assist us with our careers. So, why are we hung up on coddling the professional young women in the firm?'

How would I truly influence the actions and behaviours of male partners, who I was sure would give me initial lip service to my face only because the CEO asked them to? I worried that, in private, gender bias and reservations would emerge, mocking the initiative, perhaps even thwarting it. I imagined there would be a fair number of older, white male skeptics whose wives stayed at home. I would forever be on guard for signs of disapproval; words spoken in jest, jeers under their breath, distasteful jokes, and the always-knowing sideways glances.

I would have to watch my back. I feared what was said in front of me didn't take the same tone when I wasn't there.

'Who does she think she is insinuating we have an unconscious bias? What privileges do we enjoy? We have worked damn hard for everything we have! We treat everyone the same! This initiative is the CEO's flavour of the month. Ignore it. In time, it too shall pass.'

The Female Perspective

The female perspective was also key to understanding what needed to change.

I knew I was going to struggle with what to do or say to retain more women in the firm. Moreover, how the hell was I going to influence decisions to promote more women into the partner ranks?

I knew there were some women we would never be able to keep in PwC's ranks. I accepted a woman's personal decision to opt out of the firm. I understood the conflict to forego a career they worked very hard to achieve, to tend to a worthier cause: taking care of their children. And what could be more worthy than that?

In many ways, I envied the stay-at-home moms. Wistfully naïve, I imagined the choices, the freedom, and the flexibility I would have to take that 9:00am yoga class I was desperate to attend. I dreamed of long, leisurely walks through the park, baby in stroller, on a bright summer's day. Back in the day, I had wished to hear firsthand my child's latest adventures during our ride home from school, exploding with excitement at their accomplishments, meeting their new friends, and lending an empathetic ear to their latest challenges.

I remembered how much it stung the day I learned that my kids' favourite meal was *chicken adobo*, a dish their nanny made. Wait, what? How did this happen? I had yet to taste this dish, and damned if I could make it. These are the sacrifices even the best working moms make every week, every day, and the massive guilt we live with makes us quickly learn that we don't indeed 'have it all'.

So, how was I supposed to retain those women who firmly chose family over career? Was there a way to accommodate them?

Then there was the fact that I wasn't an expert or role model on work/life balance. But I challenge you to find any woman who says they are.

My entire working-mom career, I was in constant distress rearranging my priorities to keep the many balls I was juggling from falling. With too few senior females in the firm to confide in, I, and other women, made up the rules as we went along. We each learned to juggle work and family over and over again, and hoped we'd get the balance right 50% of the time.

But that constant problem seemed to remain in most areas: rising female stars in PwC couldn't look up and see other women who looked like them, and who they could aspire to be like.

The women partners promoted before me worked full time, took minimal time off for their maternity leaves, could afford the cost of 'live out' nannies, or used doting grandparents as caregivers. Others decided not to start a family in the first place. Despite the many qualities these talented female partners demonstrated in the office, I did not relate to their life choices outside the office. Simply put, there were too few women in leadership positions because there were too few *role models,* too few women *partners,* and too few women *leaders* to emulate!

And there was also the thorny issue of 'tokenism'—which, of course, extends to more than women—but in this case, it was how I assumed women would feel being associated with any part of this program. Women were loathe to be connected with anything that might be seen to treat them differently.

Were 'quotas' the answer to kickstart change and measure success? Many viewed quotas as negative diversity incentives because they gave unfair advantages to women based on their gender. Women selected for a promotion, a hire, or a board position over a man, often assumed a primary reason for their big break was to fill a quota, rather than *earning* their place based on merit, fit, skills, and expertise. I have never met a woman who wanted any part of being the token female, myself included. This concept often crept into my own view of my progression, my partner status, and my belonging as a leader among men.

Was I offered my position because of the skills I brought, or because I was a female?

Even today, as I sit here writing this book, when I consider the number of corporate board positions I am recruited for, I question whether it is truly my experience, skills, value, and fit that interests a company, or is it the convenience of my gender? Do I check the competency and capability box they are looking for, or am I filling a desperate board's need to meet the rules for at least 30% of their members to be diverse?

I hope it is the former, but I will never know for sure.

My Perspective

The CEO's need for greater focus on the retention and promotion of women in the firm did not fall on my deaf ears. Over the years, I had accepted my role as a coach, mentor, and sponsor for men and women rising through the ranks of PwC. I provided coaching through formal relationships, but much more of my time, especially among younger women, was spent in informal conversations.

Around this time, a recently married, newly-promoted manager would drop by my office, usually after hours, and poke her head through my open door. She felt safe asking me about her next step: having children. She needed to know how to manage this alongside her demanding career, because this was the burning question that kept her awake at night. I had navigated my path to partnership in a two-career household with two children. What advice could I share? What was my secret?

I knew all too well the struggles these women were facing because, frankly, they were a carbon copy of mine.

For me, finding childcare, keeping to a routine, and establishing stability in the home was always a match about to catch fire. If left to its own devices, I was afraid the fire would spread and destroy the house without warning. I never felt safe, even when the match was doused with water. I was fraught with anxiety and guilt.

I couldn't take care of things that *could* go wrong, because I never knew what *would* go wrong. Instead, I was forever rushing through the front door, destined to be late for my morning meeting, despite my best intentions.

I was horrible at factoring in the 'interruption of the day'. There were no instruction manuals to help me hurry up Danielle's strong-willed defiance to don clothes, any clothes, whatsoever. I couldn't rightly drop her off at school naked, could I? Moreover, I was unable to rearrange babysitting on the spot when our nanny woke up with a fever, requiring John or I to negotiate who was changing plans to stay home for the day.

And then there is my recurring, most unhelpful daily interruption, courtesy of our insolent dog, Tasha. She was a white-haired, slightly aggressive Cockapoo rescue, our second family dog, sporting the same name as the first. Tasha 2, as she was known by our vet, was famous for dashing through the open front door as I hugged everyone goodbye, escaping capture, and enjoying a few minutes of freedom chasing squirrels throughout the neighbourhood. 'Tasha, come back! Where are you? Tasha? Come! I need to get to work. Get over here. Now!' Eventually, she'd be found in a neighbour's backyard, being fed scraps. You can't make this stuff up.

It should be acceptable for men and women to interrupt their workdays to participate in their kids' activities and have a personal life, without apology. My clients understood I had a life outside of work, because so did they! They accepted and applauded my transparency when I disclosed my family priorities, and readily accommodated my requests to reschedule a work meeting.

But I only had the courage to share this practice late in my career when I was secure in my place as a leader. Staff observed my actions as positive, a shift to a better work/life balance, and by sharing my priorities, I allowed my staff (and my clients) permission to emulate it. I wanted them to have the courage to apply this practice early on in their careers, and I believed then, as I believe now, that there needs to be universal acceptance for circumstances when work can't take precedence over life.

As for the *promotion* of women side of this opportunity, I knew there were many women afraid to 'lean in' to their career aspirations; women who were unaware of their exceptional potential and refused to raise their hand. If they weren't being asked to lead a stretch assignment or offered a promotion, they assumed they mustn't be ready. Their solution was to work hard with their heads down and produce good results, and one day they would be ready, and their boss would ask them. Right? Meanwhile, their male counterparts, confident in their abilities, were not afraid to negotiate on their own behalf. It was simple—they asked for it and they got it.

I wished the list of struggles women shared were easy to solve, but I knew they were not. Women were constantly weighing the pros and cons of leaving the firm and the job they loved because they lacked the toolkit of skills to pilot their path to partnership. They wanted it all, or at least some part of it, but thought it was possible only if they sacrificed their personal lives, their relationships, and their motherhood. For many, it was all or nothing.

Over the years, I'd held emotional conversations with these souls, effortlessly relating to their challenges. I knew the questions, but I had a harder time with the answers.

What was the right answer in their circumstance? It varied, but my goal was always to broaden their perspective.

'Try to think past today's frustrations and stressors and consider the big picture, including everything you have done that has got you to this point. What makes you happy? Where do you want to be? Where is your heart telling you to be? Here, or somewhere else?' Sooner or later, every mother had to face this difficult choice.

By asking open-ended questions, with the intention of having them share their internal feelings out loud, they would validate their inner-thoughts, and could come to grips with the conflict that would not go away no matter what path they ultimately chose. Over the years, I gave them permission to accept their path, whichever fork in the road they chose. Sometimes, the answer wasn't what the firm or I wanted to hear, and they decided to leave public accounting. But if it was the right answer for them, that was all that truly mattered.

With my female colleagues, I shared my litmus test for staying at the firm for as long as I did with the following motto:

The day I wake up and find myself bored, unhappy, or not looking forward to going to work, is the day I will leave this firm.

Either way we lean, as stay-at-home moms or working career moms, we must be true to ourselves, and ultimately be content once we have made our choice. You are not a bad mother because you want to work. You haven't wasted your degree because you want to stay home. There is no right or wrong answer, there is only the answer that is right for you; the answer that is in your heart.

My Decision

As I considered the WIL/ROW role, I thought hard about the women who needed my help, especially those who I had helped in many small ways already. I thought about how I could have used that kind of help when I was standing in their shoes, and I reflected on all the fears and misconceptions I had because there was no one for me to ask.

If my CEO thought I was the right person to tackle this issue, I realized that I should have felt honoured rather than overlooked for the prestigious position I never received. I had entered the last stage of grief.

Acceptance.

The more I thought on it, the more I came to realize WIL/ROW *was* my plum role. The CEO had done me a huge favour. This was a leadership position I could sink my teeth into. It was bigger than any client proposal, a profit and loss statement, or an industry marketing initiative, because if I was successful, my leadership in this area could change the very culture and fabric of the firm, forever. If I could make an impact of this calibre, it would be purposeful, and it would align with my long-term goal:

To make a lasting difference and leave the firm better than I found it.

For this reason, I was all in.

I would be a champion for gender diversity, reporting directly to the CEO, who had placed his hopes on my leadership. Increasing awareness of unconscious biases and levelling the playing field for women was my new pot of gold at the end of the rainbow. This inspired me.

I later learned this role gave me a seat as a founding member of PwC's Global Diversity and Inclusion Council, which meant I could influence the *global* direction of the firm's diversity initiative. The thought of influencing the global directive, chaired by the Global CEO, fascinated me.

Hiring my Subject-Matter Expert

But I had a steep hill to climb. I had, in many ways, been exemplifying the change the CEO wanted to see, but I didn't know how to apply this to other women in the workplace. I needed help.

To embrace this role and be fully committed to its success, my first step was to develop a strategy—one that would resonate with men and women on *their* terms. The mandate against which my performance and success was measured, as the CEO reiterated, was, 'To retain more women in the firm and promote more women into the partnership and leadership positions.'

I couldn't do this alone, nor was I expected to. I set out to hire a full-time subject-matter expert to help me develop, inform, strategize, persuade, and positively influence the change needed. The firm needed subtle tweaks in its daily behaviours and actions, as well as several sweeping changes to firm policies and processes that would resonate with all lines of service and all levels of the organization. It was a tall order to navigate these murky waters, and I needed an extraordinary person I felt could be my ears, eyes, right and left hands.

Human Resources helped me develop a job description for a WIL/ROW Manager and posted it on PwC's website. As the resumes rolled in, I narrowed my selection to the frontrunners. Two candidates caught my attention. I set up phone and in-office interviews.

The first candidate, Marilyn, a woman in her late thirties, was a manager with the perfect resume for my needs. She had amassed human resource degrees in a wide variety of subjects (gender and diversity among them), appeared to have relevant experience in similar positions with likeminded corporations, and she was keen to apply her expertise for PwC's benefit. You could say the role had her name written all over it. It would be an easy transition for her to walk into.

My second candidate, Julie, a woman in her twenties, held a bachelor's degree in science, a master's degree in public health, and two years of a partially completed PhD in sociology. Although she had grown up in Mississauga, she had lived in the US while completing her undergraduate, masters, and PhD. Julie explained, transparently, why she had decided to come back home. She was taking a break from her PhD to get some real work experience so she could apply what she had learned in school. This would be her first full-time job.

I know what you're thinking. Why am I talking about Julie when Marilyn is quite obviously the more experienced, tried and true, safe choice?

If you have learned anything about me, you know I tend to take the road less travelled. I root for the underdog. And that's not to say there was anything wrong with Marilyn; I expect she would have fit in at PwC like a glove with her experience and expertise.

Julie, however, was in another league. She was passionate about what she could bring to this role and was (and still is) one of the most articulate individuals I have ever met. She carried herself confidently and professionally, and she was mature beyond her years. As the interview progressed, I was captivated by the thought-provoking, stimulating conversation we engaged in.

While Julie elaborated on organizational culture, she demonstrated her knowledge of gender differences and societal biases that innocently begin in the sandbox. Moreover, she was completely open to my feedback, listened to my mandate, and seemed to quickly grasp the unique attributes of a professional services firm like PwC.

I immediately knew working with Julie would be a seamless transition, and I visualized the exciting new direction the program would take under our collaborative leadership. I could learn from her as my subject-matter expert, and from me she could learn about our culture as well as the nuances of a professional services firm. This was a win-win.

I listened to my gut and didn't sell myself short. My gut was urging me to give Julie a chance just like PwC had given me an opportunity all those years ago.

I reflected on who I was all those years ago when I sat across from recruiters with a geography degree and nothing else but an Olympic swimming pool brimming with passion, determination, and drive. I saw right away that what Julie lacked in work experience, she made up for in intelligence, communication skills, and enthusiasm.

Julie was a calculated risk. She may not have been the *expected* choice, but to me she was the only choice. I saw something unique and special in her, and I was not about to let her slip through my fingers.

So, in the summer of 2008, Julie was added to the PwC ranks, and we took on the WIL/ROW initiative together with energy, passion, and a drive to initiate and create the long-term change we wanted to see in the firm. For all the reasons I've mentioned in this chapter, we knew it was going to be difficult. But we were determined, and we wouldn't be ignored.

20

Making a Difference: Retaining More Women in the Workplace

With Julie on board as my WIL/ROW Manager, it was time to build our program and give it the renewed attention it deserved.

First order of business? The formidable task of developing, from ground zero, a new and improved strategy '**to retain more women in the firm and promote more women into partnership and into leadership positions.**'

I asked Julie to forget about what had been done at PwC in the past. At the glacial speed it was moving prior to my appointment, we estimated it would be 2035 before any mandate could be achieved.

So, we ventured down a more important path:

'Why is it not working today?'

It was time to expose the firm's shortcomings. Our measures would need to resonate with men and women alike, and it would be critical to have leadership support to spread our message to the rank and file. We needed leaders to set the tone at the top.

Julie had three short weeks to develop a strategy to present to the firm's Executive Leadership Team (ELT) for their review, comments, and approval. It was a tall order for a new manager in her first professional job, but, as I expected, Julie rose to the challenge.

She was a quick study, grasping the nuances of a professional services firm, impressing the people she met, and influencing those she needed to win over, while expressing herself clearly and with authority. Her professionalism, expertise, and her oral and written strengths shone brightly throughout her draft plan. I was beyond impressed.

So, it was no surprise that her presentation to the ELT was flawless. I supported her from the fringes and was prepared to step in to deal with any backlash she may encounter. But none was forthcoming. She exceeded my expectations in what would become a recurring trademark of hers.

With the firm's leadership behind us, we first had to identify what wasn't working. So, we set out to discover the systemic barriers women faced in the PwC workplace.

We investigated the numbers of men versus women hired for our entry-level and our experienced audit, tax, and advisory manager positions. We found that, while our entry-level positions had a healthy mix, our new hires beyond the manager level were comprised of predominantly men.

This begged the question:

Were there no experienced professional women to recruit from, or did we have a recruiting bias?

Then, Julie identified several unexpected gaps in women's progression and performance by comparing them to men. We found the percentage of women *promoted* to senior manager and partner levels was significantly lower than men.

It was painfully apparent the two legs of our mandate—the **retention** and **promotion** of women—were fiercely interconnected. The challenges in one area negatively impacted the other. We felt if we could direct positive change by promoting more women, for example, it would positively impact their retention. And the opposite was true as well. When fewer women stuck around to get promoted, there were fewer women to promote. It was a vicious circle, but we knew that identifying the root causes of both could give our initiative a big lift.

So, what was getting in the way of women's progression and retention?

What we eventually discovered was a landmine. But I'll get more into that later.

First, we identified the blind spots and unconscious biases women faced in our firm, starting with each line of service—Tax, Advisory, and Audit—and learned that each department had their own set of issues to address, unique to their business and practices.

The major area of concern in Audit was retention of female CPAs once they reached the 'new manager' level. You may remember that I also struggled with this decision when I attained my CPA. So, when we dug into the numbers, we found the proportion of women leaving the firm versus men was *dramatic*. It was no surprise that this timing coincided with new managers getting married and becoming first-time parents. The similarities to my own experience were unsurprising, but I was still shocked to see the same issues decades later.

We identified the need for better support networks and programs to support women at this critical stage in their life and career. Although flexible work arrangements existed, *no one* took advantage of them, and there were very few success stories of senior women being promoted to partner after taking one (other than my own, which surprised me).

We set out to change the culture of acceptance around flexible work arrangements and to remove the stigma attached to them. We trained coaches on the benefits of alternative career development paths for women (and men, who were even less likely to ask for one), and ensured leadership fully supported the very real possibility that promotion to partner was a valid avenue for anyone who chose a non-linear career as their path to partnership.

In Advisory, where it was more common for PwC to recruit experienced candidates with specialized expertise, we found an imbalance in the *hiring* of experienced males over females. When we dug deeper, we discovered that the senior managers and partners in charge of recruiting were predominantly other men who relied on their networks to find talent. Their tendency was to hire people who they could relate to—their 'mini-mes'.

Even executive search firms PwC paid to find talent provided more men to the hiring pool, as they too were chocked full of male recruiters with predominantly male networks to pull resumes from. As a result, they had an underrepresentation of women at all levels. Not only was Advisory unable to find women to hire, but they also suffered from an inability to attract women once found.

Retaining women once recruited was also a struggle due to the nature of the advisory work itself, which included unpredictable working hours with time-sensitive assignments, and frequent travel for weeks at a time. With a dearth of role models to ask questions of, it was a constant struggle for young female professionals forging a career in Advisory.

Finally, we found the Tax department held the most enviable position for attracting young, professional women. They recruited the majority of their staff from the seasoned CPAs in Audit.

Tax, for women looking from the outside in, offered a more balanced, steady workflow. Sure, they worked overtime, but it could usually be planned for in advance. Predictability offered women in Tax the encouraging possibility of achieving a better work/life balance. There were even a few success stories of managers performing well in flexible, part-time work arrangements.

Nonetheless, the Tax department's representation of women in leadership and partner ranks was sorely disproportionate to the number of women hired, indicating they too lost women to jobs in industry and the stay-at-home alternative.

After analysing the three departments, it was clear that our current model to retain women was broken. But it was more than just internal issues, and I knew that.

For decades, the modus operandi of the baby boomer generation (*my* generation) was a hangover in perception from the post-war era, where a woman's place was not at the boardroom table. It was in the home. And I'd seen it time and time again.

During my tenure at PwC, senior women left their once sought-after professional careers faster than the firm could hire and replace them. They left not because they didn't like the work or they were underperformers, but because the delicate dance of balancing career and family was simply too hard to manage.

Worse, the work/life balance challenge was, and still is, exacerbated by the nature of the accounting profession itself. Since the dawn of auditing, tax, and consulting, the unpredictable demands of a client service industry have stolen our brightest and best women (and men!) in search of greener employment or stay-at-home pastures. No doubt, if it was easy to unscramble this riddle, the code would have been cracked decades ago.

So, what is a woman to do? With no clear path for balancing the scales of work and family pressures, women give up meaningful work to serve another passion as a stay-at-home mom. Either that, or they choose unrelated, less stressful, part-time work that allows them to be home more often so they can support their kids and their working spouse.

There was also a common trend in our industry, and others, where women re-entered the workforce full time when their children attended school full time. They try to pick up where they left off, jumping back on the corporate merry-go-round. But, more often, women fear they have lost too much time in the interim, and their skills need upgrading. Or perhaps their priorities have changed, and they can't go back to the slog they once endured.

So, with all of this in mind, Julie and I were curious as to why so few PwC women felt 'safe' taking advantage of the flexible work options available to them. In the Greater Toronto Area, for example, less than 3% of women enjoyed a flexible work program. So, we asked them.

Apparently, in some 'hard to put your finger on' way, women in flexible work arrangements felt they were not being treated the same as their full-time peers. They deemed they were sidelined for advancement, placed on a 'mommy track', and excluded from challenging assignments because they were not committed to their careers.

We often saw that their careers had stalled. These moms were stuck on a rung halfway up the corporate ladder. They weren't able to break the glass ceiling because they couldn't even reach it! Feeling their work/life balance had come at a price, eventually many part-time moms left, because that was better than the alternative: watching their peers surpass them while they were overlooked by their bosses for no apparent reason.

This was not unique to PwC. The corporate world handled many of their part-time moms this way. So much so, this situation has a name: 'The leaking pipeline'.

In order to stem the leak, we needed a commitment from leadership. To achieve equality for part-time moms, women in flexible work arrangements could not be considered to be uncommitted employees. They needed to be given the same opportunities as full-time staff. Women needed to be considered for promotion, even part-timers, as long as they demonstrated the necessary skills and attributes.

Our proposition would take time and patience.

First, and most important of all, we had to encourage women to *accept* a flexible work program in the first place, trusting that it wouldn't curtail their careers. We supported their arrangement by assigning a mentor to oversee their work assignments. Finally, we hoped that these women would stay in the firm long enough to get promoted. We weren't going to see the fruits of our labour materialize in the short term, but we hoped once we set the ball in motion, we could aim for better retention.

Another pressing issue Julie identified was a high rate of attrition after their *second* maternity leave. We knew some women left the firm after their first child, but we didn't realize how many *more* women resigned after their second. It seemed two extended leaves from the firm tipped the scales against them. A second maternity leave, not long after the first leave, left them feeling they had missed too much time to ever catch up. They felt the firm, and their clients, had moved on without them.

When I gave birth to Andrew and designed my part-time arrangement, it was to keep me in the firm. I attributed my need to slow down and stay home to my son's health, but it's possible that I was just like other PwC moms with two kids. Had I missed too much time to face the changes in the workplace that had taken place in my absence? I don't know, but I could relate to women who believed they needed their flexible work arrangement after *two* kids versus just one.

To address this issue, Julie designed a post-maternity leave transition program called 'Life Changes' and began to roll it out to the practice. It was designed to give women the opportunity to stay connected to the firm, as much or as little as they desired when they were on leave. They were assigned a friendly face, a colleague to connect with throughout their leave, as well as a coach who would keep them informed, and they would arm them with a stronger voice to ask for what they needed to be successful upon their return to work. For those so inclined, they could take whichever online or in-house courses we offered so they didn't fall behind in their technical skills.

There was also an externally facilitated program by Lisa Martin I had inherited from my predecessor called 'Briefcase Moms'. It was offered to working moms, and Lisa's program had received rave reviews, so we retained it. It took place over several months, and included a series of workshops, self-reflections, and practices. It was led by its founder, a professional outside coach and mother, to help our working moms balance their lives through her proven practices and intentional change. Over 400 working moms (including myself) attended this program.

Because I could relate to other moms, I considered myself a litmus test for our programs, questioning and assessing whether we were headed in the right direction with our solutions. As the programs continued and feedback was gathered from moms and their coaches, I believed the 'retention of women' piece of our mandate had legs.

21

Making a Difference: Promoting More Women in the Workplace

A statistic I repeatedly heard from new staff to seasoned partners was, 'Although women represent more than half of our new hires, why do we have so few women partners and even fewer holding leadership positions?'

Good question.

Over the previous three decades, an equal number of women were graduating with BComm degrees as men, and 50% of our hires were female. However, the answer we received from leadership on why we had so few women partners was not satisfactory.

'It's just a matter of time. More women will be promoted to partner one day.'

If this was true, it should have already transpired.

This was more complex than 'a matter of time'. Real change needed to occur.

So, why did women get stuck in the talent pipeline? Were women less ambitious than men? Research categorically refutes this;

men and women's career aspirations are similar, so what was getting in the way of women's progression?

This won't surprise you considering my story to this point, but when we turned to gender research, we learned that women were less likely to put their hand up and ask for an opportunity or promotion, whereas men were much more likely to do so. In part, this was because women were more likely to think that they would be *asked* to assume a new role or assignment when their manager thought they were ready. Research suggests this may be because women negotiate less often and less aggressively than men.

Women are socialised from an early age not to promote their interests, but rather to focus on the needs of others. However, by not asking, women are passed over for stretch assignments, roles, and opportunities, and research suggests this makes them appear *less ambitious*.

We were also failing to recognize the ebbs and flows of a person's ambitions. It didn't have to be the traditional male standard, because for women there is the very real issue of timing.

Imagine the conflict an ambitious woman faces accepting a leadership role while she is also in the midst of successive maternity leaves, raising a family, or dealing with the demands of eldercare. Let's face it: nature can be cruel to working moms.

Caught between the proverbial rock and a hard place, working moms are in a constant struggle and are always asked to question their priorities. When she attempts to slow down her career progression, she is considered to be on the 'mommy track', and often watches her male colleagues zoom past her. When she decides *now* is the time to lean into her career (often later than her male colleagues do) she worries whether she will be noticed or be considered past her prime.

Companies should not assume that women (and men) who say 'no' to stretch opportunities at thirty-five years old (or forty-five!) will *never* want to ramp up at some point in the future. Companies who cast a wider net in their talent pipeline to include employees at all ages and stages in their lives will be more likely to retain committed and experienced staff, which fosters capable, high-performing candidates available for promotion into leadership ranks.

A second factor holding back women being promoted in the workplace was the lack of female role models and mentors—other women who have been there and done that who can help them understand the business of climbing the corporate ladder. (*Hmmm, maybe this would make for a good book?)* Research suggests when women look 'up' in an organization, they rarely see someone they can relate to. Having fewer women to relate to shapes a woman's belief that the career path she envisaged is not open to her and, consequently, she doesn't aspire to pursue it.

As Julie wrote in her '*Gender Differences in the Workplace*' Guide:

'Expectations of rewards for hard work also affects a woman's aspirations. To the extent that her calculation of the rewards and recognition she will receive for her efforts are diminished, so too is her desire to pursue her goals. However, once a critical mass of women is in place at the top of an organization, women tend to rise through the ranks organically, as role models. These women can have a tremendous effect on engagement, retention, and progression of junior female staff.

For some women, it's not simply the position or role that they aren't interested in. It's also the process of 'getting there' shaped in part by the *likelihood* of getting there. In Anna Fels HBR article 'Do Women Lack Ambition', she explains that women find it difficult to demand appropriate support—in the form of time, money, or promotion—to pursue their own goals; they feel foolish asking for acknowledgment of their contributions, and selfish when they don't subordinate their needs to those of others.'

To Julie's point, if we had better representation of role models rising through our ranks—leaders that more closely resembled the backgrounds and faces of the staff we've hired—could we fix our gender retention issues? For three decades, I'd had trouble finding role models who looked like me, a Caucasian female. Moreover, in 2008, our demographics had become even more diverse, not less. We needed our leaders to reflect these changes.

To Anna Fel's point, it was time to pull out all the stops and deliver in ways that *actively* supported women. We needed to remove the barriers for flexible work programs, ensure high-performing women were offered (and accepted!) stretch assignments, and critically assess our performance evaluation system (which I'll get into a bit later).

Setting measurable goals for progress

With all of this in mind, we knew that setting firm goals to promote more women into leadership positions would be critical to progress, achieving gender parity, increasing our pipeline of women to partnership, *and* overall retention. I was encouraged by the CEO's constant support of this initiative, but Chris knew he couldn't do this alone. He intended to hold his senior leaders accountable for meaningful change.

He was onto something. Holding leaders accountable is a critical success factor for any initiative. Lasting change doesn't happen until leadership believes in the need for it, walks the talk, and when it's stalled, pounds the pavement to support meaningful progress.

Leadership's tone at the top cascades through an organization. It was our ace in the hole.

We discussed how we should measure progress. Quotas had gained traction in parts of the world. Norway, for example, had achieved significant success increasing the percentages of women on their corporate boards by mandating it. But this approach, in my opinion, was flawed.

Quotas *forced* change prior to gaining wider acceptance of its objective benefits; in this case, the important role that women serve on boards. It leads to greater diversity of thought and stronger than average financial performance, which is firmly backed by data from Fortune 500 companies with greater than three women on their boards. People were beginning to understand that diversity was good for the bottom line!

My contempt for quotas, and the backlash I knew they would send through both the male and female partnership, led me to recommend soft targets and call them, *aspirational goals*. Our strategy was to set goals to change the landscape for gender diversity for years to come.

Thus, our two aspirational goals, with leadership's buy-in were:

1. to increase the percentage of women partners in the next five years from 17% to 22%, and
2. to increase the percentage of women in named senior leadership positions from 16% to 25%.

With these goals in place, we sprang into action to address what was getting in our way. Julie explained the issues were bigger than us: Society's long-held beliefs and norms were working against women.

Gender communication differences

Take the female's style of professional presence, as an example. Women feel they are not seen nor heard at the leadership table or in the boardroom. Even how many women hold their bodies and their postures (i.e., legs crossed) tends to take up less personal space than men in their chairs. If women don't 'lean in' and speak up, it's easier to overlook they are even there. When a more observant Chair notices, he/she can ask for the opinions of the quiet ones. However, in the heat of a debate, when there are a multitude of voices weighing in, not every leader remembers to do this.

To make matters worse, women find their ideas tend to fall on deaf ears. Then, sometime later, their thought is seized by an astute man repeating it to the accolades of the male audience. Often, men are oblivious as to what has transpired. 'That is a great idea, Nelson! Let's jump on that!' It's so cringy to see, and I'd be lying if I said it didn't happen to me on more than one occasion.

There is a reason this happens. When women express an idea at a meeting, they are often *making a suggestion* that invites the input of others. When men express an idea, they often do so with authority, so the action to be taken is clear. As a result, women think men don't collaborate, and men think women lack confidence and leadership skills.

Moreover, women lose credibility as leaders or influencers when they speak in a feminine, higher-pitched, 'sing-song' voice, ending each statement with a rise in tone, suggesting they are asking a question. They continue, in desperation, to influence their audience, but the problem is they aren't making a statement! A woman may use the technique of ending her sentence in a question, because it is uncomfortable to take a firm stand on her own position. She softens the impact of what she has to say to avoid appearing too aggressive or unlikeable, and because of this, her communication style is met with skepticism, making her come across tentative and lacking competence. 'I'm sorry' is a woman's ritual way of restoring balance in a confrontational situation. This is an added problem for polite Canadians, who use this phrase to cover everything from an insignificant nudge in the grocery aisle to an excuse for our long Canadian winters. For men, apologizing is seen generally as an admission of fault.

A glitch in the appraisal system

So, what truly impedes a woman's influence as a leader? Is it her feminine style, her method of communicating, her confidence, the collective unconscious gender bias in the workplace, or all of the above?

Through the use of quantitative information, which you can bet your bottom dollar accountants loved to see, we found eye-opening differences. The glitch in the matrix of PwC's 'tried and true' appraisal system was the most insightful to me.

PwC's performance appraisal system was based on *self-evaluations*. The self-evaluation was sent to the person they reported to (the 'evaluator') to provide their comments, a numerical rating, and to agree with their assessment or change it.

This process has its merits. A self-evaluation ensures the evaluatee provides their personal, detailed account of what they accomplished, how and why they were successful, and what they could have done better. Human nature supports this process as well, because the busy evaluator can often only recollect the most important and/or annoying specifics once a job is complete. He or she may move on to their next crisis without giving much thought to the individual and what their impact on the completed project was.

So, it is in the best interest of the evaluatee to create a true and candid account of their performance. Makes sense, right? It's an efficient process offering a convenient and timely review by their evaluator.

That is, until you compare the differences in how men and women document their performance. I have a feeling you won't be surprised with our findings.

Gender research demonstrates females tend to *understate* their achievements and prediction of their performance in a self-evaluation process (Daubman, Kimberley A., Heatherington, L., and Alicia Ahn. 1992 'Gender and the Self-Presentation of Academic Achievement. Sex Roles, 27(3/4): 187-204). Women typically attribute a good performance on the job to the attributes and hard work of *their team*, not themselves as individual contributors.

On the other hand, and this is important—if asked to judge where they can improve, women are quick to disclose their failings and areas for improvement, while laying very little blame on the team. Some of these 'failings' are often so minor that their supervisor was completely unaware of them! Women are also prone to share attributes that are missing from their current skillset. What kind of picture does this self-deprecating evaluation paint on the true performance (or potential) of that woman?

You would think she was average at best, and, without too much of a stretch, an under-performer! She leaves you thinking, *Thank goodness I gave her a strong team to cover for her; a team that has, apparently, been managing themselves!* You might think this can't be true; it's too extreme to be real. But time and time again, we came across evaluations like this written by our top-performing females! Incredible.

In contrast, research on men in the workplace indicates—and we discovered this in practise to confirm it—that men tend to *overstate* their individual performance on the job. They are less likely to give credit to their teams, citing their strong suite of technical and interpersonal skills as the catalyst for success as managers. Moreover, men are typically reluctant to provide areas for their personal improvement, because they don't see their minor inconsistencies as faults. Who needs to broadcast tiny flaws or shortcomings to superiors anyway? I tend to agree with them!

If you can tell which of the men drafting their self-evaluations were 'average', 'below average', or 'above average', you're more astute than the average bear. To the naïve, uninformed evaluator, most men look like 'above average' high performers. They demonstrate the skills needed for our future leaders, ready to accept a stretch assignment and a promotion.

Or are they?

In the examples above, both male and female evaluatees' self-reflections are misguided. That is, neither reflect their true, unbiased performance. So, armed with the knowledge of gender differences existing in our system, we set out to calibrate the process so that ratings were a better reflection of reality.

As we dug deeper into the quantitative ratings given to male and female managers and above, we stumbled upon another unexplained difference. The performance ratings assigned to senior female professionals was troubling. There was an unexplained lack of women rated '1' at the experienced manager and senior manager level. It is important to understand that the '1' rating represents PwC's highest performance level, reserved for only the top, outstanding performers: *our future leaders.*

The more senior a woman became, the fewer female's rated '1' we found. And this was disproportionate to the number of female managers that should have been highly rated based on their feeder pools. That is, there were plenty of outstanding female staff assistants, accountants, and senior accountants in the firm, but inexplicably, once a woman was promoted to manager, they rarely retained their 'outstanding' rating. They were rated as 'average' or 'very good' at best. Yet, their male counterparts, at the same level, retained their high-performing '1' ratings, and this remained in proportion to the number of men in their feeder pool. In fact, men retained their outstanding performance ratings up to and including their promotion to partner.

Statistically, this didn't make any sense. We were staring down the barrel of an issue but couldn't explain what caused it. Few 'outstanding' female managers meant few 'outstanding' experienced female senior managers, and even fewer on a confirmed path to partnership. With only a handful of partner openings in any office, these coveted spots were taken, as you might expect, by the most highly rated senior managers: the '1' rated, outstanding *men*.

As we examined the discrepancy further, it dawned on us that two things had changed:

1. The firm's transition to a self-assessment evaluation process for a manager's job-based performance.
2. The shift in the firm's focus on subjective 'soft' managerial skills at the higher levels, including their style as a leader, their communication, and their client relationship skills. (At the more junior levels, performance criteria were focused more on technical skills that could be applied objectively across genders.)

Curiously, women at the manager levels were more often evaluated by their supervisors as 'Has a style that isn't quite right—she's not confident with clients,' or 'She is too overbearing or abrasive with clients,' while men at these levels received feedback such as, 'He's amazing with clients—they love him!' So, women who were once rated '1' slipped to a '2' or '3' because the performance criteria were stacked against them. And the disparities in ratings—and thus promotions—started to emerge.

Moreover, the habitually *understated* self-evaluations of female managers were taken at face value. No one corroborated their comments and ratings with their actual performance. No one noticed how incongruent these evaluations were to their previous stellar performance. In comparison to their potentially *overstated*, high-performing males doing their own evaluations, these females *were* average on paper!

Women were sabotaging their opportunities, their promotability, and their future by unintentionally downplaying their performance, while emphasising their areas for improvement. Women were passed over for challenging assignments to build on their strengths, because they didn't look good enough on paper. Even women who stayed with the firm, waiting for a shot at a long-term career at PwC, were stuck in the pipeline at the experienced manager level with unconscious bias playing out big-time.

We shared our insights with Human Resources, the leadership team, as well as all partners and coaches. Julie identified the issue and began to wrestle it to the ground. We delivered training to all employees to increase awareness of the gender differences we'd identified, and we engaged with partner and manager coaches by showing real examples to help them critique written comments and ratings provided by self-evaluations. We raised their awareness of how two seemingly comparable individuals—one male, one female—could describe their performance so differently, and more importantly, what we could do about it. This resulted in many instructive moments with many people saying, 'I never knew about these dynamics, but now that I do, I can see it!'

Then, we took it one step further. We used the annual summary evaluation meetings process to calibrate or 'true-up' inconsistent self-evaluations by asking 'gender monitors' to attend and apply a gender lens to our discussions. More often than not, they called out unconscious biases when they reared their ugly little heads.

For example, any time a statement like, 'Her style with clients isn't great' was made, the evaluators had to scrutinize and unpack that statement. What, exactly, 'isn't great'? What are the specific examples? Is it that her style is simply different from our preconceived notions of what a good (i.e., male) client relationship style looks like?

This ensured performance evaluations were fair, grounded in reality, and not simply a reflection of unintentional but harmful biases. We also created a short framework for coaches with three simple questions they had to answer before attending a performance review meeting. The questions specifically pushed coaches to ask, and therefore know, the aspirations of *every* person, not just the men who happily volunteered their goals (even when not solicited!).

We asked HR to track the nature and reasons for changes made to ratings and promotions, and we armed managers and partners with greater awareness of gender differences, then augmented the evaluation review process with discussions using a gender lens.

So, with all these initiatives, did anything actually change?

Discussions were more robust and transparent, and probing questions were asked by both male and female evaluators. Gender lens champions and other influencers were not afraid to call out a discrepancy that didn't mesh with their understanding of a person's performance. The solution was often, 'Let's investigate this further to make sure we have the correct facts.'

Comments on a female's performance and her stated aspirations were no longer the status quo. We questioned statements such as:

'She's not ready for this role; she told me this herself.'

'She doesn't want more responsibility; she's happy where she is.'

'Thank goodness for her high-performing team; they did all the heavy lifting.'

Similarly, comments raised on a man's performance and aspirations were held under a microscope:

'He really wants this promotion; he says he's ready for it, and I believe it.'

'We all know he is an outstanding performer; just look at these glowing evaluations.'

These statements, taken at face value, begged further questions. Were societal norms speaking through us, or were we speaking the truth? By allowing discussions to dig deeper, we uncovered the truth around an individual's actual performance. On occasion, women's ratings were adjusted upwards. Some women initially overlooked for promotion were merited a second chance and were given a stretch assignment to prove they were ready. Of course, some situations warranted no change from the original assessment, but what we found was that, overall, leaders felt satisfied with the process, the results, and the decisions made. Everyone believed a more transparent, fair, and unbiased review of both men and women's performance was carried out. I was proud to see others playing by the new rules.

But where were the female leaders?

Next, we dug into the issue of women not being awarded leadership roles once they were promoted to partners—the second piece of our mandate. Societal norms and gender differences again explained what might have been getting in the way of a woman's progression up the corporate ladder.

First, there is the 'high competence threshold' women are held to. Typically, women must meet higher standards than men to prove they are capable leaders. Women need to manage their reputation to appear competent but still feminine, but when women act in stereotypically feminine ways, they are disadvantaged to the extent that these behaviours are not as highly valued, nor rewarded. Then, when women act assertively, decisively, ambitiously, or take a stand, they can be met with resistance and be perceived as unlikeable, unfeminine, too aggressive, or threatening. Women leaders are stuck between a rock and a hard place, often seen as either competent or likeable, but not both. This is the double bind phenomenon I described earlier in this book.

Second is how women see their accomplishments. Julie explained to me that women often ground their self-assessments in what tasks they *actually* execute and what skills they *actually* exercise. Men are more likely to ground their self-assessments not in what they accomplished but base them on their *perceived future potential.* While men's perceptions of their potential are more likely to be inflated, women are more likely to downplay theirs.

Adding to this is the fact that women do not perceive themselves to be 'ready' for the next promotion unless they have completed or feel competent performing *100% of the tasks and skills expected of them* at the next level up. Men, on the other hand, perceive themselves to be ready for their next promotion based on the perception that they possess the *potential to succeed.* They deem themselves ready for the next promotion when they have completed or feel competent at performing less than 70% of the tasks and skills needed.

Gender differences don't always translate into biases skewed in favour of males, because frankly, not every male or female acts this way. However, knowing these unconscious differences can and do exist provided us with valuable data to level the playing field for all staff.

The plethora of gender differences Julie identified were enlightening. Up until now, the lights were on, but nobody was home. I became acutely—no, embarrassingly aware—of how often I demonstrated many of these same behaviours, saying 'sorry,' avoiding confrontation, letting others take credit for my ideas, not raising my hand, and feeling inadequate. You've heard this before, but I can't stress it enough. I brushed them off as *my* problem, but what I didn't know was my problem was not just common but pervaded our workplace and countless others.

I thought my school of hard knocks upbringing had shaped me to be a strong, independent woman, but society's values on women and their place seemed to run deeper. Armed with this realization and my increased self-awareness, I started to look out for familiar gender traps and attempted to stop myself from stepping on them. I hoped other women would eventually do the same.

With this in mind, we set out to increase the firm's awareness of gender differences, and to help everyone understand how and why gender discrepancies arise. Our hope was to alert them to potential biases holding women back, without judgment or blame.

To do this, Julie developed a concise, matter-of-fact guidebook to address the societal differences that arise in the workplace, based on extensive research and science around how we are brought up, what we are rewarded for, and how we are encouraged to play. Julie addressed how these differences shape how we view ourselves in the world, how we work, and how we lead others, then she developed a '10 Simple Things' list of what men and women can do every day to foster gender diversity.

'10 Simple Things' (reproduced with permission from PwC LLP):

1. Don't assume. Think a great assignment that involves travel will be more stressful for a woman with children than for a man? Ask first. Open the dialogue to create an opportunity for a woman to stretch and develop.

2. Be a mentor—formal or informal; share your own experiences.

3. Encourage networking. Engage women in your networks, especially during business hours. Invite a woman to lunch or an important client meeting.

4. As a coach, encourage strategic, long-term career planning. Ask: where do you see yourself in two years, five years, ten years from now?

5. During performance reviews, deal with facts, not assumptions for both men and women.

6. Be authentic.
   Women: You don't need to present yourself as 'superwoman'.

Men: Women value authenticity—personalize the conversation, and talk about your family, your hobbies, and your interests outside of the office.

7. Support work/life flexibility. Actively support women requesting flexible work arrangements. Be proactive in finding a way to 'make it work'.

8. Be passionate about women advancing. When a choice assignment opportunity presents itself, think about the talented women you know who would be great to take on the role.

9. Appreciate different styles. Better yet, embrace them.

10. Live by your values. Put yourself in each others' shoes.

We hoped to increase awareness of gender differences and how they impacted decisions and unconscious biases, so we could set the stage for a more inclusive culture where women felt supported and *chose* to stay with PwC because they foresaw a career where they would be recognized, promoted, and rewarded as respected leaders. If we could open eyes, everyone could be looking at the same song sheet, even if they weren't ready to sing the song.

It seemed to women their path to partnership was a bumpy dirt road, while the path for men was a smooth, fresh-paved, four-lane highway. Too many women didn't appreciate how societal tendencies had shaped them to understate their true capabilities. While they waited to be asked for a promotion, once given a stretch opportunity, they felt unprepared or undeserving. They didn't have the inside scoop on how leadership decisions were made, they didn't understand the politics, nor did they fully grasp the importance of networking. And how would they? You can't understand leadership decisions when few, if any, of your female peers are leaders.

I may sound like a broken record, but this is and was so important. Women needed what men had always had: **Mentors to show them the ropes.**

They needed to speak with partners who had stood in their shoes and made it, and not in the typical up (or out) linear way, but with periods of career on- and off-ramps, so they could learn how to progress at their speed on *their* terms. They needed confidants to ask questions of, and sponsors to advocate for them.

So, we invited women to come together across all levels to 'lunch and learns', 'fireside chats with leadership', and other opportunities to network with each other. One such event featured a panel of high-potential/high-performing managers. They talked about their personal experiences through the lens of the gender issues they faced, and I could immediately tell that their stories resonated with the all-female audience.

Panelists told stories about the time they didn't get an early promotion they thought they would absolutely get and deserved, but in the same breath shared that they had never expressed wanting it. They thought, *Of course my performance will be recognized* but were crushed when they didn't get it because no one thought they wanted it early. Something about spotlighting these real stories—of the real colleagues we worked with every day—was so powerful, because it brought the research to life. The sessions also provided a welcome opportunity for junior women to meet and network with other senior women of the firm, while the impactful stories they told raised awareness of how these dynamics played out at PwC.

We also sought to address these challenges by revitalizing an in-house program called 'Mentoring Connections' which was designed by my predecessors to help experienced managers and above. We paired women with senior men and women partners whose job it was to provide guidance based on their own experience with their path to promotion and partnership. We enlisted 85 partners to mentor 135 women. It was a welcome addition to our suite of intentional programs to address our key performance indicators and our mandate.

Passing the Baton

I knew the day would come when Julie would decide to return to the US to complete her PhD. It was a risk the day I hired her, but I couldn't stand in her way. She had created a program that was a household name at PwC, awareness of gender differences in the workplace was at an all-time high, and we were making good progress with our goals and strategic plan. I wished her well, knowing our friendship would last forever. I knew that when this woman spread her wings, she would achieve greatness. I couldn't wait to witness Julie enter other organizations and galvanise business strategy, talent, culture, and change. I was confident she would go on to influence more companies and their leaders in the years to come.

With Julie's departure, and more work to be done, it was time for me to advertise for my next WIL/ROW Manager *internally.* With the groundwork laid, I saw this a perfect role for an experienced manager who understood the firm's culture. I needed this person to take the reins, implement the programs Julie started, and continue to socialise gender awareness while engaging with the practice. I positioned the role as a high-profile, two-year secondment working full-time with myself and the CEO; one that would be equally as rewarding as it was challenging.

I was blessed to have several candidates come forward, and ultimately, I chose Monica; a high-performing, second-year Audit Manager with subject-matter expertise from a Gender Studies specialty (bonus!) from Queens University. I was struck by her can-do, fresh perspective with the passion to match.

How could I have struck gold again? Monica was articulate, intelligent, creative, easy to work with, committed, an independent thinker, and a self-starter.

Although I knew I could hand over the program (my work baby) to her and not give it another thought, I just couldn't do it. I enjoyed her company and our brainstorming too much! My days were brighter under the magic and glow of her creative process. Her strategic input would take this program (now *her* program) to the next level, and I had a front-row seat to this blossoming rockstar.

In hiring Monica, I saw my unconscious bias at work in wishing to hire my mini-me. I realized how easy this was for any man or woman—many of whom I had disparaged in the past for doing the same. Although Monica was an exceptional professional on so many levels, she struggled with a lack of self-confidence, harboured a case of imposter syndrome, and routinely thought her outstanding performance deserved barely a passing grade, which, ironically, Julie and I had *indicated as factors holding the women in PwC back*. She had a poor work/life balance because 'no' was not a word in her vocabulary, and to add icing to the cake, she was a perfectionist. She took things hard and expected so much of herself.

Remind you of anyone? Don't answer that.

I couldn't wait to take Monica under my wing and teach her all the things I wished I had known earlier in my career. As my protégé,

I wanted nothing more than to watch her excel. I offered her stretch assignments and exposed her to our CEO and senior leadership on a regular basis.

But I'm getting ahead of myself!

There was one final piece of the puzzle to be put in place before we slapped our initials on this initiative.

22

Men: The Final Piece of the Puzzle

Monica was the architect of involving men in WIL/ROW in a way that we had not done before. This was the instrumental, final piece of the puzzle. In my opinion, this was the tipping point for the greatest, most lasting contribution Monica made to the culture of PwC during her tenure as WIL/ROW Manager.

First, Monica took the lead updating our annual quantitative analysis of male and female statistics. She identified where we were not moving fast enough, and then introduced herself to senior leaders to push our key performance indicators. As she communicated her innovative ideas to advance the strategy, placing her stamp on it, she gained instant credibility with the staff, partners, and leaders because she was a professional, an Audit Manager from the practice, and a high-performing female who was living this reality herself.

Next, Monica assisted the Line of Service leaders (Tax, Advisory, and Audit) with tweaks to their WIL/ROW plans and made a key change to our approach. It was time to take the 'no boys allowed' sign off the door and ask our male staff and partners to join in our commitment for change *together* alongside our women. She designed a clever plan to do just that, though, despite all the positive signs I'd seen from the men at PwC to this point, I still wasn't sure they would take up the program as Monica hoped.

For the past eight years of the firm's WIL/ROW journey, events and programs to assist women with their work/life and career challenges (Briefcase Moms, Mentoring Connections, and Life Changes) had been open to women only. We now know this strategy was flawed. While it is unproductive to ignore 50% of the population (women) in a company's hiring and promotion decisions, it is equally ineffective to address a gender initiative without the support and commitment of the other half of the population (men). We also recognized that, as men took on more responsibility at home and with childcare, they too wished to take paternity leaves and to not have their dedication to PwC and personal ambition questioned. Working dads and husbands were looking for answers to similar issues faced by our working women.

It was time to right this wrong.

Catalyst, 'a global non-profit company whose mission is to accelerate progress for women through workplace inclusion' demonstrated through their research and practical experience that engaging both women and men in culture change was critical to its success. Without the support of men, progress toward ending gender disparity was unlikely, if not impossible. Why didn't I think of this? Suddenly, I was dear Watson receiving feedback from Sherlock Holmes on how *elementary* this was.

Together, Monica and I approached the Line of Service leaders to ask for their help in identifying the most respected, influential, gender-aware men in the firm, and after searching every nook and cranny across all offices and service lines, we found them. We looked them up, sprinkled fairy dust at our feet for good luck, and began recruiting them to our cause. If they were willing to champion our initiative, we assured them Monica and I would stay close by for support. We armed them with the tools they needed to be knowledgeable and effective subject-matter experts.

We brought them together in small groups to allow them to share their fears and ask their questions. We gave them the cold hard facts, the inequities demonstrated by our analysis, the strides we were making using metrics, the research on gender, how supporting gender equality benefitted both men and the firm, and finally, why we needed their help.

We successfully sold our cause to forty brave men, all of whom agreed to advocate for the WIL/ROW mandate and show their support for women in the firm. But before we left them to influence their male colleagues to join the parade, we had one more area to explore.

We couldn't resist asking, 'Why did you agree to sign up for this?'

What they told us made me want to hug them! Our male champions supported gender diversity because it was the right and fair thing to do. Some were influenced by their courageous, trailblazer moms who were their role models, while others wanted gender parity and a future without bias for their daughters. Sometimes, their wife's negative experience pushed them to support our mandate; they witnessed firsthand how their spouse faced inequalities, and they had felt powerless to help. They wanted to end gender bias to give women unfettered access to opportunities for advancement.

Finally, there were some men who could relate to our plight. They knew what it felt like to be the only one in the room and feel excluded as a visible minority, a member of the LGBTQ+ community, or a person with disabilities. Supporting our mandate put their heart and mind toward a much broader goal: to reduce discrimination and biases beyond gender; to be open and mindful of race, religion, culture, ethnicity, age, and sexual orientation.

I was blown away by their candour, which begged me to ask an even tougher question. 'I need you to be honest and vulnerable. Can you share your personal story of understanding with others?'

For these men to truly make a difference in the perceptions, behaviours, and attitudes of other male partners and staff, we required their authenticity and their vulnerability. Understanding the business case for diversity was not enough; the desire to make change had to be linked to their personal story. We asked them to be prepared to talk openly and often about their journey to understanding. Our male champions were asked to hold themselves and others accountable for managing personal and unconscious bias; to call out inequalities when they saw them, to stop them in their tracks, and, finally, to mentor and advocate for the women on their teams.

I was struck by the commitment and empathy we received from all the male champions, but one story sticks out in particular for me.

He was a first-generation Italian in Canada. He remembered how isolated and uncertain he felt as the only hire at PwC from immigrant parents, with English as his second language. He felt like an imposter in a sea of white, upper-class Canadian men.

I couldn't believe it!

In all the years I worked with this man, I never saw him as an outsider, or a part of a minority, but as he shared this with me, my eyes were opened. He related to a woman's plight, not because of his mom, or his wife, or his daughters, but because of how *he* felt growing up in Canada and the experience of his early years in the workplace.

These men's stories of why change was meaningful and important to them were powerful and impactful to their male colleagues. The male champions, and the firm leaders who held themselves accountable, were fundamental to the success of the WIL/ROW initiative; they were the secret sauce propelling our efforts forward.

So, once we had enough men squarely on board from the most senior levels of the firm, it was time to put our money where their mouth was. The CEO, Monica, and I drafted our response; an executive sponsorship program to support the advancement of PwC's highest-performing, high-potential female senior managers and partners. We asked all executives to sponsor at least one woman from our list of stars. This was not the same as our 'Mentoring Connections' program. This was aimed at sponsors actively advocating for our brightest and best female partners—our future leaders.

Executives were asked to stake their reputation (and influence with senior male colleagues) on the women they chose to sponsor. When a leadership opportunity arose in which the sponsor believed his protégé should be considered, he was not to take 'no, she is not ready' or 'she's not what we are looking for' as an answer.

We trusted that the sponsorship program would level the playing field for senior women who may have been overlooked or discounted by leaders in the past. We wanted to eliminate bias in favour of predetermined preferences for mini-mes, the usual suspects, drinking buddies, or the up-and-coming male partners.

There was no turning back. If we were ever going to reach our aspirational goal of 25% named leadership positions being held by women, everyone needed to step up. Male leaders could no longer make excuses, say they didn't know, or find another way to divert attention away from our high-performing women.

When influential male sponsors advocated for the merits of considering capable female superstars for open leadership positions, we saw a new, diverse face of leaders begin to emerge. But this was always a long-term plan. We hoped these new female leadership role models would inspire new recruits to stay with PwC (retain!) and then confidently strive for promotion. As the program transpired, we did see a fair, more representative slate of candidates competing for the leadership positions offered.

After five years of holding my leaders and myself accountable, measuring results against aspirational goals, and tweaking our strategic plan, I can confidently say Julie, Monica, and I did move the needle on gender diversity. We promoted more women into partnership and leadership positions and achieved our aspirational goals two years ahead of schedule. Setting targets, and holding leaders accountable for achieving them, blew the doors off gender inequity for promotion and positioned them in leadership roles.

But don't take my word for it. Because numbers tell a powerful story (and I love numbers!) here are PwC's statistics (reproduced with permission from PwC LLP) regarding female staff hires, women partner admissions, and women in named leadership roles as of July 1, 2022:

- **54%** of PwC's firmwide staff are women and **46%** of all professional staff are women.

- **30%** of PwC's partners are female. (Recall, in 2008, at the start of my WIL/ROW tenure, only 17% of the partnership was female, and we set a five-year aspirational goal to achieve 22%.)

- **52%** (10 of 19 positions) of PwC's Extended Leadership Team are held by women. (In 2008, only **16%** of the named leadership positions were held by women, and our five-year aspirational goal was to promote **25%** of our women into senior leadership positions.)

- Female partners now lead business units, geographic markets, and industries.

- PwC has women partners serving some of the firm's most coveted, high-profile clients.

- Women partners hold strategic, transformation roles for the firm in positions such as Vice-Chair, CFO, Chief Legal Counsel and National Managing Partner. Two of six (**33%**) of the most Senior Leadership Team members are women.

- Validating the support and value of women in the partnership has also been demonstrated by the partners themselves. PwC partners *elected* 4 women to serve on PwC's Partnership Board, representing **44%** of the board's partner composition (or **35%** of the full board, including the CEO and invited external directors).

Looking to the future, PwC's diversity and inclusion journey is not done or dusted. PwC's Trust Roadmap, which shares key performance indicators, publicly disclosed new five-year targets (to 2026):

- to employ at least **50%** female professional staff.

- to have at least **50%** of the Extended Leadership Team be women.

- to have at least **50%** of the Partnership Board be women.
- to have at least **35%** of the partners be women.

Our initiative, and the work of those who eventually took over from us, resulted in unequivocal change throughout the organization. I truly believe involving men in our quest for fairness and awareness, and having them state their advocacy for diversity, opened dialogue to make it safe for everyone to voice their opinions—one of the many advantages of diversity of thought.

We reduced bias embedded in our performance evaluation processes, increased awareness of gender differences in the workplace, and amplified male mentoring and the sponsorship of women by making this a recognized, formal program.

My unlikely, upward career trajectory and success in the firm beat the odds of my upbringing. That much you know. My many positive experiences with my male mentors and sponsors shaped my perspective, as well as how I viewed the firm and the opportunities presented to me. This felt like a final step for me. By paying it forward, I brought other women under my wing, into my influence.

At first, however, I took my promotion and success as a female partner somewhat for granted. 'If you work damn hard enough, and you have aptitude for the job, eventually you will get there!' was my mantra. It wasn't until I championed gender diversity, and the retention and promotion of women, and learned of other capable, hardworking women's discouraging experiences, that I realized how much of my success was not due to my persistence and capabilities alone. The equation works best when the three groups are in sync: **Support systems, supporters, and influencers.**

This trio during my first thirty years in the firm consisted of men who performed their deeds without my knowledge, asking for nothing but my trust in them (and myself!) in return. My champions and sponsors offered me challenges, stretch assignments, and secondments, using their influence to speak about me and my capabilities, on my behalf. Mentors supported me with empathy and patience. They were there when I needed them most.

Yet, my experience shaped the programs Julie, Monica and I introduced, implemented, socialised, and reinvested in. We focused on the importance of mentors, sponsors, flexible work programs, and understanding gender differences to help retain and promote women. It was not a coincidence that these things helped propel *me* forward in my career with PwC.

We had opened Pandora's box. As the program unfurled and started to show real results, it then shifted to shine a lens on improving opportunities for men and women of colour as well as the LGBTQ+ community, with the mantra, 'Bring your whole self to work'.

I could not ignore a staff member entering the profession who had the courage to share, 'I don't see myself as a woman in accounting. I am a (brown, Asian, disabled, etc.) woman, dealing with a different kind of unconscious bias. I am more than my gender. Why should I be encouraged to work at a place where there is no one like me in leadership?'

With momentum gained on gender diversity, it was time to address the nuances of intersecting identities, as well as the behaviours, decisions, and actions that impacted marginalized communities. Diversity, equity, and inclusion is not a one and done initiative. It evolves on a continuum with persistent focus, education, awareness, measurement, and assessment.

I felt the moment was right to pass the baton to a new leader with fresh ideas, time, and energy for the broader mandate in our journey. As a proud parent keen to see our initiative expanded and flourish, once again I watched from the sidelines just as I had with the CEO V2R Conference.

In recognition of my five years spent improving women's retention and advancement, in 2013, I was acknowledged with two prestigious external awards.

The first was the 'Business Leader Champion' award presented to me at Catalyst Canada's Honours Awards in front of 500 senior Canadian businessmen and women in attendance. My acceptance speech was my legacy for the remarkable forward-thinking Mississauga office partners who supported and promoted me. My highest tribute went to Don. He was the partner who talked me into staying at PwC with the 'Sue, you would be bored in a month' speech, the one who gave me an all-important stretch assignment while I was part time, and the one who was always in my corner, believing I could be more. You can view my five minutes of fame (AKA my acceptance speech) on YouTube. Then, in a shocking twist, later that same year, I was named one of the 'Top 100 Most Powerful Women in Canada' by the Women's Executive Network.

Say what?

I have to give credit where it's due, and this isn't just the woman in me trying to celebrate the team's accomplishment while ignoring my own contribution!

Because neither of these awards would have been possible without hiring two incredibly talented women, back-to-back, to support me. Julie and Monica were the foundation. They developed, socialised, and implemented the strategy and my God did they make me look good. So, I attribute much of my success to Julie and Monica, whose passion and pursuit of excellence were awe-inspiring.

Although the awards showcased the firm's diversity efforts and distinguished PwC from the competition, what made it all worthwhile was the sweeping change that occurred within PwC in the years to come. I believe the WIL/ROW initiative contributed to the acceptance and recognition of a broader diversity and inclusion mandate. By embracing our initiatives, increasing awareness among staff, partners, and senior leadership, we not only achieved the step change our CEO asked for, we knocked it out of the park. Not one to rest on their laurels, today the firm is committed to continuous improvement and believes there is more work to do.

Through my leadership journey, I discovered something new, something unexpected. *The job you apply for isn't necessarily the job you want, nor the job you are meant to do.* Sometimes, the job comes to you.

When it does, seize the moment, let passion guide you, and extraordinary things *will* happen!

REFLECTION

Blazing your trail

With the support and buy-in of firm leaders and male allies, Julie, Monica, and I advanced the firm's diversity journey, and it contributed to a significant change in the fabric of the firm's culture. Inclusion & Diversity at PwC is now much broader, underpinning both market-facing and internal areas of people strategy with a focus on making the firm a more just and equitable place for all. It's a lasting legacy with my fingerprints on it. Looking back (and to the future!), it is beyond satisfying.

I encourage you to refer back to these meaty chapters whenever you find yourself afraid to put your hand up for a promotion or a stretch assignment, whenever you find yourself understating your performance in your self-assessments and job evaluations, or when you are expecting to have mastered 100% of the attributes before you are ready to apply for a new job or position. Furthermore, give your head a shake if you are making yourself small in a meeting, are overcome with imposter syndrome, have a nasty case of perfectionism or mom guilt. Listen to yourself when you are speaking—is your voice lilting up in tone when you are meant to be making a statement!? (I dare you to say that out loud without raising your voice.)

If you find yourself between a rock and a hard place (as you are bound to), learn to navigate the female double bind dilemma—that tightrope we walk between nasty and nice, competent and likeable. Can you learn to communicate in a way that lands somewhere in the middle? Can you refocus your evaluators on the concrete impact you have made and the way in which you will bring that to your next stretch assignment?

I believe this starts with being an authentic leader. Don't be afraid to assert your authority, voice a contrarian view, and own it. Find the style that you are comfortable with and grow into it. If you take yourself seriously, so will others. Watch for ways you may unconsciously undermine your perspective. Be self-determinate no matter what that looks like.

In case you were wondering but were afraid to ask, I am pleased to announce that Monica is a high-performing PwC Audit Partner. I predict she will be a future leader in the firm. Julie is a new mom, who is busy juggling motherhood while transforming the culture of Corporate America, one company at a time. As a new partner and global head of learning and leadership development in an international advisory firm, Julie is a highly-sought-after facilitator, educator, and coach who is challenging the status quo. *I told you so.*

Reflection Questions

1. Next time you raise your hand for a stretch assignment or promotion (which you **are** going to do), can you accept that you haven't mastered 100% of the attributes/skills required?

2. Reflecting upon your workplace, is there a culture of diversity and inclusion? If so, are there leaders and males buying in and recognizing its importance?

3. How will you increase your and others' awareness of unconscious bias? What actions will you take to reduce these biases in your own life and workplace?

4. Are you aware of actions, beliefs, and societal norms (gender differences in the workplace) that are holding you back? What can you do to change this?

5. Do you understate your performance in evaluations? How will you change your behaviour?

Part VIII: Completeness

"Retirement is like getting home ice advantage. You worked hard for it, you earned it, now it's time to do something extraordinary with it."
—optimistic Toronto Maple Leafs fan, Susan Allen

Auditors love the concept of 'completeness'. We use it to ask ourselves, 'What's missing? What should have been recorded and disclosed in the financial statements?'

However, I believe the concept of *completeness* has a more profound meaning in life.

When I think of completeness, I am reminded to stand back, look at the big picture, take stock of what I have lived through, and consider what lessons I must impart upon you. When it came time to conclude this book, I asked myself, 'Has anything been inadvertently omitted? What are the most meaningful pieces to share of the last stage my career?'

As you may have noticed in Part VII, in my latter years, the thought of using my knowledge and experience to widen my influence and maximise the impact I could have on others was central. I did not realize that with this goal came opportunities that allowed me to smash the glass ceiling and defy heights that even my most optimistic young self could never have imagined. Cheerleading squad be damned!

In accepting the road that let to my retirement, three lessons emerged.

First, I was invited to explore impactful and strategic global opportunities because I was in the right place at the right time. This is not to say I was *lucky*. Performing these coveted roles was possible because I was the best person for the job—I was *in the right place*. Dovetailing with this was how seamless my personal circumstances—the priorities I sought and my ambitions—placed me squarely to accept them *at the right time*.

Second, armed with an in-depth knowledge of gender differences championing the WIL/ROW initiative, and a bolstered sense of self-worth and confidence, I acted in ways that would *not* sabotage my career, my progression, nor my prospects. I practiced what I preached.

And third, when it was time to listen to my heart and retire, I did.

I encourage you to accept stretch opportunities at the right place and right time for you. And for those of you approaching, or even thinking about, the conclusion of your life's journey in business, I challenge you to consider how you will complete the following statements with conviction and passion:

'My legacy is...'

'I am famous for...'

'I have made a lasting contribution on...'

'I have touched lives in these ways...'

Come to think of it, these statements could apply to anyone at any stage of their life's journey. You don't need to be my age to consider them!

And now, for completeness, I present you with the final chapters of my journey.

23

Global Enrichment

For seven years, my office was on the fifty-second floor of one of Toronto's six well-known, black steel and stained-glass buildings: the TD Bank Towers. One of these, the PwC Tower, sits on the northeast corner of Bay and King, smack dab in the centre of the city's financial district. Although it took me *forever* to commute to the TD Tower each morning, once I parked underground and picked up my Starbucks latte, I was comfortable and ready to go. How couldn't I be? I was sitting among my TICE colleagues—industry experts, skilled professionals, lunchmates, confidantes, and friends. And it was here, looking out of my window office on the world below, that I discovered how wide my wings could spread.

No longer the insecure geography grad fearing anyone sporting the insufferable BComm degree, I had faced my insecurities. I was transformed, and I was now a confident professional with personnel, managerial, and technical skills. I had slain my many dragons in the Land of Firsts.

The Mississauga office partners saw me fit to be their *first* female partner. Moreover, moving to the Toronto office from San Jose offered me leadership roles as the *first* Regional and National CWEP Leader. Accepting the reassuring nudge from the CEO gave me the opportunity to win my *first* external awards in recognition of the role I played in PwC's Advancement of Women and Diversity.

My first appointment on PwC's global stage was my next gamble. Our Global CEO, a passionate, extraordinary speaker, and an inspiration to me, was the Executive Sponsor for the Global Gender Advisory Council I was a member of. He was an immigrant Italian living in the US who may have been small in stature, but was bigger than life in charm, personality, and influence. My positive experience with him and the Global Gender Advisory Council as Canada's WIL/ROW Leader must have been why, in a weak moment, I exposed myself to an entirely new challenge.

This opportunity came from a senior female leader and fellow partner, Diana, who carried more weight and obligation with her title than her slight frame should have been able to hold. She was PwC Canada's first female partner, and it doesn't get any tougher than that in my books.

She will forever be seen as the trailblazer, with all eyes watching, no mistakes allowed. And, thankfully, she chose to be a mentor to many up-and-coming female partners, including me.

Diana was nearing the completion of her eight-year term on the Canadian firm's Partnership Board (probably the first woman there too), and in an effort to retain gender diversity on our Canadian board, she asked me to consider running in the upcoming election. She would nominate and support me in any way she could.

How could I reasonably say no to this considering my history of pushing my female colleagues outside their comfort zone? If I didn't put my money where my diversity mouth was, I wasn't walking the talk. She knew this and was counting on it. So, with a gentle nudge, I threw my hat into the ring. *What's the worst that can happen? I'm a big girl now; I can take rejection.*

Two months later, the results were in, and my partners decided I was worthy of their vote! I was one of eight board members, and one of two women elected thanks to the sponsorship of Diana, her powers of persuasion, and her enduring belief in me.

My role as a Canadian board member was to objectively represent all partners, regardless of line of service, region, age, or gender. Leadership came to us for input on many aspects of the operations of the firm, including its current and future strategy. This included, but was not limited to, potential acquisitions, divestitures, mergers, growth objectives, target markets, annual budgets, capital allocations, the partnership admissions process, partner retirement funding, partner performance, special bonuses, CEO and leadership evaluation, and succession planning. To sum it up, there wasn't a whole lot that we didn't oversee.

Yet, it was a delicate balance governing with 'noses in and fingers out.' I learned how critical it was to not step over the invisible boundary separating leadership's autonomous decision-making and unwarranted board-meddling. That was none of my (our) business. This could have presented challenges to the auditor in me—the detail-oriented Columbo type, whose career MO was to *ask a lot of questions*—but I controlled myself.

My four years was as rewarding as it was informative. I was on the leading edge of every important decision leadership was making, whether it be a major issue, a risk, an opportunity, a global firm matter, or strategic planning for the future. I had the inside track, my input was sought, and my opinion valued, and as I neared the end of my term on the board, I reflected on how much I had enjoyed my role. I was considering whether I should run for a second term or leave on a high after one season, like a good Netflix series. I was seriously pondering my future for the first time.

Had I been asked to leave the firm and my career at that moment, I would have said, 'Great! Where's the door? And please don't let it hit my butt on the way out!' I had accomplished more in my career than my younger self could have ever imagined. I was grateful for the opportunities, the friends I made, the life I lived, and my personal growth. I was content to move on with the next stage of my life.

Then, one day, I looked up to see Chris, the firm's CEO, step inside my office and stand behind one my guest chairs, leaning his body on the chair back. *I never see him on my floor. What could he want from me?* He didn't sit to make himself comfortable. *Okay, he won't be here long.*

I could tell he was itching to tell me something, but before I could ask him, he burst out with, 'I want you to think about running for PwC's Global Board in the election next month.'

'Are you kidding me? How many hours does that take?' I looked at him with the most disapproving grimace I could form. 'I don't have time for this, I'm already waaaay too busy.' I came across much more direct than I intended, my knee-jerk reaction. Too late to take it back, I decided it was better to let him down gently. 'I just don't think this is the right time for me, Chris. Thanks for thinking of me. Maybe next time.'

Then, he went on his inevitable rant. It was as if he'd expected this reaction from me. The rant was a carbon copy to the one I heard four years earlier from Diana, and I immediately knew where this was going.

'You, of all people, should be saying yes to this opportunity. You have experience on *our* board, you are at the right time in your career, and you have time do this. We need a female partner on the Global

Board. You mentor women, ask them to put their hand up for stretch assignments, and now, when it comes to you, you don't practice what you preach? Tell me why not? What's holding you back?'

All I heard was, 'Blah, blah, blah, blah, blahhhh.' My brain was playing catch up with his proposal.

Run for election on the Global Board? That's absurd!

Chris continued, for emphasis, 'I want you to consider this. Seriously. When you have made your decision, come see me... Oh, and by the way, you need to submit your CV, and why you want to stand for election, to the Canadian board nominating committee... in the next 72 hours.'

He turned toward the door of my office to leave me, speechless. Then, remembering he left something out, he turned back and looked at me with genuine concern and understanding. 'Oh, and Sue? Don't worry about the time. We will find time in your program. We can take something away if we need to. Time is not something you should worry about.'

This last point got my attention. *If I can't fit this in my schedule, you will take something off my plate? Interesting.* This ask had priority.

'You know, you still have to get elected!' he teased.

I stared at my computer, mulling his crazy idea over. *I could sit on the Global Board?* He was right. I would bring a unique lens to the global firm. They needed a woman. I felt honoured to have him think of me for such a significant, strategic role.

This was a coveted leadership position that only eighteen partners in the world held. More than 10,000 PwC partners world-wide voted to elect members to this board. The Global CEO, as well as the CEOs of the four largest PwC territories in the world (US, UK, China, and Germany), would report to me if I landed this role. This was PwC Canada's board discussions on steroids!

How stimulating would it be to discuss the firm's strategic priorities, staff and partner affairs, mergers and acquisitions, and line of service matters at a global level?

I can't say no; not to this. It's too big, it's too... global.

As you may have guessed, barely a week later, I was one of thirty-six partners from the PwC network (spanning all corners of the globe) nominated to stand for one of the eighteen positions for the Global Board.

I learned Canada would earn one seat on the board *if* the majority of the Canadian partners voted. But there was no guarantee. Canadians not only had to cast their vote, but they also had to vote for me, and I had to beat eighteen other worthy contenders.

Over the next few months, the votes were cast. When the results were in, it was the responsibility, and privilege, of the outgoing Global Board Chair to call each candidate with the outcome. However, I missed his call, and twenty-four hours passed before a voicemail from Australia landed in my phone.

What I didn't miss was another personal visit from Chris.

He came charging in, confident smile planted, his pride beaming through in an 'I told you so!' moment. 'Did you hear? You got elected! Congratulations!'

I was delighted to hear the news from him. 'Wow, really? That's amazing!' I stopped mid-thought. 'Wait, what are you going to take off my plate so I can actually do this?'

'What do you mean?' he replied, head cocked to one side like I had suddenly sprung five heads. 'Where would you get a silly idea like that from?' I watched the man with his Cheshire Cat grin slip out of my office to avoid further discussion.

Great.

As the news settled in, I realized, as grateful as I was to have won a seat, this was not the 1950's and we were not living in the world of *Father Knows Best*. I couldn't understand why it had taken women so long to land a seat on the Global Board. Why was I the first? *It was about bloody time.*

Still, I wasn't upset. I was honoured. My fellow partners, more than 10,000 of them globally, saw it fit to elect a woman to the board, and that woman was me.

Unfortunately, I was the *only* woman elected. Thoughts began swirling in my head, juggling the added weight of this responsibility I carried. I thought of Diana's plight. *I am the first and only.*

Must I be a role model and champion for all women in the firm? My euphoria of winning was weighed down by the responsibility I felt. Was I overthinking this? *I cannot make a mistake... but what does that even look like? Eyes will be watching, ears will be listening, minds will be made up. I may be the first, but I must pray that I'm not the last.*

The new slate of global board members was a balance of newbies and returning veterans elected to their second four-year terms. Similar to my experience on the Canadian board, regardless of where we called home, we were to act as *independent* board members objectively representing all partners, with the goal of bringing our strategic minds, as well as our diverse experience and skillsets, to the table for the good of the network.

There was only one female leader in the extended leadership of the global firm—the Global Diversity Leader. She was a veteran trailblazer herself who I had occasion to meet on the Gender Advisory Council. I admired her stamina and how she carried herself as a confident, articulate equal among the throngs of men she encountered at every turn. I knew from experience that her mandate to promote female retention and advancement was no easy task. I hoped she was making a difference, but I knew it was a struggle.

Which was moving faster: Advances in gender diversity at the leadership level, or icebergs receding from global warming? I think we both know the answer to that... and neither is helpful.

However, in time, it became second nature for me to overlook my place as the only woman with a seat at the big boys' table. I had found my voice and took my place as one of them. (It didn't hurt that a second female partner was appointed to the board within the first twelve months of my term from a vacancy created by one of the men.)

My four-year term on the Global Board is one I will cherish forever. I was proud to be a member of a high-performing team, applying best practices to board decisions and governance matters. The friendships made and the places visited will remain at the top of my fondest career memories. Being able to hold my own as an equal among my peers, at the highest level of leadership in the firm, was a defining moment for my growth as a professional, a partner, and a woman.

But at 54, and with my plan to retire at 57, I had the itch for one last hurrah before I hung up my shingle. I wanted to try something new before the sands of time seeped through the hourglass of my career. How would I ride out my last couple of years? Would it end with a flicker or a flame? What would be my swan song, the culmination of my career, my legacy?

As seems to be my way, an opportunity came knocking at my door when I needed it to. I was presented with another global leadership role, reporting to a former colleague of mine from San Jose. Coincidence? I think not.

Never underestimate how your past, your connections, and your reputation can provide you with exciting avenues to pursue. In other words, never burn bridges. Your past, how you left, what you said, and what you left unfinished, will remain in the minds of your industry's influencers long after you are gone. Do you want to be remembered as a positive or a negative contributor? It's largely up to you.

The newly appointed global leader from San Jose was chosen to monitor and assess the firm's audit quality for our 150 member firms around the globe. Auditors were no longer self-regulated due to the SEC's response to the fallout of Enron and demise of Arthur Andersen. The profession faced strict, independent regulators and new rules which were overseen by objective watchdogs carrying big sticks. This kept auditors up at night.

I said 'yes' to becoming one of ten hand-picked, experienced, and respected senior Audit Partners, called International Team Leaders (ITLs), because I saw how I could make a difference for the execution of audits and audit quality. It truly was my bread and butter.

But before I could accept this, my Canadian Audit Leader warned me of its downside. Business travel was a 'dirty' word to Canadians, and this role involved *a lot of it*. He also warned my new boss that 'Canadians don't do travel well.'

Even though my current global board travel took only six weeks of my year, it did feel like I had spent most of my time hopping in and out of planes, packing and unpacking, sleeping in unfamiliar hotel rooms, and winding my watch backwards or forwards to adjust my mind and body to the different time zones. That was the downside of travel.

However, the upside was undeniable. I was treated like royalty! Seated comfortably in business class, staying in luxury, five-star hotels, dining in the best restaurants in the world, and touring places

I never dreamed I would visit? This was one of the best gigs around. I would be livin' the dream.

Nonetheless, my boss's point was well taken. Canadians, in general, are homebodies who are born, grow up, get married, work, and retire in the same city.

'What countries are they thinking of giving me?' I asked with some trepidation.

'The Nordics: Denmark, Finland, Sweden, and Norway, as well as Luxembourg, Belgium, and Switzerland,' my boss said proudly. *His* partners would be hard-pressed to accept any country located more than an eight-hour flight away. *Well, that's promising*.

In the end, travel did not deter me from this role. I saw it as my last hurrah before retirement, using the culmination of my experience as an auditor, a teacher, a mentor, a coach, and a leader to make a difference on a broad scale to the *most* important aspect of PwC's audit practice and future: *quality*.

My kids were older, at university, doing well and (sadly) requesting less of my time. *They grow up too fast.* They were excited for me to accept this adventure, unlike John, who would be home alone at frequent intervals under my new regime. But, as was typical of John's way, he too was on board, hoping to see the world with me on weekends, and he was supportive and encouraged me to announce, 'I'm in! You have your Canadian!' I was the only female appointed to the team.

No sooner had I accepted the position when several new countries were added: South Korea and two firms in Japan. I waved goodbye to my short flights across the pond before they had even started.

This global role was not for wimps. Essentially, we were PwC's internal quality monitors (AKA police) assessing quality just like the external guys. I very much doubt any audit partner or manager, anywhere, was glad to see us. We were the auditors' auditor, an emotionally draining assignment for anyone with empathy. (i.e., *me*)

I surprised even myself, sticking to my career choice for four years, and extended my term for another year. It was exhausting. I often felt completely used up after so few hours of rest on my overnight flights. As I trudged to my hotel room, I would collapse, useless to anyone unless I had my siesta. Waking up groggy, I ventured outside for an evening stroll in the 'old town' of whatever city I was in, ordered a light dinner, and found that my mood and energy soon lifted. By morning, I would almost be back to my normal self.

I wouldn't have been able to do this if I wasn't passionate about improving audit quality. It was deeply satisfying to watch my member firms advance and improve. It was the most fulfilling part of that job.

Working with the other ITLs on the team was never dull. We played just as hard as we worked. We were the firm's nomads, living out of suitcases for the good of our firm and its partners. We needed and depended on each other. We were a decent, hardworking, fun-loving group, even if we *were* the audit police.

As I neared the completion of my ITL term, I was asked whether I would be returning to the audit practice or staying another year or two in this global role. The global leader was happy to have me stay on as long as I liked. Similarly, the Canadian firm said they would take me back. I was, after all, *their* Canadian partner. So, as my planned retirement year approached, I considered my future.

I would miss the PwC friends I made at my member firms; the kind hospitality and the support I received made my job infinitely easier.

But the constant fatigue and loneliness of my business travel was difficult to ignore. Moreover, returning to the audit practice to build a client base from scratch, *again*, would take more energy and effort than I was willing to give. Neither option appealed to me.

As I trudged down the long, international departure hall at Terminal One in Toronto's Pearson Airport, I thought about my nomad life as an ITL. This was my typical route on a typical Sunday evening for my typical flight to Copenhagen. It was leaving in an hour, and then I would be gone for three whole weeks. I dragged my carry-on suitcase and my tired body into the business class departure lounge. I couldn't even look at the food or listen to the news on the TV monitor overhead. I flopped myself down in a seat and waited till it was time to pick myself up, then wait in line at the departure gate, again, for the hundredth time.

I don't want to take this flight. I don't want to leave John at home. I don't want to have another sleepless night. I don't want to wake up on the other side of the world after having slept terribly for only two hours on a plane.

I was sad, and feeling my private sadness made me sadder. *What am I doing here? Why am I doing this?*

'The day I wake up and find myself bored, unhappy, or not looking forward to going to work is the day I will leave this firm.'

They were my words, my motto, said to many a young CPA or manager when they felt lost.

I saw my thirteen-year-old self listening to my grandad. He was whispering in my ear, *'To my dearly loved and first granddaughter... may she always be true to herself.'*

The time had come. All roads pointed in the same direction. *My someday is today. It's time to leave PwC.* No regrets.

As I look back on my 34 years with PwC, I feel pride and wonder. What started out as an interesting pursuit became a lifelong career; a passion that never felt like work. I truly feel like it was something I was meant to do.

After years of uncertainty and doubt, I eventually set out to make a difference for those who came after me and to leave the firm better than I found it. Did I accomplish this? Yes, I sincerely believe I did.

As you reflect upon what you have come to learn from my life's journey, and you have absorbed the stories of my failures, my self-doubts, the curse of my perfectionism, or the sacrifices I made to find a suitable solution to balance work and family, know that I have shared this with the highest regard for you. Deep memories and the negative inner voice that plagued me for so many years have been unleashed for your benefit.

No, I don't have all the answers, but I have my truths, my beliefs, and my reality. As I attempt to pay it forward, like so many have done for me, I hope I have helped you ask the right questions and search for the answers that will help you navigate the path you wish to pursue.

I have been vulnerable and honest in my thoughts, in order to liberate you *from you*. I need you to know you are *not* alone in your ideas and judgements. I daresay it's not even your fault.

When you are awarded a seat at the table beside those you admire and respect, see yourself as others do: a leader who has earned the right to be there! It doesn't matter if you've only been at your current workplace for a few years and advanced quicker than you or others thought possible. You were placed in your role for a reason, so take it on and be a role model and a mentor for those who come after you—especially those who may not have the privileges you enjoy. It doesn't matter if you're 28 or 58; the responsibility is still yours.

When you catch yourself thinking, *I'm not comfortable asking for that raise, stretch assignment, promotion, or flexible work arrangement*, take a deep breath, write it down, say it out loud, and ask for it! The worst you may hear is 'no'. You know that word. Make sure you use it to stand your ground.

You possess the courage and strength to take a risk, take that fork in the road, and correct a wrong turn. Believe in yourself, be gentle when you stumble, and take the time you need to recover from disappointments or setbacks that threaten your resolve.

Please, don't make the same mistake as me and overplay failures in your head. This is a waste of energy that drains you and gives those often-meaningless mistakes more weight than they warrant. Instead, spend your energy on the positives: your accomplishments, successes, competence, emotional intelligence, and all of the good qualities you possess and spread to others.

It *is* possible to pursue your wildest dreams. Now follow your heart and achieve them on *your* terms.

24

Reflections of Life in the Present Lane

'I'll wager a bet… I can beat you straight up,' I say, ignoring the twenty-point difference in our handicaps. Unlike auditing, my competitive nature in golf eludes my actual skill.

As John and I begin our game, I am peppered with his incessant putting advice *on every hole.* This tests my resolve. Do I listen to my supportive spouse in my time of need? He reads greens better than anyone I know. *Or is he secretly sabotaging me?* This is a winner-take-all match; the loser makes dinner.

As we approach the 18th green, drenched from the sun and heat, I am suddenly more interested in spiritual recovery than beating John once I look down at the scorecard. *I'd rather be sipping on Rombauer Chardonnay.* Soon I will watch the Sonoran sunset transform day into night with breathtaking shades of deep crimson and yellow billowing through cumulous clouds.

I never tire of nature's serenity in paradise. It calms my soul. I am at peace here. I sleep like a baby.

John and I have settled in North Scottsdale, five months of the year, as Canadian snowbirds. We bought our house in 2008 and now spend our winters golfing, hiking, mountain biking, and finishing it all off with a glass or three of wine.

Back home in Mississauga, we are empty nesters, and my house is so much better than the materialistic one I dreamed of owning in my early days at PwC. It is the home where my children were raised, lasting memories were made, treasured traditions were established, friends are welcomed, parties are hosted, and my grandkids are spoiled.

Retirement, the next chapter of my life, is also my chance to do the gazillion things I've always wanted to do but never found time to prioritize. Now, I attend weekly yoga classes and have an in-home personal trainer. I have joined not one, but two golf courses, and I golf three times a week with John's golf buddies, who I have adopted as my own.

More than anything, I finally have time to slow down and *think*—to reflect and choose what I wish to pass down to those faced with the challenges I confronted and overcame. It was a big reason I chose to write this book.

So, as I think back to my last day at PwC in 2016 on February 29 (a leap year, yup!), I am reminded of the many cherished memories and lasting friendships I made as a CPA and PwC partner.

I needn't look too far to find memories of my years at PwC. I type this page with my brand-new ThinkPad computer, a gift from PwC Canada, and think fondly of my retirement dinner expertly organized by Jill, my assistant, who corralled twelve of my best friends and family members together in the thick of their busy season.

Under my backyard gazebo are four black and white Carlsberg blankets, a gift from my Copenhagen colleagues. As I wrap this blanket around me every October, watching the leaves fall along with the temperature, I remember how these blankets comforted me as I sat down in the outside cafés of Nyhavn, Denmark.

My hutch proudly displays my Iittala designer serving dish from my Finnish friends, and every Christmas I carefully place my Georg Jensen snowflake ornaments from PwC Sweden's CEO in a prominent place on my Christmas tree. Each night as I climb into bed, I catch a glimpse of my Korean inlaid mother of pearl jewelry box sitting on my dresser.

These gifts, and the many other mementos adorning both of my homes, are as special to me as the celebratory, farewell dinners with my global family and friends of PwC because of the memories they represent. In return, I brought my global colleagues and friends a bottle of Canadian maple syrup and a copy of John's famous pancake recipe to remember me by. It was my way of saying thank you for their incredible support over the last four years of my career.

In close, and in reflection, I wish to leave you with the most significant tipping points of my career and life.

I must start with the wonderful world of accounting—the great unexpected surprise—and how it was unlocked for me when I accepted a junior position at college as a Cashier. While I was figuring out what I wanted to be when I grew up, my aptitude for math knocked me over the head with the discovery of a new field: auditing. I learned that **while you navigate your winding road called life, let its inevitable twists and turns lead you in directions you never imagined.** Your choices may take you down a much different path than mine did but know there is more at play than just the decisions you make. Let that internal compass guide you. Trust in it because it may lead you on your most exciting journey yet!

As you've read, my passion for auditing led me to pursue and obtain my CPA, be promoted to partner in a global professional services firm, take on senior global leadership positions, and break several firsts as a woman and an executive in business. Yet, it still stings to recall the moment, after I had built up the courage to finally *ask* for a promotion, to be flatly turned down.

Just as I was feeling the agony of defeat and regretting the very moment I opened my mouth, I was shocked and dismayed to be offered another position with the big, fat 'HR' tag written all over it. But I soon came to learn that my WIL/ROW leadership role was the role I was better suited for, the role I could excel at, and the role I was *always* meant to do. I made a difference, left a lasting legacy, and you will too.

But that opportunity was still preceded by the **painful lesson of rejection**, and oh, how much it stings! It never gets easier either!

Still, when you reach higher, take a risk, and apply for a stretch assignment or a role that you don't get, please don't feel defeated. You too will be offered or will find something better, something you are more suited for, and something you will excel at. I saw it happen again and again over my many years at PwC, and I continue to see it today.

When I think about being rejected from the cheerleading squad, failing my US CPA exam, and even the trauma of my son's tumultuous birth, I now realize that some of life's setbacks seemed worse in the moment than they ultimately were. Time truly heals all wounds, and these unexpected blows are served to make you stronger, so you can build resilience and appreciate life's simple, precious moments.

My third lesson is the most emotionally draining to personally experience, but in time, I have come to appreciate its meaning, tenfold. When things don't go your way (or go absolutely terribly!), just STOP, take a breath, sit back, and **take stock of the blessings**

you may have taken for granted. Reassess your priorities, and rather than dwell on the negative, pursue what makes you happy and gives you purpose, knowing that, in time, you *will* get through this.

Speaking of blessings, how fortunate was I to be surrounded by forward-thinking male mentors and sponsors who protected me, steered me straight when I got lost, and supported me throughout my impressionable years and, really, throughout my entire career? These incredible men propped me up, believed in me, and stood beside me. I now know how many times they saved me from myself. Imagine prodding a high-performing woman to declare, 'I want to be a partner!' like it was root canal! Just one of many examples.

That is why this next lesson may be the missing link to your career success. **Understand gender bias in your workplace. Understand those gender norms that were programmed into you from childhood and don't let them hold you back. I implore you to fight against them and rise above.**

When I think back to the heavy blanket of fog that descended upon my first marriage, draining my body as well as my soul, it took me some time to realize I was living a lie, trapped and seemingly helpless. I needed to find strength to pick myself up, change my future, and start fresh, even if I had no idea where this would lead. Similarly, as I learned the hard way from four plus years of international travel, I missed being home with John, and the exhaustion of circling the globe at least a dozen times had chewed me up and spit me out.

Thankfully, in time, I followed the advice I had often preached to others when they shared their internal conflict and pain with me.

If you wake up in the morning, distraught by the fog that has befallen, forgive yourself, find the strength to move on, and

make necessary changes to create a better tomorrow for yourself.

And finally, my last lesson for all of you, my dear readers, comes from the prophetic words of my grandfather:

'May you always be true to yourself.'

Afterword

There is one more important subject to be addressed that I'm sure many of you are wondering about.

How did the three people closest to me manage the turmoil (and excitement) I created for them, while I followed my dreams?

You have read how John and the kids embraced my career and supported me. Decisions my family encouraged me to accept took my kids to new schools, transferred my husband from his role as chief financial officer to chief domestic officer, and the move required all of us to make new friends in a new country. They stood by me, cheering from the sidelines when I made partner, received awards, and accepted global roles that took me to every corner of the world and back for weeks at a time.

But did my definition of work/life balance meet theirs? How were their lives shaped in their childhood by in-home caregivers? Was I present for them?

Although I admit I was afraid to ask Danielle and Andrew this, it is only fair to get their perspective on this for your benefit. If I didn't, how can you trust that the advice and lessons I provided throughout this book actually worked?

Here is what Danielle had to say about these questions:

Thinking back on my childhood, I rarely reflect on what could have been, since having two full-time, working parents was all I ever knew.

What I do reflect on is how my parents made me feel during my childhood, and what I've taken with me throughout my life as a result. The amount of time we spent together mattered far less to me than the values they instilled when we *did* spend time together.

The two most important values I gained from my upbringing was confidence and unconditional love. My parents had an unwavering confidence in me that made me believe I could do anything. This was ingrained in me, in part through their constant encouragement, as well as through the example they set—in particular, seeing my mother persevere in her career. I also feel strongly that much of my confidence was gained by having parents that worked outside the home while I was being cared for by multiple caregivers: nannies, grandparents, etc. Having that time without my parents each day fostered a sense of independence that has served me well.

I also felt loved unconditionally by my parents, and while I took it for granted most of my childhood, I am now most grateful for it as an adult. My parents made me feel seen, heard, and understood. My feelings, life, and accomplishments, no matter how big or small, mattered to them. They took a genuine interest in my life, and I noticed how much they sacrificed to give me a life any kid would dream of. For this reason, it didn't matter how much time we spent together, because the time we *did* spend together was special, and even at a young age, I felt important.

And here is Andrew's take on my parenting and his childhood:

I don't have a comparison point to definitively say whether my childhood was better/worse than anyone else's. But what I can say is that I always felt like my mom was there when it counted. She was there to read me bedtime stories and sing me a lullaby; she was at my sports games to cheer me on; she was in the audience to hear me give my 'Tower of Pisa' speech to the entire school; and I saw her smiling proudly at my graduations and all my important milestones. I always felt my mom knew what was important to me and made sure that these were her priorities as well. It was a running joke when she said, 'I'll be home at 7pm.' but when we called (at 7pm) to see how close to home she was, she hadn't even left the office. Honestly, I was probably playing on my computer anyway.

An aspect of my childhood that certainly shaped my life is the experience of being uprooted in grade seven and moving to California. Without that experience, I don't think I would have been able to leave my family and friends behind to begin my career as a software developer in Seattle (not to mention the formative tech camps I attended in California that introduced me to the tech industry).

I would be remiss not to mention my heart condition. That was (obviously) not part of my parents' plan for me, but it is also something that certainly shaped my childhood. The annual tests, my parents avoiding putting me in hockey, my parents' nervousness when I decided to take up rugby; it all impacted my childhood in various ways. When all was said and done though, I look back fondly on my childhood. And now, as an adult, I feel that the mentorship from my parents has positively impacted my adult life in many ways. I am driven to be successful. When looking for a partner, I looked for someone who was driven and passionate about their career, just like my mom. As a parent, I see myself trying to emulate some of my parents' behaviours—for example, reading to my son every night before bed, or talking to him about his day at the dinner table. I just hope that I can be as successful a parent as I believe my parents were to me.

I made a huge mistake by asking them these questions *after* I wrote the book, so thank God they didn't reveal that I'd royally screwed them up! And just imagine, they typed all that without any veiled threats or blackmail!

As far as how John has dealt with my work habits, my extensive travel, my retirement before him, and my improving golf handicap, I have this to report: John has recently retired from the company he acquired upon our return from San Jose. He sold it to his management team, and had the original founders been alive, they would have been proud to hear this. It was really a full-circle moment—their legacy continues. As I expected he would be, John is happy in retirement, settling into his new stage of life and playing more golf than you can shake a seven iron at.

The apple didn't fall far from the tree for strong and independent Danielle. As both a CPA and a proud alum of PwC, I was elated to be the one to tell her she passed her CPA exams as we sat in our kitchen anxiously awaiting her results! Siding with her dad's view, however, she refused to board the 'I love auditing' train and left PwC to pursue her business career in industry. Since then, she has been working her way up the corporate ladder, accepting more demanding finance roles at each place she leaves her mark. Inspired by the greater impact she feels she can make with early-stage start-up companies, she has chosen to work for tech organizations with extraordinary potential; some of which I had personally surveyed and learned so much from.

One of those start-ups, where she was the first finance hire, is now a successful billion-dollar tech 'unicorn' powering consumer experiences in the healthcare space. Danielle is the Chief Financial Officer and the first woman to sit on their senior executive team. As her mom, I worry about how hard she works. What is it they say about history repeating itself?

She is also a new mom to my beautiful granddaughter, Owen, who is the spitting image of her mom. It is surreal to hold my granddaughter and see myself looking down at my own daughter from thirty-five years prior. I've already noticed that Danielle is a much calmer and competent mom than I ever was. She's married to Evan, a hands-on, supportive husband and father, and I couldn't be prouder of them both.

Andrew is a PEng, married, a father of two, and is living with his professional wife, Nicolette, in Kirkland, Washington. He too, is entrenched in the technology industry and accepted a job with a tech giant upon graduation from Queens University over ten years ago. While he rejected the accounting route (picture both his index fingers crossed in front of his body), he used his extraordinary aptitude and interest in math (Aha! Gotcha!) to pursue a difficult Applied Math and Engineering degree. He is now a Lead Software Engineer with Salesforce. If you recall, this was that infamous start-up technology company that impressed me so much in 2005!

A benefit I completely overlooked as a by-product of my working-mom career has really played out in my son's life. While I did my best to be a positive role model for Danielle and show her that she could follow her dreams and reach for the stars, what I didn't realize was how deeply my career, John's support of my career, and our home dynamic influenced Andrew's views on his role as a father and husband. It was a proud mom moment when I heard Andrew say, 'Of course I will be taking my paternity leave! I'm looking forward to spending time with my son, Liam.' And his company was no slouch either. They gave him a promotion just prior to his leave, despite knowing he would be off for the next three months. Andrew is currently enjoying time off with his second child, a daughter, Daniella, as he tries to keep up with his active two-year-old, Liam, on his second paternity leave. Atta boy!

Since you've made it this far, I may have a surprising piece of news for you. By now, if you put two and two together, you realized I married a man with the dreaded BComm degree. For the past 36 years, we've stuck it out, for better or worse. But here's another fun fact: guess who I count among the four dudes to *grab* lunch at the men's only club in those first two weeks with PwC?

Oh John, how could you...

As for me, my friends say I have yet to retire. In truth, they are not far off. I have joined four corporate boards as an independent director and Audit Committee Chair. You can take the woman out of the audit, but you can't take the audit out of the woman. Honestly, I find board work fulfilling and stimulating, a natural extension of my audit partner career. I am most often pursued to fill vacancies created by the retiring, white, male audit committee chairs.

I find it ironic that it has taken thirty-four years of reporting audit findings to clients before I have been able to move my seat to the other side of the boardroom table: auditors reporting to me! I relish in the debates with fellow directors and management, and I find a thrill in discussing strategic alternatives and potential acquisitions, as well as helping solve complex business problems. I know this second career will keep my brain from turning to mush, and I'm also proud to report...

I'm not the *only* woman seated at the boardroom table!

Amen.

One More Thing…

Dear reader, I hope you will take the time to reflect upon the questions posed in this book. When you are ready, armed with your toolkit and courage, I invite you to exchange your ideas and dialogue with your peers, trusted colleagues, mentors, friends, and sponsors. Be the change you need to see in your world.

Do not be afraid to collaborate with others who wish the best for you. Seek answers to the issues and challenges you will face, and find support, encouragement, safety, and comfort in the men and women of your community at every age and stage in your life.

I invite you to visit www.countmein.info for additional resources and information. What you find there will continue to assist you with your career in business as well as your life's journey.

Let's keep the conversation going! I welcome your thoughts and questions.

Connect with me at: susan.allen@outlook.com

LinkedIn: http://ca.linkedin.com/in/sueallenauthor

Acknowledgments

As I reflect upon the thousands of winners who have accepted their little gold statues over the past ninety-three years at the Academy Awards, I am astonished at how often they go over their prescribed time limit. They babble on as the conductor cues the orchestra, microphones are turned off, and lights are dimmed. Ignoring these subtle hints, they are dragged off-stage waving their Oscar at the audience shouting, 'I have so many people to thank—you know who you are!'

I now empathize with this scene. With my book baby in my hands, three years and a global pandemic later, I am the one ignoring the signs, shouting, 'I have so many people to thank!'

I am overflowing with gratitude for the support I have received in my life and career. I apologize if I miss someone in this large connected global village of support I have received. *You know who you are!*

Mom and Dad, you provided me with the foundation to trust in myself. Thank you for introducing me to a lifelong love of dance and for fostering an interest in math which led me to pursue my passion. For these gifts, and many more, I am forever grateful. Your love and belief in me guided the disappointed cheerleader into becoming the determined young woman who dared to think, *I can figure this out. I can do better. I can* be *more.*

John, your love and support is as constant and extraordinary as the Sonoran sunset. Although our lives have traversed many winding paths to arrive at where we are today, I wouldn't want to experience this with anyone else. Thank you for being there, always. You are my biggest cheerleader, my trusted co-pilot, our kid's all-star Dad, Mr. Mom, and my fastidious 'Honey do list' completer. Thank you for saying 'yes' to stretch when I didn't have the courage to do so myself, regardless of how this impacted you.

Danielle and Andrew, watching you build your lives with your awesome partners and raise your little ones with love and affection, all while managing your thriving careers, gives me proud mom moments every single day. As new parents, you will appreciate what I am about to say next, 'You are the greatest achievements in my life.'

To my high school friends, Sandy, Diane, Suzanne, and Fab, and to the PW colleagues I met in the bullpen in those first days and years, Kathy, Jane, Carol, Laurie, Mary, Debbie, Mary Jo, Hector, Peter, Andros, Vik, and Agako, thank you for making me laugh (till I snort), keeping me grounded, and never letting the sands of time change our enduring friendship.

To Christiane, your warm heart, generous soul, and positive outlook is infectious. Thank you for being a good listener, and a great golf partner! Salut, my friend. Here's to more HIOs! (For you anyway...)

To Mr. Hamill, thank you for your mentorship, support, and encouragement. You helped me find my way when bumpy roads could easily have veered me off course.

How do I begin to thank the many, many members of my global, national, and local PwC family? During my thirty-four-year career with the firm, you were my esteemed colleagues, ardent supporters, personal confidants, advocates, coaches, mentors, and sponsors. You were my home away from home, a global community of the most intelligent, committed, insightful group of problem-solving, client-serving, math-loving, bean-counting men and women I have ever had the pleasure of calling my friends. You find humour in unusual places, care deeply when hearts are heavy, party hard when times are tough, and always do the right thing. I am indebted to your steadfast belief and support in me. Thank you for giving me space to make mistakes and to grow into the businesswoman I am today. Thank you for giving me wings to soar and igniting my love/hate relationship with travel.

I would like to name all of you, but that would fill chapters, so I will settle on a shout out to the following true partners of mine from my former career: Nicolas, Chris, Bill, David, Mike, Don, Ian, Monty, Laurie, Paul, Rick, Diana, Allan, Rob, Dave, Gino, Harish, Nick, Bob, Larry, Wayne, Marshall, Lee-Anne, Anne, Cathy, John, Anita, Marelise, Kevin, Judy, Martin, Vik, and Lisa. You, and the rest of my PwC family, are my heroes! Without you, there would be no content, no stories, no career path, no successes, and no lessons learned. I am grateful to all of you, my second family. That is to say, I am *PwC proud*.

To Monica and Julie, thank you for making me look good. Your sound judgement, strategic vision, and deep expertise is top shelf. You are highly analytical, articulate professionals and I value the knowledge I gained working with you during our influential Women in Leadership/Retention of Women days together. You inspired me then and you inspire me now. As I watch your careers flourish as rising stars, I take pride in watching your limitless potential and the small part I played in your early days as future leaders. What I cherish most, however, is that I now count you among my dearest friends.

This book would not have been written, or at the very least would have remained trapped in my computer, were it not for the brilliant editing, guidance, and advice from Dustin Bilyk of the Author's Hand. Dustin, you saw potential in that dreadful, messy first draft. When I was riddled with self-doubt and questions, you served up a dollop of patience, direction, and encouragement. You teased out buried memories, coaxing me to share those I held closest to my heart, then you took that lump of clay and molded it into the book I hold in my hands today. Focus, brevity, relevance, and reflection was the result of your guidance and collaboration. Thank you for your prowess with a pen and unparalleled talent as an editor. I am indebted to my friend and fellow author, Janna, who introduced me to you, so that I too could reap the benefits of your expertise.

To Emily of Emily's World of Design, thank you for your responsiveness, passion for creativity, and professionalism. I love everything about the cover design you created! You nailed it.

To Emily Jackson, journalist extraordinaire, thank you for your willingness to step in with flair and finesse on the finishing touches. Your sound guidance was invaluable.

To speaker author and business book strategist, Cathy Fyock, and author/publisher, Amy Waninger from A Page Beyond, your master classes and writer workshops, your timely influence to get my words on the page, and heartfelt support while I dipped my toes in the first-time author ocean, is much appreciated.

To friends and colleagues who generously gave of their time to read all or parts of earlier drafts of my manuscript, you pushed me forward with your indispensable judgement and compelling feedback. You are rockstars! A most sincere thank you to Molly and her brilliant mom, Carolyn, my long time NCE friend from across the pond, Francine, my 'L'air du Temps' book club partner in crime, Janna, my ultra-supportive accountability partner, Evan, my favourite son-in-law, Trang, who is like a daughter to me, and, finally, my heartfelt thanks to Cheri, Rachel, Amy, and Masumi.

... cue the orchestra, kill the lights, and for Pete's sake, take that microphone off her!

Manufactured by Amazon.ca
Bolton, ON